United in Death

United in Death

Roy Pargetter

YOUCAXTON PUBLICATIONS
OXFORD & SHREWSBURY

In memory of my Mum and Dad

When we are all conceived
We are all born to die.
It's all for a known reason
But no one really knows why.

Everyone lives their own life
Whether it's for good or bad.
Some of us are so gifted
For others it all so sad.

Whether you like it or not
You really have no say.
Whatever road you must choose
It's in your D.N.A.

Never take anything for granted
Pause and take a breath.
Life is a gifted miracle
Before we're all united in death.

Contents

Chapter One

Listening to Childhood Stories

As a lad growing up with my family during the late fifties, early sixties, I was told a lot of stories about my ancestors by my parents, my grandparents, uncles and aunts as well as friends who visited now and again. They were great times back then, especially during the early sixties when I was growing up – there was so much for youngsters within the community to do in those days and we easily made our own fun and entertainment.

In 1960, fifteen years after World War II ended, the country was still getting back to normal and there was plenty of work to be had, many people regularly changed jobs – security didn't seem to be an issue. I remember that lots of people used to come round to our house and they would often sit and reminisce in one of the rooms or in the garden during the summer months while enjoying a cold drink. I didn't pay much attention to what they talked about; I wasn't really interested in what they had to say, playing was far more appealing to me! But if I made a comment, my father would often respond with, "When I was a lad," and would tell me snippets of information about his childhood – they had this or they didn't have that – he was part of a very large family and I didn't realise at the time how hard it had been for him as they had very little.

As I got older, I grew to love music and listened to the bands in the charts, often imagining myself playing with them. I also gradually started to ask my mother or father questions about the family (I have to admit this was often when it was time to get ready for bed so as to prolong my time before going upstairs to sleep). They recounted stories to me – some parts I'm sure must have been true, but I think as the tales were passed down from generation to generation, quite a bit of embellishment was added over the years. Even so, they made for very good listening and I guess a seed of interest was sown in me.

In the late sixties music was a big thing and my fascination with the bands grew and grew. I soaked up all the information that I could – I still remember to this day how high in the charts the popular bands got to. When I wasn't tuned into the radio I would often spend time with my father as he was repairing my bicycle or pottering around the garden, and he would tell me stories about his family and about what he remembered being told about World War I.

My mother came from Prussia, Germany and often talked about her family there when I watched her in the kitchen or helped her to bake cakes. I would watch her for ages baking these wonderful German delicacies and cooking her traditional food which I loved as a boy. She used to tell me stories of how her relatives had taught her to cook or about what life was like for her as a child growing up in Germany and the hardships they had suffered. But there were also stories of joy and of love – I took it all in and still remember them. I have included some of the stories in this book along with photographs.

One of the stories that my mother told me that I remember very vividly was about an incident during 1944 in Germany, before she knew my father and had come to England. She lived with her step-mother, who treated her harshly, and farmed her out to other people quite often and she grew used to fending for herself. When my mother was 28, and my sister was four, my mother once again had to find somewhere to live and ended up in a place called Bomblitz with a family called Ottens. She worked hard for her board and lodgings and ended up marrying their son – this was her first marriage. On one occasion, she was out walking and came across some German officers. They asked for her name and she replied, "Helene Eugenia Finger". This aroused the officers' suspicions because they classed the name Finger as being a Jewish name, so they took her to a holding within one of the camps. Obviously my mother was very scared and upset – she knew about the death camps and what went on inside them and had seen the thick black smoke coming out of the chimneys several times.

She was kept in the holding building all night despite her protests that she was born a German and had German parents. Eventually, as my mother pleaded, the officers decided to find her father and he was taken to the building where she was being held and was able to prove that she was in fact German. The name Finger is still thought to be of Jewish origin in many countries around the world, especially in America, which is where many families with the surname Finger ended up after the war. Although the family is recorded as Prussian and they came from Prussia, the name Finger could be of Jewish origin.

My father used to tell me about how large families were very common in those days and how many of the children would die because of disease, illness and poverty. A lot of his relatives came from Wordsley, Kingswinford and Dawley Brook in Staffordshire and as he got older, he had a longing to visit these places. It didn't mean much to me at the time – they were just names – I was only interested in listening to the stories that he told.

I couldn't have known that one day my interest in my family history would be so great that I would spend almost seven years researching it and building up my family tree, collecting information about my ancestors and enjoying the whirlwind journey that my research would take me on.

It was not an easy task! At the beginning, I thought I would just need to go to the local library or archive, look at a couple of documents or so, find everything I needed to know, and that would be that. How wrong I was!

That was about twenty years ago – my research and dedication only lasted a couple of days. I found a few names, but had no patience so gave up at the first hurdle when things started to get tricky. I thought no more about it until, in 2007, I went to a church that my nephew was redeveloping into apartments. He mentioned the family tree and asked me if I wanted to carry on with it and research some more. I really had no interest in it so I told him no.

However, a while later he brought up the subject again and, surprising myself, I decided to carry on. With my nephew's help I thought we may have a better chance of unearthing more information. I explained to him that there would be no point in doing it though unless we were both prepared to put the time in and do it properly. He agreed and I was happy with that.

We started the very next day and over the following couple of weeks I regularly went round to my nephew's house to compare and exchange the information that we had collected from the Internet. However, a few weeks later we were getting nowhere and I opted to go it alone. I realised that we wouldn't get very far just sitting in front of a computer screen and trawling through the Internet. I needed to get out and research properly. The Internet can help with some things, but it can also lead you on a tangent, as I found out to my cost. With my new enthusiasm to develop my family tree, I found many original records and documents that are so old they are virtually falling apart. Microfilm and microfiche was successfully used to find copies of other documents and information. This research has been the best thing that I have ever done in my life.

The Pargiter Coat of Arms

There are many ways to spell the name: Pargetter, Pargeter, Pargiter, Pargitor, Pargetaur. The surname, founded in England, is occupational in origin. In early times, names such as Baker or Butcher were given according to the occupation pursued, the bearer being recognised and referred to by their profession. After a time occupational names became hereditary even though the bearer no longer followed this trade or vocation. In the case of my surname, it comes from the word Pargeter, i.e. plasterer – one who coated castle walls. There is a typical example at Corfe Castle in Dorset. The interior walls of the castle were all plastered by Stephen the Pargeter. This tradition was recognised by many as an art, which it is, and Pargettering is known throughout the country if not the world. This artistic trade is still active today and the work can be seen all round the country especially in big country houses and town halls. Ornamental plastering is a specialty and some of the work is amazing, as I've seen myself. It's a remarkable skill that has to be learnt over many years.

Not everyone has a coat of arms; it is usually only seen with families who had power, wealth and respect. Fortunately our name does and at present, after lying dormant for a long time, the Pargeter coat of arms can be bought for a price. There are several versions of this coat of arms as it has been changed and developed over time; the one opposite is a drawing of a fine example.

THE PARGITER COAT OF ARMS

Key dates to look out for regarding parish records

Parish records from the start

The year 1538: Thomas Cromwell's injunction establishing the registration of baptisms, marriages, and burials.

The year 1598: Entries are now to be written into parchment registers and copied. These copies are known as Bishops' Transcripts and they are to be deposited with the diocesan Registrar.

The year 1653: Civil registration of births, marriages, and deaths during the commonwealth begins.

The year 1678: The Burial in Woollen Act, stating that corpses had to be buried in shrouds of pure wool only; this act was later repealed in the year 1814.

The year 1754: The Hardwick Marriage Act; this act was to prevent any secret marriages and introduced standardised marriage registers.

The year 1812: Rose's Act; this act introduced printed standardised registers for baptisms and burials.

The year 1837: Civil registration for all births, marriages and deaths stating more information than ever before; also, a new marriage register was issued.

Baptisms in most registers: Date of baptism, child's name (sometimes parents' names, father's occupation and date of birth).

Additionally from 1813: Parents' names, father's occupation (mother's if the child was illegitimate), abode (and sometimes the date of birth).

Burials: Date of burial, name of deceased (sometimes age, occupation); (in case of a child: names of parents); cause of death, marital status, biographical details.

Marriages: Most registers, all periods: Date of marriage, names of parties (sometimes whether the marriage was by license or banns), name of parish, also if one party was from another parish.

1754–1812: Additionally: Parish of both parties, whether the marriage was by license or banns, signatures or marks of the parties (usually marked with 'x'), also signatures or marks of the witnesses, the signature of the minister officiating. Sometimes it would also state whether the parties were a bachelor or spinster and whether the marriage was with the consent of the parents or guardians.

Additionally from 1837: Age (sometimes only 'Full' or 'Minor'), whether they were a bachelor or spinster, occupation of both parties, also names and occupation of fathers.

The Ancient Pargeters

Sulgrave Manor was the home of George Washington's ancestors, including his seven times grandson, Lawrence Washington, who married my great aunt Amy Pargitor. The house today is jointly owned by both English and Americans. The historians of America researched parts of this and today thousands of visitors come to Sulgrave Manor in Northamptonshire.

The history of the Pargiter family is very easy to trace back before the sixteenth century due to some research that was undertaken by the Americans. Robert Pargiter of Greatworth, or Gretworth, as it has been spelt in many ways over the centuries, was a very rich and important land owner. He was influential in the machinery of the government aristocracy and control in the Middle Ages.

The beautiful village of Greatworth still exists but sadly the Greatworth estate went into decline and was broken up for three main reasons. The first reason was that the Pargiters had the misfortune of choosing the losing side in the dispute of the state crown and government. This was disastrous for them and resulted in the family losing their power, influence and of course their wealth. The second reason for the break up of the estate was that there were several generations who failed to produce a male heir. The Pargiter name did not disappear but property went to female heirs and so the Pargiter association with the house at Greatworth was lost. The final reason was that the house burnt down in a disastrous fire in the year 1793 on Christmas Eve. I uncovered several stories about the fire during my research, both written sources and also from the many people that I spoke to, wealthy and well known people as well as normal families and even the poor.

Two of these stories really intrigued me and made me wonder which version was correct. In the Civil War of 1642 to 1647, the Pargiters' choice to support and fight on the side of the Royalists caused animosity with some very influential people and the hatred and anger remained for many years. An unexplained fire broke out at the house on the Greatworth estate, which spread rapidly, destroying room after room at frightening speed. Everything inside the house was lost, including family heirlooms and important papers and documents which would have charted the past history of the family and would have been a valuable resource to me in my research.

The other version of the story of the destruction of Greatworth House I somehow find rather less believable. It was said that the fire started in the kitchen as a result of some unattended cakes catching fire. I am unconvinced that, in such a grand house with so many people and staff working there, the kitchen would have been left whilst cooking was in progress. But, the story goes, the burning cakes alighted their surroundings and soon the fire became out of control and tore through the rest of the house, setting everything ablaze.

The only remaining clue in Greatworth today of the Pargiter history is the fact that one road is called Pargiter Close. Having never been to Greatworth I decided to go there and see it for myself. So one clear and bright Sunday in August 2009 I took my family and set off. It took about fifteen minutes on the A423 to reach the M40 motorway, then a further forty minutes to reach our exit. We first went to the beautiful village of Cropredy in Oxfordshire to find Saint Mary the Virgin church which I had discovered during my research had a connection with my family. Apparently on 1st May 1616 the wedding of John Pargitor and Alice Carpenter was held there – they are my ten times great grandparents. We found the church and walked around the grounds – I wasn't sure whether it was open to the public or not (not all are these days unfortunately), so I decided to go to the Rectory and talk to the vicar. It was just at the end of the road and a lady vicar answered my knock on the door. I asked if I could take my family inside the church and look around, and she was pleased to agree. I have since found and obtained the wedding certificate of John Pargitor and Alice Carpenter.

The vicar walked back to the church with us and told us about its history as we walked quietly around the interior. It had been built in the ninth century and very little had been altered in the years since. It is a beautiful church, with stunning stained glass windows and solid oak altar plinths and pews. I could sense and smell the age of the place and remarked upon the lectern to the vicar. It was fashioned in the shape of an eagle-like creature with a large eagle's head and lion's feet and is used to hold the Bible as it is being read during services. The vicar told us that the lectern dates back to the pre-reformation times and according to tradition it was hidden in the River Cherwell on the eve of the battle of Cropredy Bridge (1644) in case it was found by the Puritans. When the lectern was later recovered from the river, parts of it were badly discoloured and one of the three feet was missing, so a replacement foot had to be made before it was returned to the church. The original foot had been made of bronze, but unfortunately the replacement was cast in brass so doesn't quite match. Some lecterns are made of wood, even a rare few of stone, but this one was made from solid bronze. The beak of the eagle's head may have been used to collect Peters' Pence which was a tax paid to Rome. The coins had still been there when the lectern was recovered from the river, but they were then removed and the beak is now soldered up.

The thick stone-tiled floor of the church told of the many people who had walked on it over the years by the indents and uneven surface. As we walked towards the font I told the vicar about the marriage of John Pargitor and Alice Carpenter in May 1616 who probably lived not far from there at the time. In fact I know that John Pargitor came from Greatworth, just a couple of miles away, with his rich and powerful family. Greatworth is not actually in Oxfordshire, but in Northamptonshire.

I let myself get swallowed up in the tranquil atmosphere of the church as I imagined the wedding ceremony that had taken place there all those years ago. I tried to picture the clothes that they would have been wearing and the joy that they must have felt on that day, and here I was, today, in that very same place – I felt a shiver travel down my spine, almost as if I could feel their presence. It would be something to find out what hymns had been sung at their wedding. The churches of yesteryear are as beautiful as the day they were built and I believe that the new ones that are built today will not stand the test of time nor will they even get close to the beauty of the old ones.

I took my family for lunch in a pub and we then went to Sulgrave

Manor which is half way between Cropredy and Greatworth. I had discovered a connection between the Pargitors and a family called Washington, who had eventually ended up in America and are still there to this day, and I wanted to know the reason for the American interest in Sulgrave Manor and Greatworth.

Robert Pargitor of Greatworth bore a daughter whose name was Amy (or Amie, there are various spellings). Amy married Lawrence Washington, the son of John Washington and Margaret Kitson. The Washingtons, at the time, were another important family and were well known just like the Pargitors. We had gone to Sulgrave Manor because this was the Washington's ancestral family home and it still survives today. It's a beautiful place and is open to the public. Lawrence Washington's great grandson went to Brasenose College. He became the Reverend Lawrence Washington around 1634. Conditions became politically impossible for the Washington family and the Reverend's son John was forced to emigrate. He settled in Virginia, America, where his grandson Augustine Washington and Mary Ball had a son named George Washington. Many people believe that he was forced to go to America because he was a transatlantic trader, but there were rumours about a murder connected to the Washingtons and so some believe that this was the reason why John emigrated, although there are no records about a murder. The Washingtons were originally called Hertburn, taken from Hertburn in County Durham England where they lived and they retained this name until the 12th Century, about 1180. When the family moved to Washington, Northumberland, they changed their name to reflect this.

George became the first US President. He was seven generations directly descended from Amy Pargitor and Lawrence Washington, hence the reason why many Americans also visit Sulgrave Manor whenever it is open to the public. Catherine Kitson, a cousin of Amy Pargitor, married Sir John Spencer (of Badby, Northamptonshire) in 1486. Fourteen generations later, Lady Diana Spencer was born, so the next but one in line for the throne to be the King of England is distantly related to the Pargiter family – not directly but by marriage. The same Spencer family line also spawned Winston Spencer Churchill, thirteen generations directly down from Sir John Spencer. I discovered this from a family tree published in the Daily Telegraph on 18th September 2002. That means we are also related to none other than George W. Bush through the Spencers.

Chapter Two

The Washington Link

Ancient Pargiter Ancestry Down to George Washington
(Notice the 'o' in the surname has been replaced with an 'e'.)

Descendents of Richard Pargiter:

Generation No. 1

Child 1: Richard Pargiter, born 1460, died 1527. Richard Pargiter married Ann Coles in 1488. Ann Coles was born about 1470 in Preston, Northamptonshire. Parent of Ann Coles is Richard Coles, born about 1425 in Preston Northamptonshire, year of death unknown. I know the names of his parents and grandparents, but the documentation is proving hard to find even though I've tried and am still trying – it will lead me back to about 1360 or even earlier.

Generation No. 2

Child of Richard Pargiter and Ann Coles:

Child 1: Robert Pargiter was born about 1490 in Greatworth, Northamptonshire, and died on 31st January 1558. Robert Pargiter married Anne Knight, date of wedding unknown. Anne Knight was born in Charwelton, Northamptonshire, about 1482. Anne Pargiter (nee Knight) died in 1560. Anne's parents were John Knight and Ann Hely.

Children of Robert Pargiter and Anne Knight:

Child 1: William Pargiter, born about 1510 in Greatworth, Northamptonshire, and died on 6th July 1584.

Child 2: Antony Pargiter, born about 1512.

Child 3: Edward Pargiter, born about 1514.

Child 4: George Pargiter, born about 1516, died 1565.

Child 5: Ann Pargiter, born 1518, married John Blencoe.

Child 6: Mary Pargiter, born 1520, married William Mole.

Child 7: Cicely Pargiter, born 1522, married Edward Nanley.

Child 8: Amy (or Amie) Pargiter was born about 1524 in Greatworth, Northamptonshire and died on 7th October 1564. Amy's first marriage was to Master John Tomson, date unknown. Amy later married Lawrence Washington in about 1540 and was later to become a very wealthy widow. The seven times great- grandson of Lawrence Washington and Amy Pargiter was none other than George Washington who would become the first official President of the United States of America. Before George Washington, there were many Presidents as originally there were only going to be thirteen states (the actual countries were the 13 colonies, which are now states). Each of these Presidents would only be the President of one state. George, on the other hand, was the President of the whole of America which would eventually have fifty states and Washington DC.

The church below is the beautiful Parish Church of Saint Peter, situated in the lovely surroundings of Greatworth. Built in the 13th Century, with the bell tower not being added until 1300. Architect, H. R. Gough, rebuilt the chancel arch in 1882. In the last fifteen or so years Saint Peter's has undergone extensive restoration work inside and out, as repairs were badly needed.

ST PETERS CHURCH, GREATWORTH

The Washington Family Tree

Lawrence Washington was born in Northampton about 1500, the son of John Washington. Lawrence married Amy (Amie) Tomson (nee Pargiter), about1540/1544. They had eleven children together. Lawrence Washington died on 19th February 1584.

The list below shows a child from each generation directly related to George Washington.

Child 1: Robert Washington, born about 1540 in Sulgrave, Northampton. Robert married Elizabeth Light. Elizabeth Washington (nee Light) was born about 1540 in Radway, Warwickshire.

Child of Robert Washington and Elizabeth Light:
Lawrence Washington, born about 1568. Lawrence married Margaret Butler on 3rd August 1588 in Aston-le-Walls. Margaret Washington (nee Butler) was born about 1570 in Tighes, Sussex.

Child of Lawrence Washington and Margaret Butler:
Lawrence Washington, born about 1602. Lawrence married Amphyllis Twigden in 1633. Amphyllis was born about 1600. Lawrence was a church warden and he was educated at Brasenose College in Oxford.

Child of Lawrence Washington and Amphyllis Twigden:
John Washington, born about 1634 in Yorkshire. John married Ann Pope, date unknown. Ann Washington (nee Pope) was born about 1635. John Washington emigrated to America in 1657. Ann Pope was the second wife of John Washington and the couple lived in Virginia, America.

Child of John Washington and Ann Pope:
Lawrence Washington, born about 1659 in Bridges Creek, Virginia. Lawrence married Mildred Warner, date unknown. Mildred Washington (nee Warner) was born about1660 in Gloucester County.

Child of Lawrence Washington and Mildred Warner:
Augustine Washington, born about 1695 in Bridges Creek, Virginia. Augustine's first wife was Jane Butler and they married in 1715. Jane Washington (nee Butler) was born about 1700. Augustine's second wife was Mary Ball who he married in 1730. Mary Washington (nee Ball) was born about 1700 in Leicester County, Virginia.

Child of Augustine Washington and Mary Ball:
George Washington, born on 11th February 1732 in Bridges Creek, Virginia, died on 14th December 1799 in Mount Vernon. George married Martha Dandridge in 1759. Martha Washington (nee Dandridge) was born about 1732 in New Kent County and died on 22nd June 1802, and the rest is history!

Going back this far in time is hard work but not as hard as going forward to find relatives. It took me on a roller coaster ride up and down half of the country but I loved every minute of it. Paperwork for individuals and families can be easy to find if you know where to look as parish records can go back as far as 1538 and in some cases even further than that. However, some records and paperwork no longer exist and this can be a nightmare to prove your connection to your family tree. But I never gave up and have found nearly all the connections which lead me right back to 1360, and I intend to go back even further if I can. The Internet is great for research and can save you many hours of footwork, but don't be fooled by this – researching a family tree online can very easily take you in the wrong direction. Names and dates have to be checked and double checked to ensure that the correct information is documented.

Generation No. 3

William Pargiter was born about 1510 in Greatworth, Northamptonshire, and died on 6th July 1584. William married Agnes Light in 1550. Agnes Pargiter (nee Light) was born about 1532 in Horley, date of death unknown. Agnes' parents were Christopher Light, born about 1500 in Oxfordshire, died on 9th October 1546, and Elizabeth Warde, born about 1504 in Pillarton, Warwickshire, date of death unknown. Christopher Light's father was Thomas Light. Parents of Elizabeth Warde were Henry Warde and Ann Bishop.

Children of Christopher Light and Elizabeth Warde:

Child 1: Richard Light.

Child 2: Thomas Light.

Child 3: Sir Walter Light of Radway, born about 1520, died 22nd April 1597.

Child 4: Christopher Light, born about 1528. Christopher married Elizabeth Dale about 1546.

Child 5: Johanne Light, born about 1530. Johanne married Henry Savage about 1548. Her second marriage was to John Harford about 1548–1550.

Child 6: Agnes Light, born about 1532. Agnes married William Pargiter about 1550.

Children of William Pargiter and Agnes Light:

Child 1: Robert Pargiter, born about 1551 in Greatworth, Northamptonshire, died in 1595.

Child 2: Ursula Pargiter, born in 1552 in Greatworth, Northamptonshire.

Child 3: Christopher Pargiter, born in Greatworth, Northamptonshire.

Child 4: Susan Pargiter, born in Greatworth, Northamptonshire.

Generation No. 4

Robert Pargiter, born about 1551 in Greatworth, Northamptonshire, died in 1595. Robert married Margaret Samwell on 29th May 1574. Margaret Samwell was born about 1553 in Upton, Northamptonshire, and died in 1594. Margaret's parents were Francis Samwell and Mary Bill or Anne Spencer.

Children of Robert Pargiter and Margaret Samwell:

Child 1: William Pargiter, born about 1577 in Greatworth, Northamptonshire, died in 1661. William married Abigail Willoughby in 1601 in Brington. Abigail was born about 1576 in Wollaton, Nottingham, and died on 12th October 1654 at Wormleighton. Abigail's great-grandmother, Elizabeth Talbot, was the great- granddaughter of John of Gaunt. John was the son of King Edward III.

Child 2: Walter Pargiter, born in 1579 in Greatworth, Northamptonshire.

Child 3: Francis Pargiter, born in 1580 in Greatworth, Northamptonshire.

Child 4: John Pargiter, born in 1582 in Greatworth, Northamptonshire.

Child 5: Dorothy Pargiter, born in 1584 in Greatworth, Northamptonshire.

Child 6: Ann Pargiter, born in 1587 in Greatworth, Northamptonshire.

Child 7: George Pargiter, born in 1592 in Greatworth, Northamptonshire.

Generation No. 5

As the baptism records of the children below cannot be found, I was lucky enough to find and obtain Alice Pargiter's will to connect this generation.

John Pargiter was born in 1582 in Greatworth, Northamptonshire, date of death unknown. John married Alice Carpenter on 1st May 1616 in Cropredy at the Virgin of Saint Mary's church. Alice Pargiter (nee Carpenter), date of birth unknown, died in 1658 in Worcester.

Children of John Pargiter and Alice Carpenter:

Child 1: John Pargiter, born about 1625, died on 11th January 1675

Child 2: Richard Pargiter, born about 1627, date of death unknown

Child 3: William Pargiter, born about 1629, date of death unknown.

Child 4: Elizabeth Pargiter, born about 1631, date of death unknown.

Chapter Three
The Staffordshire Families

Generation No. 6

John Pargiter, born about 1625, whereabouts unknown, died on
11th January 1675, is buried at St Giles Church, near Dudley, West
Midlands. John married Elizabeth, surname unknown, about 1650.
Elizabeth was born in 1629, whereabouts unknown, and died on
5th March 1694, aged 65. John Pargiter was a silk stocking maker in
Spitalfields, London. I discovered that John and Elizabeth travelled
from Rowley Regis to London and then back again where they eventually
settled after having worked in many different parts of the country.

Children of John and Elizabeth Pargiter:
Child 1: William Pargiter, born about 1653, died before 7th September
1718. William married Ann Shirt on 24th July 1707 in St Thomas
Church, Dudley. Ann Pargiter (nee Shirt) died on 10th December
1725 and is buried at St Thomas Church, Dudley.

Overleaf is a photograph of St Thomas Church, Dudley. This
church replaced a previous church in 1815 by order of the vicar at the
time, Dr Luke Booker. St Thomas's was built between 1815 and 1818
in the gothic style and was designed by William C. Brook. It was one
of the first buildings in the world to use cast iron and timber in the
construction of its rafters. The stone used to build the church was at
first very pale grey in colour but it darkened over the years due to the
pollution within the Black Country. However, the church was restored
in the 1990s and the stonework was cleaned, bringing it back to its
former glory. The top of the spire was also rebuilt. The spire is 175
feet high and is a familiar landmark all around the community; it is
known locally as 'Top Church'.

ST THOMAS CHURCH, DUDLEY.

Child 2: Richard Pargiter, born in baptism[1] on 7th December 1655, died before 28th February 1729, buried at St Giles Church, Rowley Regis. Richard married Margaret Hawksford on 28th April 1678 in St Giles Church, Rowley Regis. Margaret Pargiter (nee Hawksford) died before 6th August 1726.

Opposite is a drawing of St Giles Church which is located at Hanover Street in Rowley Regis. The earliest church that stood on this site was just called Rowley Church and this was in the reign of King John (1199–1216). There were other churches built on the same site over the centuries. In 1800, it was documented by Curate George Barrs in his journal that when it rained the church roof leaked so badly that the floor turned to mud. Eventually a new church was built in 1840, but it was to be short lived because by 1894 there were major

---

1 'Born in baptism' was a phrase used in records prior to 1st July 1837 when the actual date of birth was not recorded. Baptism was usually performed very soon after birth.

subsidence problems due to mining and the church was condemned in 1900. The construction of the next church on the site began in 1904 and was completed in 1907, only to be burned down on 18th July 1913 by suffragettes campaigning for the vote. Apparently a lot of records were destroyed too, including birth, marriage and death records along with irreplaceable items of the church. There are photographs of the devastated church taken the morning after the fire. Luckily a lot of records would have been copied according to the practices of the time – these were called Bishops' Transcripts and they would have been kept, or should have been, at a different church in case something like this did happen. The current St Giles Church was built in 1923 and because it is 700 feet above sea level with breathtaking views all around they say that on a good day you can see the Black Mountains in Wales.

Child 3: Elizabeth Pargiter, born about 1656 in Rowley Regis. Elizabeth married Thomas Broun on 18th April 1672 in St Giles Church, Rowley Regis. Thomas was born in Kingswinford.

Child 4: John Pargiter, born in baptism on 10th December 1657, at St Dunstan's Church Spitalfields, Stepney, London. John married Sara Waylesby on 16th September 1679 in St Stephen's Church, Hatton, Lincolnshire.

ST GILES CHURCH, ROWLEY REGIS.

ST DUNSTAN'S CHURCH, STEPNEY.

Above is an image of St Dunstan's Church, Stepney, London, around the 1800s. I've never been to the church, but I hope to one day – to think that one of my great, great grandfathers was baptised there in 1657! I did some research into methods of transport at that time – I assumed that people probably didn't travel very much back then and would stay in one place. But I was wrong, people travelled all over the country looking for work to feed their families or they would starve. If they had some money, they would travel by horse and cart, but if not, they walked. Sometimes people travelled by ship to the nearest port. There were no canals until the mid to late 18th Century; the first was built about 1757 and ran from St Helens Coalfield to the River Mersey – it was used to supply the coal for Liverpool. Also the tradition was that when a man got married, they would hold the wedding in the bride's city however far away it was. Some people still follow this tradition today, but sadly very few. St Dunstan's Church sits in eight acres of grounds. At the time of the plague, in one year a total of 6,583 people died, 154 being buried in just one day in September 1665. The church now standing on the site was built in the 15th Century, the chancel, however, dates back two hundred years earlier to the 13th Century. In AD 952, the first wooden church was replaced by the second one which was constructed in stone.

Generation No. 7

John Pargiter was born in baptism on 10th December 1657 in Spitalfields, London. John married Sara Waylesby on 16th September 1679 in St Stephen's Church, Hatton in Lincolnshire. Sara was born about 1657 and died before 20th June 1700. John Pargiter's second marriage was to Mary Homer on 1st September 1703 in Oldswinford. John died on 5th October 1712 at the age of 55.

Below is an image of St Stephen's Church in Hatton, Lincolnshire.

ST STEVENS CHURCH, HATTON.

This old medieval church was replaced by a new one in 1870. The architect, James Fowler (born 1828, died 1892), designed the church and many more like it. He used bricks for the construction and revived their use as a construction material. I have seen a photograph of this church and it is truly a beautiful design. The walls are of red brick, probably mined locally, and show thick bands of green sandstone. Some of the bricks were most likely salvaged from the original church and are now in a pretty bad state of repair, but there are no original bricks remaining to replace the damaged ones.

From medieval times, many churches were used as court rooms, the heavy doors locked while the proceedings took place. Stories tell of the barbaric way in which a person's fate was decided when they were taken into a church to face a judge and a court, even for crimes such as stealing a sheep to feed their family. A large pot would be filled with boiling water or hot oil and a stone placed at the bottom of the pot. The accused then had to put their arm into the pot and retrieve the stone. If the person's arm, when pulled clear from the pot, had suffered no damage, he was deemed to be innocent. Not much chance of that! One man is reputed to have put his arm into the pot and when he brought it out, the skin all the way up his arm was melting away and because of this he was found guilty and he would have then been sentenced, if he hadn't died in the meantime of course. Stealing or rustling sheep was a hanging offence. Incidents such as this have been documented from church court rooms many years ago. People will find it hard to believe that such things went on within the walls of a church, but it is true.

Children of John Pargiter and Sara Waylesby:

Child 1: Thomas Pargiter, born before 1st December 1679, died before 2nd June 1680.

Child 2: Sara Pargiter, born before 11th June 1681, date of death unknown.

Child 3: Mary Pargiter, born before 19th February 1686, baptised in St Giles Church, Rowley Regis. Mary married Edward Harris on 10th February 1715 in the same church.

Child 4: John Pargiter, born before 8th July 1689 in Rowley Regis, died before 2nd February 1758, buried at St Mary's Church, Kingswinford, Staffordshire.

Child 5: Jane Pargiter, born about 6th March 1693 in Rowley Regis, died before 15th June 1715, buried at St Giles Church, Rowley Regis. I have a copy of her will.

Generation No. 8

John Pargiter, born in baptism about 8th July 1689 in Rowley Regis, died before 2nd February 1758. John married Ann Philips on 4th July 1723 in Stone, Worcestershire. Ann was born about 1692 to 1694, location unknown, but probably Stone, Worcestershire. Ann Pargiter (nee Philips) died on 5th January 1772 in Kingswinford, Staffordshire.

OLD STONE CHURCH WORCESTERSHIRE.

Above is a photograph of an original pencil drawing, dated 1795, of the old church at Stone in Worcestershire. According to the Worcestershire archives, there are no pictures of the old church, but after three years, I eventually tracked this one down. The church was built in 1269 and had a thatched roof. It burnt down in early 1830 and work on the new church started straight away in the same place and was completed in 1831.

Apparently historians can spend a lot of time and money trying to track down pictures such as this for their records and often fail – luckily I was successful with this.

Children of John Pargiter and Ann Philips:

Child 1: Richard Pargiter, born before 8th March 1723, baptised in St Thomas's Church, Dudley, died before 13th June 1750, buried at the same church. Richard married Sarah Nicklin on 5th November 1744 in St Thomas's Church, Dudley. Sarah Pargiter (nee Nicklin) was born on 21st August 1726 in Dudley, date of death unknown. Sarah's father's name was William Nicklin and her mother's name was Ann Nicklin (nee Troman).

Child 2: Mary Pargiter, born before 18th September 1726, baptised in St Thomas's Church, Dudley, died on 31st December 1757 in Kingswinford at 31 years of age. Mary married John Pearson on 14th June 1749 in Holy Trinity Church, Wordsley. John Pearson was born on 9th March 1719 and baptised on 11th March 1719 at Oldswinford, Worcestershire. He died on 16th February 1767 at 48 years of age and was buried at Holy Trinity Church, Wordsley. John's father was Joseph Pearson and his mother was Sarah, maiden name unknown.

Child 3: Hannah Pargiter, born before 31st May 1730, baptised in St Thomas's Church, Dudley, died on 1st March 1763, aged 32. Hannah married Thomas Westwood on 27th March 1758 in Holy Trinity Church, Wordsley.

Child 4: Sarah Pargiter, born before 14th January 1732, baptised in St Thomas's Church, Dudley, died 12th September 1793, aged 61. Sarah married Francis Westwood on 27th March 1758 in Holy Trinity Church, Wordsley. Francis Westwood was born about 1728 in Dudley.

Note that Hannah and Sarah were married on the same day at the same church.

Opposite is a photograph of Holy Trinity Church in Wordsley. There is a painting of the interior of the church, painted in oil colours by Martha Alice Richardson about 1900. Martha was the granddaughter of Benjamin Richardson and the great niece of William Haden Richardson, the glass pioneers. I have visited this church several times, but have been unable to go inside to see the stunning interior – the door has been locked on each occasion and the vicar unavailable. Many relatives of mine are laid to rest in the graveyard at Holy Trinity, some graves are marked with a headstone, but sadly some are not. On one occasion when I was walking around the graveyard searching for my relatives' graves, it was snowing; the snow lay on the ground as it had been coming down for quite a while before I got there – everywhere was so quiet and peaceful – and I managed to locate many graves that I was looking for despite the cold.

Child 5: Philip Pargiter, born before 26th June 1735, baptised in St Thomas's Church, Dudley, died before 21st March 1824 in Stourbridge, buried at St Michael's, Brierley Hill. Philip married Mary Westwood on 4th January 1758 in Holy Trinity Church, Wordsley. Witnesses at the wedding were Edward Allchurch and John Scriven. Mary was born about 1734, died before 4th October 1769 and is buried at St Michael's, Brierley Hill.

HOLY TRINITY CHURCH, WORDSLEY.

Below is a drawing of St Michael's Church, Brierley Hill and it really is up high on a hill. Brierley Hill is where the town derives the name from. St Michael's Church is of red brick and was consecrated on 29th September 1765 during the reign of King George III. The first minister there was the Rev Thomas Moss who also wrote poetry. One of his books, The Beggar's Petition, was to become well known as it was used by Charles Dickens in the classic novel Nicholas Nickleby. I visited St Michael's on the same snowy day that I went to Holy Trinity Church. Looking at the photograph of St Michael's Church below it reminds me exactly how it was on that day – very cold yet very clear and bright. At the top of the hill, I stood and gazed at the incredible view stretching out around me. My great uncle John Pargiter lies here, at peace within the grounds with other relatives.

The Church after the alterations in 1837.

ST MICHAEL'S CHURCH, BRIERLEY HILL.

Philip Pargiter also married another Mary Westwood, who was possibly a cousin of his first wife, on 16th April 1770 in Holy Trinity Church, Wordsley. Witnesses at the wedding were William Brettel and William Hunt. Mary was born about 1733, died before 7th January 1774, and is buried at St Michael's, Brierley Hill.

Philip Pargiter's third marriage was to Ann Nash, born about 1730. The wedding took place on 13th December 1776 in Holy Trinity, Wordsley. Witnesses at the wedding were William Brettel and William Hunt. Ann Pargiter (nee Nash) died before 5th August 1810 and is buried at St Michael's Church, Brierley Hill.

Child 6: John Pargiter, born before 27th November 1737, baptised in St Thomas's, Dudley, died on 27th July 1796 in Kingswinford. John married Mary Baker on 24th February 1754 in St Mary's Church, Kingswinford.

Child 7: Thomas Pargiter, born before 2nd June 1742, baptised in St Thomas's, Dudley, died before 20th June 1802, buried at St Michael's, Brierley Hill. Thomas married another Mary Westwood on 27th October 1762 in Holy Trinity, Wordsley. Witnesses at the wedding were John Partridger (Thomas's brother) and William Hunt. Mary was born about 1745, died before 19th January 1785 and is buried at St Michael's, Brierley Hill.

Notice how Thomas's brother John's name is spelt. The vicar at the time of a baptism, wedding or death would just write down the name as it was pronounced to him. Thus misspellings were a common occurrence as many people were illiterate.

Generation No. 9

John Pargiter, born before 27th November 1737, died 27th July 1796. John married Mary Baker on 24th February 1754. Mary was born before 29th December 1727 and was baptised at Holy Trinity Church, Wordsley. Mary Pargiter (nee Baker) died on 28th November 1805 and is buried at Saint Mary's Church, Kingswinford.

Overleaf is a photograph of Saint Mary's Church which is located in Kingswinford. This church dates back to the 12th Century, about 1150, and is still in good condition today. The crypt however can be dated back even further to Saxon times. There is about a thousand years' of history on the site of Saint Mary's Church. Some of the basement rooms are blocked, apparently 'filled in', possibly due to subsidence. Many of my relatives were buried here over the centuries, and I have documentation to show the family baptisms and weddings as well. Churches around the country were built on the highest point of a hill to show power and authority and to be easily seen and the graves at Saint Mary's go right down to the bottom of the hill – I would think they cover about four acres in total.

ST MARY'S CHURCH, KINGSWINFORD.

Children of John Pargiter and Mary Baker:

Child 1: Sarah Pargiter, born before 15th January 1755, baptised at Holy Trinity Church, died 1774. Sarah married John Peaton on 20th November 1774 at Holy Trinity Church, Wordsley. Witnesses at the wedding were Joseph Pargiter and William Hunt. Date of birth and death of John Peaton unknown.

Child 2: Thomas Pargiter Westwood, born before 9th October 1757, baptised at Holy Trinity, Wordsley, date of death unknown. Thomas married Sarah Smith on 22nd March 1776 in Brierley Hill.

Child 3: Ruth Pargiter, born before 18th March 1759, baptised at Holy Trinity Church, Wordsley, died on 29th October 1794, aged 35. Ruth married William Wood on 5th July 1778 at Holy Trinity, Wordsley. Witnesses at the wedding were Joseph Pargiter and Samuel Peaton. Date of birth and death of William Wood unknown.

Child 4: Mary Pargiter, born before 8th November 1761 and baptised at Holy Trinity, Wordsley. Date of death unknown. Mary married Charles Sowter on 18th June 1785 at St Mary's Church, Oldswinford, Stourbridge.

Child 5: Thomas Pargiter, born before 15th July 1764, baptised in Holy Trinity Church, Wordsley, died on 31st December 1819 and buried at Holy Trinity Church, Wordsley.

Child 6: Phillis Pargiter, born before 7th December 1766, baptised at Holy Trinity Church, Wordsley, died before 24th January 1768 and buried at Holy Trinity Church, Wordsley.

Child 7: Elizabeth Pargiter, born before 25th December 1774, baptised in Saint Michael's Church, Brierley Hill, Worcestershire. Elizabeth married Edward Beddard on 18th March 1896 in Wombourne, Staffordshire.

Chapter Four

Kingswinford, Dawley Brook and Wordsley

Generation No. 10

Thomas Pargiter, born before 15th July 1764, baptised at Holy Trinity Church, Wordsley, died on 31st December 1819 at the age of 55. Thomas married Ann Bullas on 23rd July 1786 at Holy Trinity Church, Wordsley. Ann Bullas was born before 6th May 1759, baptised at Holy Trinity Church, Wordsley. She died on 5th February 1806 and is buried in Wordsley. The name Bullas is derived from Bullhouse, signifying people who looked after bulls.

Children of Thomas Pargiter and Ann Bullas:

Child 1: Phillis Pargiter, born before 21st September 1788 and baptised at Saint Michael's Church, Brierley Hill, Worcestershire. Phillis married William Pearson on 8th April 1806 at Holy Trinity Church, Wordsley. Witnesses at the wedding were Elizabeth Seager and Ben Bullas. Phillis Pearson (nee Pargiter) died on 28th October 1817 at only 29 years of age.

Child 2: John Pargiter, born before 3rd January 1790, baptised at Saint Michael's Church, Brierley Hill, Worcestershire. Died on 31st March 1833 at 43 years of age and is buried at Brockmoor Holy Trinity Church, Wordsley.

Child 3: Philip Pargiter, born before 4th November 1792 and baptised at Saint Michael's Church, Brierley Hill. Philip died on 31st May 1851 aged 58 in Townsend, Kingswinford. He was buried on 5th June 1851 at Holy Trinity Church, Wordsley. Philip married Susannah Richardson on 3rd January 1814 at Saint Thomas's Church, Dudley.

Child 4: Richard Pargiter, born before 17th January 1796, baptised at Saint Michael's Church, Brierley Hill, Worcestershire. He died in 1799 at just three years old.

Child 5: Mary Pargiter, born before 12th November 1797, baptised at Saint Michael's Church, Brierley Hill, Worcestershire. She died before 2nd January 1802 and is buried at Holy Trinity Church, Wordsley. Mary was just four years old.

Child 6: Sarah Pargiter, born before 27th October 1800, baptised at Saint Michael's Church, Brierley Hill, Worcestershire, died on 30th April 1883. Sarah married Edwin Cook on 24th December 1818 at Saint Thomas's Church, Dudley. Witnesses at the wedding were Samuel Cook and L. Paskin. Edwin was baptised on 28th July 1801 at Saint Mary's Church, Kidderminster, Worcestershire, date of death unknown. Edwin's father was William Cook and his mother was named Sarah, maiden name unknown.

Child 7: Richard Pargiter, born before 8th June 1803, baptised at Saint Michael's Church, Brierley Hill, Worcestershire, died before 2nd March 1806 and is buried at Holy Trinity Church, Wordsley.

The spelling of Pargiter was to change in the next generation.

History of Wordsley and Kingswinford

Wordsley is located not far from Dawley brook and Kingswinford and all of them are located within a few miles from each other and are easy to get to. Wordsley is full of history and it has a long-distance foot path which runs for a distance of 610 miles. The path, or part of it, is apparently loosely based on an escape route of the future king Charles 11 during the English civil war. It is said that Charles stopped at a house in the area which was on the corner of Kinver Street by the main Stourbridge Road in Wordsley, during the night following the battle of Worcester which was on 3rd September 1651. He then took bread and beer for himself along with a group of about 50-60 cavaliers. Also in Wordsley the glass-work industry was operational from as far back as 1776 till the 1930s.Wordsley had its very own workhouse there which opened in about 1903 and it was fully operational in 1907. It became a military hospital in World War I and was still used in World War II. Eventually, in 1945, it became a civilian hospital. As the years went by many extensions of different kinds were added on to the buildings in and around the grounds and the final extension came in 1988 when by that time it had a state-of-the-art maternity unit. It closed in 2005 with all the service's being transferred to Russell's Hall in Dudley. Most of the buildings were demolished in about 2007 to make way for much-needed housing within the area due to the increase of the population. Part of the hospital, the chapel and the workhouse, was kept and. I've been past the Wordsley Workhouse a couple of times when I've been on my travels either grave hunting, visiting churches or collecting information on my family tree and a few members of my relatives who are mentioned in the book spent time living and dying there along with their children and I bet that place could tell a few stories from within.

Kingswinford, originally known as Swinford Regis, also has a great history to it and records on the area go back to the Doomsday Book. Its name is derived from a Ford for the king's swine making it 'Kingswinford' but without the letter 'e'. One of the most historic things to come out of Kingswinford is the historic connection to the Gunpowder plot on 5th November 1605. Near Kingswinford town, formally Kingswinford village, there is a place called Holbeche House or Holbeach House. This is a large mansion located about one-mile north of Kingswinford which was originally in the Staffordshire area but is now in the parish of Dudley. Some of the main protagonists associated with the Gunpowder Plot were either killed or captured at Holbeche House. The final end came for them on the 8th November 1605 a couple of days after the failed plot to blow up the Houses of Parliament which eventually saw a victory for the government. Four of the conspirators were killed on that day including their leader, Robert Catesby [1572-1605]. Within the house walls you can still see the bullet holes but exactly where it all happened all them years ago unfortunately is not open to the public which is a shame as this is great history and I'm sure it would attract a lot of people from all over the world. There are many houses within the community of Kingswinford where lots were built there in the 70s. Some of the streets are named after the gunpowder conspirators who were killed or captured on 8th November

1605: Catesby Drive named after [Robert Catesby], Digby Road named after [Sir Edward Digby], Keyes Drive named after [Robert Keyes], Tresham Road named after [Francis Tresham], Ambrose Crescent named after [Ambrose Rokeham], Rokeham Close named after the same person, Monteagle Drive named after [Lord Monteagle-William Parker]. I wonder if people know about that?

There has been a lot of housing development over the decades in Kingswinford, especially during the 50s and 60s, and the original beauty of the area has been destroyed with time and the only good thing it brought with it was an enormous amount of wealth into the area. I've been to Kingswinford several times over the years and, like so many other areas, it has seen better days. It started declining in the late 1980s and early 1990s and although a lot of people attribute this to the opening of the Merry Hill Shopping Centre, which is partially true, how we live and our attitude along with the internet have a lot to do with it. Another place within Kingswinford is a place called Townsend which dates back to the 19th century. Townsend was centered on the seat of the Bradley family from the 17th century right up to the early 20th century. John Bradley of Townsend [1678-1768] was an ancestor of John Bradley FRCS and John Haden Bradley the centenarian educator and founder of the Bedales school. In 2001 the population of Kingswinford was 25,808. Looking for old documentation is great and to date I have looked at and researched around 400,000 documents including parish records, wills, census, and much more.

Chapter Five
Finding Old Photographs

Generation No. 11

Philip Pargeter, born before 4th November 1792 in Wordsley, baptised at Saint Michael's Church, Brierley Hill, died on 31st May 1851, aged 58, in Townsend Kingswinford, buried on 5th June 1851 at Holy Trinity Church, Wordsley. Philip married Susannah Richardson on 3rd January 1814 at Saint Thomas's Church, Dudley. Witnesses at the wedding were John Walton and Mark Bond. Susannah Richardson was born before 3rd April 1794 in Kingswinford. She died on 18th December 1868, aged 74, and was buried on 24th December 1868. Susannah was the daughter of Joseph Richardson and Martha Haden. Philip Pargeter was a boatman on the canals and then later he became a stock taker. Notice how the name is spelt in a different way again, this time the 'i' has been replaced with an 'e', whereas before the 'o' was replaced with an 'e'. This fluctuates up and down the centuries.

Children of Philip Pargeter and Susannah Richardson:

Child 1: Thomas Pargeter, born before 15th January 1815 in Wordsley, baptised at Holy Trinity Church, Wordsley, died on 23rd November 1867 at Norfolk Street, Sheldon, Stoke-on-Trent at 52 years of age. Thomas married Mary Anne Beddard on 31st March 1834 in Wombourne, Staffordshire. Witnesses at the wedding were Edward Beddard and Hannah Capewell. Thomas was a manager at the glassworks. Mary Anne Beddard was baptised on 6th December 1812 at Holy Trinity church, Wordsley, died in 1888 in Dudley. Mary's father was Edward Beddard and her mother was called Mary, maiden name Cooper. Edward Beddard was a Clerk.

The 1841 Census:

Wordsley

Thomas Pargeter – Head, age 25, Kingswinford

Mary Pargeter – Wife, age 25, Kingswinford

Ann Pargeter – Daughter, age 2, Kingswinford

The 1851 Census:

Wordsley Wall Heath Village

Thomas Pargeter – Head, age 36, Foreman – Glassworks, Kingswinford, Staffordshire

Mary Pargeter – Wife, age 35, Kingswinford

Ann Maria Pargeter – Daughter, age 11, Scholar

Joseph Pargeter – Son, age 8, Scholar

The 1861 Census:

22 Norfolk Street, Shelton, Stoke-on-Trent

Thomas Pargeter – Head, age 46, Manager – Glassworks, Kingswinford, Staffordshire

Mary Pargeter – Wife, age 45, Kingswinford

Joseph Pargeter – Son, age 18, Warehouseman, Kingswinford

Richard Evans – Nephew (Son of Susannah, Thomas's sister), age 11, Scholar, Kingswinford

Living next door was Ann Maria Pedley (nee Pargeter) and her husband, George Pedley

The two letters that follow were sent between Agnes Pedley and her sister Mary Anna Sarah Pedley who lived in New Jersey USA. Agnes and Mary Anna were the children of Ann Maria Pedley, wife of George Pedley. Ann Maria Pedley (nee Pargeter) was the daughter of Thomas Pargeter and Mary Beddard.

Letter 1 reads:

No. 6 Havelock St
Jan 29th [1893]

My Dear Sister

We were so glad to get your letter it seemed such a long time since we had one. I am very glad indeed to know you are getting about again and hope you will soon get strong again and the baby too. I received the order at the same time as your letter. Thank you very much for it, it is very good of you, only I'm afraid you can't spare it very well. What a funny card you sent, thank you. Things seem very dull where you live, your bonnet was dear. I got a hat this winter, black straw with a brim trimmed with black and scarlet velvet and two quills. It cost about five shillings and five pence, the black velvet was two shillings and three pence a yard and the scarlet four shillings and three pence a yard and I thought that was too much. Grandma is very poorly and has gone very little and sunk. We have not heard anything about her pictures, she refuses to sit again. I'm very sorry we should all like one. I should like to have mine taken but Grandma grumbles so I can't do a bit as I want. We have had a very bad winter, snow and frost and now it's raining very hard. Grandma has got a new pair of boots and goes clumping about to let us know they are new. Aunt Polly is still at Gorsty Hill with Cissie. I do not know what to make of Uncle William, he keeps on at Harpsfield, with Clara there it is a strange tale about him and some woman, it is a pity he should do so. It puts Grandma about very much. It is Grandma's birthday on Thursday, she is 78. Aunt Polly's given her a new cap. Cissie sent word you must name the baby Eulalie Inez. Dorothy is a very nice name, only do not call her Dolly. It is my second favourite. George is not jealous is he yet? I had my purse stolen last night, there was a stamp for this letter and a penny stamp and some coppers and the key to that box that was Mother's, not much altogether but more than I could lose. You will see by the paper there has been a fancy dress ball at Hanley. Frank went as Charles II, Jimmie as Minnie Palmer and Jimmie's sweetheart as a troubadour. It was a grand success. Frank has lost all his money in his photographer's failure, he is a regular swell. Trade is very bad all about here. I've not heard anything of Mother since Christmas, I've not much time. Fanny is getting to be a nice big girl, you would hardly know Uncle Theophilus, he is such a little old man. Grandma sends her love to you and hopes you will be better soon. Aunt Emma is doing very well and Aunt Lizzie very badly; there does not seem much news this time. Give my love to Georgie and Jim and the baby and accept the same yourself from your loving sister Agnes.

How do you get your letters? Are the houses numbered, does the postman bring them or do you have to fetch them?

Letter 2 reads:

35 James Street
March 31st [1897]

My Dear Sister

I dare say you will be wondering how I am going on. I am very thankful to be able to say I am better and can get about and go out. I had a dreadful time, was ill two days before baby was born and then the doctor used his instruments twice and afterwards I flooded. I thought it would be bad but I'd no idea anything could be as bad as it was. There was no one with me but the doctor and the nurse. I would have been so glad if you would have been here. But I was looked after. He is a very clever doctor and the nurse I could not tell you how good she was and kind and then my dear husband waited on me night and day when he was in and made me all sorts of drinks. (I was kept on a low diet.) He was always ready to get up and do all he could for me. I dare say you will be surprised when I tell you I had not any milk. I was disappointed so baby has to have the bottle. He looks a boy all over and is a proper Pedley. He is very much like Uncle Harry. He is rather cross. We had him baptised last week. Mr Derrick and Will were godfathers and Fanny was godmother and we called him Eric George. Do you like it? It is my choice. Mr Derrick bought him a little printed frock and Fanny and Daisy a hat and veil and a pair of wool toots and Fanny has knit him two pair of socks. She thinks a lot of him and fusses over him like an old woman.

Following on are some old photographs of my relatives – note the style of clothing that they wore. The photographs are in remarkably good condition considering their age. Below is my great aunt, Mary Ann Sarah Pedley. The one on the top right is my other great aunt, Agnes Pedley, and below is a family photo of, from left to right, second wife Margaret Ada Pratt with her step-daughter, Mary Ann Sarah Pedley, her husband, George Pedley and their other daughter Agnes Pedley. These are all great photographs and I'm proud to have them in my collection especially as it was not easy to get them. I'm not certain of the year, but from looking at the census and a little bit of detective work, I think they are probably late 1880s or very early 1890s. You can see by the clothes that they are wearing and the furniture in their house that they were fairly well off and were living a comfortable life. Having said that, there were many families that I came across during my research that had money, but at the end of their lives they had nothing to show for it and in some cases they died in the workhouse.

MARY ANN SARAH PEDLEY.

AGNES PEDLEY.

MARGARET ADA PRATT, MARY ANN SARAH
PEDLEY AND GEORGE PEDLEY.

Below is a newspaper article about Joseph Pargeter. Joseph was the son of Thomas Pargeter and Mary Beddard and the uncle of the sisters shown above.

Birmingham Daily Post, Tuesday January 18th 1876
Sad Death through Drink

Yesterday afternoon Mr Hawks [borough coroner] held an inquest at the Duke of York Inn, Duke Street, on the body of Joseph Pargeter, aged thirty five, who died early on Sunday morning last, in a cell at the Duke Street Police Station. Superintendent Sheppard of the 3rd Division was present on behalf of the police. From the statement of Mr James Pargeter, the deceased's cousin, and Police Constable Moseley, it appears that the deceased was well educated and very

respectably connected. His father, who was manager of a large glassworks, died some five or six years ago, and since that time the deceased had gradually fallen in the social scale. What money his father had left him he squandered away in drink and he had not worked for years past although had he chosen to persevere he could have earned four or five pounds a week. Instead of doing this he went about the streets begging, and at night slept in the common lodging houses in John Street and Litchfield Street. Lately he had got into a wretched condition. About twenty minutes past two on Saturday morning, Police Constable Moseley found the deceased lying drunk in the gutter, in John Street, Dale End. The lower parts of his body were quite nude, the rags which had covered them having fallen over his heels. There was a sharp frost, and the deceased appeared to be suffering greatly from the cold. The constable elicited from him that he had consumed seven or eight half pints of ale given to him during the previous night, but hadn't had anything to eat. He was so helpless that the police were obliged to convey him to the Duke Police Station in a perambulator. Once there he was allowed to warm himself up by the fire and Inspector Fletcher very considerately gave him some warm tea and food. He was subsequently placed in one of a range of cells which are heated by means of hot air pipes, and after being wrapped up in a rug was left there, apparently comfortable. About a quarter to three, Police Constable Staplos, who was on reserve duty, went to the cell and found that the deceased was ill. Staplos informed Inspector Fletcher who at once sent for Mr Drummond, the surgeon. Pargeter died before the arrival of medical aid. Mr Drummond stated that a post mortem examination revealed the fact that the deceased's brain, lungs and kidneys were diseased and his liver presented the appearance of what is called nutmeg or gin-drinker's liver. There was no food in the stomach and the body was very emaciated. Death had resulted from syncope. The coroner, in summing up, remarked that the circumstances of the case depicted a deplorable story of the pernicious effects of drink. The jury returned a verdict that Pargeter had died from the affects of drink and exposure to the cold.

Children of Philip Pargeter and Susannah Richardson continued:
Child 2: Ann Pargeter, born before 10th December 1815 in Wordsley Green, baptised at the Holy Trinity Church, Wordsley. Ann married John Jones on 23rd June 1835 at All Saints Church, Sedgley. Witnesses at the wedding were John Newton and Stephen Cox. Ann Jones (nee Pargeter) died on 29th July 1849 in Wordsley, Kingswinford and was buried on 3rd August 1849. Ann was just 33 years of age. John Jones was born in baptism on 26th December 1813 in Kingswinford, Staffordshire and died on 31st March 1859 at the age of 47. I was unable to find the 1841 and 1851 census for John and Ann Jones and their family but I did track down their birth dates. John Jones was a glass stopperer and an organist and later he worked up to be a glass cutter. John's father's name was George Jones and his mother's was Elizabeth Jones (a.k.a. Betty), maiden name unknown.

Children of John Jones and Ann Pargeter:
Child 1: Ann Maria Jones, born in baptism in 1836. Ann Maria married John B. Lloyd and when Ann Maria died in 1906, John married her sister (child 2), Sarah Haynes (nee Jones) in 1910.
Child 2: Sarah Jones, born on 25th February 1840, baptised on 22nd March 1840. Sarah married William Haynes on 22nd February 1864. Witnesses at the wedding were Thomas Haynes and Mary Jones.

Child 3: Mary Jones, born on 29th April 1842, baptised on 5th June 1842.

Child 4: John Jones, born on 20th December 1843, baptised on 21st December 1843.

Child 5: George Handel Jones, born on 2nd April 1845, baptised on 27th April 1845.

Child 6: Ellen Jones, born in 1846.

Child 7: Edward Pargeter Jones, born on 30th July 1849.

When Ann Jones (nee Pargeter) died on 29th July 1849, her husband John Jones went on to marry Jane Brown on 24th June 1850. Witnesses at the wedding were Edward Hennifer and Eliza Maybury.

Below are two very rare photographs of my great aunts, daughters of Ann Jones (nee Pargeter). The one on the left shows either Anna Maria Jones or her sister Sarah Jones, taken around 1855 to 1860. The photograph on the right is of their other sister Mary Jones, taken at the same time. The photographs were confirmed by a costume expert who I went to see at the Herbert Art Gallery in Coventry and were dated correctly. I was delighted to have come across such old photographs in such good condition.

ANNA MARIA OR SARAH JONES   MARY JONES

When Ann Jones (nee Pargeter) died in 1849 the family was split up and only John Jones, her son, was mentioned on the 1861 census out of the whole Jones family.

Children of Philip Pargeter and Susannah Richardson continued:

Child 3: Joseph Pargeter, born before 4th May 1817 in Kingswinford, baptised at the Holy Trinity Church, Wordsley, died on 10th January 1869 in Level Street Brierley Hill, buried on 17th January 1869 at Holy Trinity Church, Wordsley. Joseph Pargeter married Ann Hillman on 16th May 1840 at Saint Martin's Church, Tipton.

Child 4: Martha Pargeter, born before 20th September 1818 in Wordsley, baptised at the Holy Trinity Church, Wordsley, died on 10th July 1904 at 85 years of age, buried at Saint Eve's Church. Martha married Henry Unitt on 8th November 1846 at Saint Edmund's Church, Dudley. Witnesses at the wedding were Philip Pargeter and Ann Bailey – by banns.

Henry Unitt was born on 29th August 1823, baptised on 28th December 1823 in Dudley, Worcestershire, and died on 23rd December 1885, aged 63 years. On his baptism certificate the name Unitt is spelt with an 'e' (Unett) instead of an 'i', another instance where a spelling error was recorded in someone's name. The vicar would have been literate, but they never asked if they had spelt a name correctly or not, they just wrote it in the book without checking it. Henry Unitt was a Mill Maker and later on in life he became an Engine Fitter. Henry's father's name was also Henry Unitt and his mother's name was Sarah Unitt (maiden name unknown).

The 1851 Census:

63 Springs Gardens, Dudley, Worcestershire

Henry Unitt – Head, age 28, Engine Fitter, Dudley, Worcestershire

Martha Unitt – Wife, age 33, Walsall, Staffordshire

Sarah Unitt – Daughter, age 3, Scholar, Dudley, Worcestershire

Philip Henry Unitt – Son, age 1, at home, Dudley, Worcestershire

The 1861 Census:

Vicar Street, Dudley

Henry Unitt – Head, age 37, Engine Fitter, Dudley, Worcestershire

Martha Unitt – Wife, age 42, Dressmaker, Wordsley, Staffordshire

Sarah Unitt – Daughter, age 13, Scholar, Dudley, Worcestershire

Philip H. Unitt – Son, age 11, Scholar, Dudley, Worcestershire

Ann Unitt – Daughter, age 9, Scholar, Dudley, Worcestershire

Charles Unitt – Son, age 5, Scholar, Dudley, Worcestershire

Joseph Unitt – Son, age 2, Dudley, Worcestershire

The 1871 Census:

91 Queen's Cross, Dudley, Worcestershire

Henry Unitt – Head, age 47, Engine Fitter, Dudley, Worcestershire

Martha Unitt – Wife, age 52, Wordsley, Staffordshire

Sarah D. Unitt – Daughter, age 23, unmarried, unemployed Boot Fitter, Dudley, Worcestershire

Charles Unitt – Son, age 15, unemployed Boot Fitter, Dudley, Worcestershire

Joseph Unitt – Son, age 12, Scholar, Dudley, Worcestershire

The 1881 Census:

102 Queen's Cross, Dudley, Worcestershire

Henry Unitt – Head, age 57, Fitter at Works, Dudley, Worcestershire

Martha Unitt – Wife, age 62, Dudley, Worcestershire

The 1891 Census:

28 Brewery Street, Kingswinford

Martha Unitt – Head/Widow, age 72, Living on own means, Wordsley, Staffordshire

Sarah A. Harper – Granddaughter, Bretell Lane, Kingswinford, Staffordshire

The 1901 Census:

40 Court Street, Wordsley, Kingswinford, Staffordshire

William H. P. Richardson – Head, age 52, Glass Engraver and Merchant, Finsbury, London

Ann Richardson – Wife, age 49, Dudley, Worcestershire

Martha Unitt – Mother-in-Law/Widow, age 82, Wordsley, Staffordshire

MARTHA UNITT (NEE PARGETER)

Memorial Inscription, Saint James Church, Eve Hill, Dudley. Description showing a grave with an ornamental cross inscribed: Thy will be done. The memorial reads: In loving memory of Henry Unitt of Dudley who died December 23 1885 in his 63rd year. Also of Martha his beloved wife who died July 10 1904 in her 85th year. They died in peace.

It is uncertain why this photograph should appear in the Richardson collection. However, there is an etched jug at Broadfield House Glass Museum, Stourbridge, signed by Alfred Unitt. It appears that the Unitt family had links with the glass trade and possibly with the Richardson Company.

Information about the Unitt Family

Charles Henry Unitt a relation of the above.

Charles Henry Unitt (1871–1936) married Clara Jane Melosh. Charles Unitt moved to Seward, Seward Co, NE, with his family sometime in 1894 to a ranch nine and a half miles south of Harrison, Sioux Co, NE, between Running Water and White River. The family decided to trade at the ranch for a hardware and lumber business and called themselves Unitt Hardware and Lumber, which Charles operated until his death with his sons Philip and Wayne. At that time it was the oldest business in Harrison. In his later years, Charles Henry Unitt's favourite hobby was using the native cedar and turning it on his lathe in his workshop to make useful and beautiful articles. I have obtained two large photographs, A4 in size, of the Unitt families which are in really good condition which I've had copied for my folders. One is around the 1920s the other is around the 1890s.

Child 5: Susannah Pargeter, born before 14th January 1821 in Wordsley, baptised at the Holy Trinity Church, Wordsley, died on 26th February 1856 in Wordsley, Kingswinford. Susannah married Edward Evans on 1st April 1845 at Holy Trinity Church, Wordsley. Witnesses at the wedding were William Elcock and Sarah Pargeter.

Edward Evans was born on 22nd January 1819 and baptised on 30th May 1819 at Saint Thomas's, Dudley, died on 5th June 1865 at Brettell Lane, Wordsley at the age of 46. Edward was a Brass Founder and later on became a Master Shoemaker. Edward's father's name was John Evans, and he was a Whitesmith. Edward's mother's name was Maria Evans (maiden name unknown).

Children of Susannah Pargeter and Edward Evans:

Child 1: Phillis Evans, born in 1846.

Child 2: Jane Evans, born in 1847.

Child 3: Ann Evans, born in 1848.

Child 4: Richard Evans, born in 1850.

Child 5: George Evans, born in 1853/4.

The 1851 Census:

Wordsley

Edward Evans – Head, age 32, Glass Mould Fitter, Dudley, Worcestershire

Susannah Evans – Wife, age 30, Kingswinford, Staffordshire

Phillis Evans – Daughter, age 5, Kingswinford, Staffordshire

Jane Evans – Daughter, age 4, Kingswinford, Staffordshire

Ann Evans – Daughter, age 3, Kingswinford, Staffordshire

Richard Evans – Son, age 1, Kingswinford, Staffordshire

Susannah Evans is not mentioned on the 1861 Census below as she died on 26th February 1856 in Wordsley, Kingswinford, aged just 35 years.

The 1861 Census:

22 Norfolk Street, Shelton, Stoke-on-Trent

Thomas Pargeter – Head, age 46, Manager Glassworks, Kingswinford, Staffordshire

Mary Pargeter – Wife, age 46, Kingswinford, Staffordshire

Joseph Pargeter – Son, age 18, Warehouseman, Kingswinford, Staffordshire

Richard Evans – Nephew, age 11, Scholar, Kingswinford, Staffordshire

George Evans – Nephew, age 7, Workhouse

Edward Evans is also not mentioned on the 1861 Census.

Child 6: Sarah Pargeter, born before 14th July 1822 in Wordsley, baptised at Holy Trinity Church, Wordsley, died on 13th July 1907 at 79 Lawnswood Road, Wordsley, aged 85. Sarah married Isaac

Whitehouse on 27th June 1852 at Saint Mark's Church, Pensnett. Witnesses at the wedding were George Whitehouse and Elizabeth Pargeter. Isaac Whitehouse was born in baptism on 21st February 1813 in Tipton, Staffordshire and died between 1871 and 1881. He was a Glasscutter. Isaac's father's name was Joseph Whitehouse and his mother was Jane Whitehouse (maiden name believed to have been Patrick). Joseph Whitehouse was also a Glasscutter, probably within the Pargeter or Richardson family.

The 1841 Census:

Vicar Street, Dudley, Staffordshire

Isaac Whitehouse – Head, age 29, Glasscutter

Hannah Whitehouse – Wife, age 30

Joseph Whitehouse – Son, age 9

Mary Whitehouse – Daughter, age 6

Louise Whitehouse – Daughter, age 3

George Whitehouse – Son, age 1

Isaac's first wife, Hannah, is mentioned on the 1841 Census, but not on the 1851 Census. Hannah Whitehouse (nee Cashmore) died about 1848 to 1849. Isaac married Hannah Cashmore in 1837 in West Bromwich, Staffordshire.

The 1851 Census:

Vicar Street, Dudley, Staffordshire

Isaac Whitehouse – Head, age 39, Glasscutter

Joseph Whitehouse – Son, age 20, Pin Turner

Mary Whitehouse – Daughter, age 16

Louise Whitehouse – Daughter, age 13

George Whitehouse – Son, age 10

William Whitehouse – Son, age 6

Isaac Whitehouse – Son, age 3

The 1861 Census:

Cross Street, Dudley, Staffordshire

Isaac Whitehouse – Head, age 49, Glasscutter

Sarah Whitehouse – Wife, age 38

George Whitehouse – Son, age 21, Glasscutter

James Pargeter – Son-in-Law, age 19, Glasscutter

William Whitehouse – Son, age 17, Pill Box Maker

Isaac Whitehouse – Son, age 13, Porter

Caroline Whitehouse – Daughter, age 9, Scholar

Child 7: Maria Pargeter, born in baptism on 20th December 1824 and baptised at Holy Trinity Church, Wordsley. Maria married William Elcock on 19th November 1843 at Saint Michael's Church, Brierley Hill. Witnesses at the wedding were John Ridgley and Ann Hobson. Maria died on 28th August 1901 at No. 29, High Street, Wordsley at 76 years of age.

William Elcock was born in baptism on 18th August 1822 in Townsend, Kingswinford. William died on 5th November 1861 in Townsend, Kingswinford at just 39 years of age. William was a Glasscutter. His father was William Elcock, a carpenter, and his mother's name was Sarah Elcock (maiden name unknown).

The 1851 Census:

Wordsley

William Elcock – Head, age 28, Glasscutter, Kingswinford

Maria Elcock – Wife, age 27, Wordsley, Kingswinford

Eliza Elcock – Daughter, age 6, Scholar, Wordsley, Kingswinford

Mary Elcock – Daughter, age 4, Scholar, Wordsley, Kingswinford

John Elcock – Son, age 2, Wordsley, Kingswinford

William Elcock – Son, age 2 months, Wordsley, Kingswinford

The 1881 Census:

Brewery Street, Wordsley, Kingswinford

Maria Elcock – Head/Widow, age 56, Kingswinford, Staffordshire

William Elcock – Son, age 30, unmarried, Flint Glasscutter, Kingswinford, Staffordshire

Susannah Elcock – Daughter, age 24, Flint Glass Decorator, Kingswinford, Staffordshire

The 1891 Census:

26 High Street, Wordsley, Kingswinford

Maria Elcock – Head/Widow, age 65, Living on own means, Wordsley, Kingswinford

Susannah Elcock – Daughter, age 34, unmarried, Forewoman in Glass Room, Wordsley, Kingswinford

The 1901 Census:

26 High Street, Wordsley, Kingswinford

Maria Elcock – Head, age 75, invalid, Wordsley, Kingswinford, Staffordshire

Susannah Elcock – Daughter, age 44, unmarried, Attendant on mother, Wordsley, Kingswinford, Staffordshire

Sarah   Pargeter – Niece, age 33, Living on own income, Kingswinford, Staffordshire

Child 8: Philip Pargeter, born on 13th February 1826 in Wordsley, baptised on 12th March 1826 at Holy Trinity Church, Wordsley, died on 19th December 1906 and was buried on 22nd December in Stourbridge Cemetery.

The 1881 Census:

Rose Cottage, Amblecote

Philip Pargeter (Jnr.) – Head, age 55, unmarried, Flint Glass Maker, Kingswinford

Elizabeth Pargeter – Sister, age 45, Housekeeper, Kingswinford

The 1891 Census:

South Street, Stourbridge, Worcestershire

Philip Pargeter (Jnr) – Head, age 65, Retired Glass Manufacturer, Wordsley, Staffordshire

Elizabeth Pargeter – Sister, age 55, Housekeeper, Wordsley, Staffordshire

Ann White – Servant, age 22, unmarried, General Servant Domestic, Kinver, Staffordshire

The 1901 Census:

Heathfield House, South Street, Stourbridge, Worcestershire
Philip Pargeter (Jnr) – Head, age 75, Retired Glass Manufacturer, Wordsley, Staffordshire

Elizabeth Pargeter – Sister, age 65, Housekeeper, Wordsley, Staffordshire

Eliza Watkins – Servant, age 20, unmarried, General Servant, Stourbridge, Worcestershire

Overleaf is a rare photograph of Philip Pargeter, which was probably taken at his home, Heathfield House, some time between 1904 and 1906 just before his death.

Over one hundred and five years later I finally managed to track it down in a private collection after many hours of research and after making a large number of telephone calls to follow up leads. The collection it belonged to was owned by a great uncle of mine who had several other photographs which were of interest to me that had been hidden away for decades – people used to put them in a box and store

PHILIP PARGETER.

them away and they would be lost or forgotten about. Luckily I was able to obtain copies of the photographs. I met with my great uncle, John Pargeter, several times and reawakened his own interest in our family history. I also have a good photograph of the large Heathfield House, but sadly the house has been knocked down and replaced by another building.

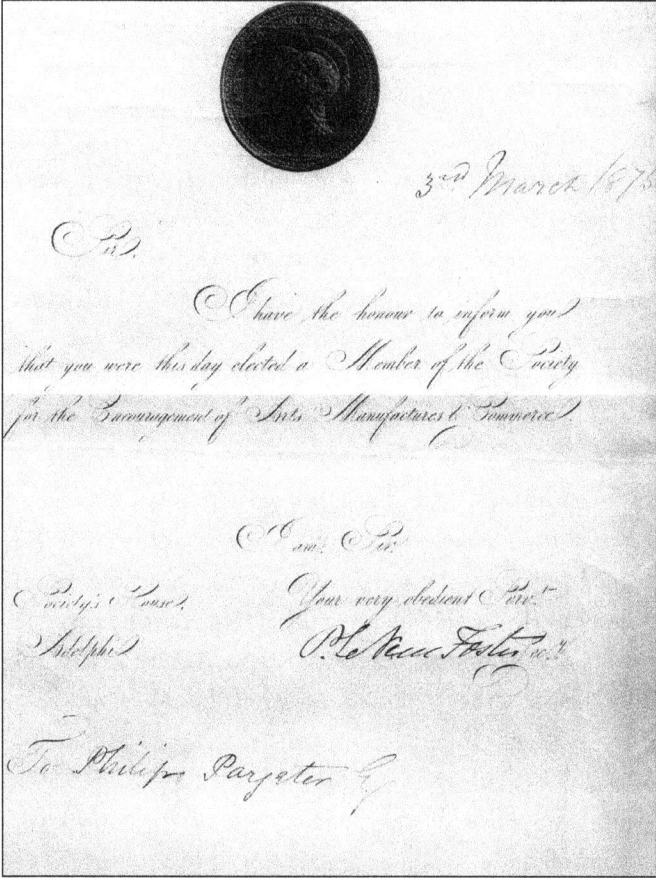

> 3rd March 1875
>
> Sir
>
> I have the honour to inform you that you were this day
> elected a Member of the Society for the Encouragement of
> Arts Manufactures and Commerce.
>
> I am Sir
>
> Society's House   Your very obedient Servant
> Adelphe   P. LeNeve Foster
>
> To Philip Pargeter Es

Philip Pargeter's life was a genuine rags to riches story. He was a Philanthropist and an Entrepreneur. Philip never married and remained a bachelor all his life. However, on several occasions, I found his name linked to a woman called Jane Turtin. Jane was named as a witness, along with Philip Pargeter, at family weddings and is also mentioned on other old documents as well. Philip left a large amount of money, property and other assets in his will. The sum of thirty thousand pounds is stated in his will, which equates to about one million, seven hundred and forty thousand, five hundred pounds today. In addition to this, he left several houses and other assets and personal belongings, which would make the total value of his estate very much more. He was well liked by many people and his memory lives on to this day – people still talk about all the good he did for the community in the surrounding areas. He was also a member of the Board of Guardians within the area along with many of the people he knew; it is clear that he cared deeply about the poor, having also experienced poverty himself during his early life. I believe that a statue or a plaque should be built in either Wordsley or Kingswinford to commemorate his life and am looking into how to secure this.

Philip Pargeter's will was made on 16th August 1895, which I have a copy of.

Obituary of Philip Pargeter

Philip Pargeter was one of the great names in Stourbridge glass. He is perhaps best known for his collaboration with his cousin John Northwood over the reproduction of the famous Portland Vase, but this was just one aspect of a life spent working in the local glass trade. By political conviction he was a staunch liberal and he played a prominent part in local politics, particularly after his retirement from the glass trade in 1882.

Following his death in December 1906 at the age of 80, numerous obituaries appeared in the local press, a testimony to the high regard in which he was held in the Stourbridge area. The extract below is taken from the obituary that appeared in the Brierley Hill Advertiser dated 22nd December 1906. There was to be another extract in a later edition in the Cameo.

Death of Mr Philip Pargeter

Men of all sorts and conditions in Stourbridge and the neighbourhood will be ready to acknowledge today that the public life of the district is greatly the poorer by the death of Mr Philip Pargeter. It seems about three weeks ago Mr Pargeter did not feel very well and with the weather being very cold and raw he kept to his house. A few days later he was feeling no better and Dr Collis was called in. The doctor ordered him at once to keep to his bed as there was an indication of inflammation on the lungs and he also had pneumonia. Two trained nurses, one for the night and one for the day, were engaged and remained in constant attendance on him to the last. From the very first outcome it was clear that his illness was of a grave character, but he had his ups and downs and at the end of last week there seemed to be a decided improvement. They thought that the pulmonary trouble was now overcome and clear, but the weakness was still there. On Tuesday night it was evident he was still weakening. Wednesday morning saw no improvement, and at a quarter past four in the afternoon he passed peacefully and painlessly away. His last public appearance was at the Stourbridge Liberal Club on 29th November 1906. Philip Pargeter was a Justice of the Peace, Chairman of the Stourbridge Urban District Council. Social meetings took place at his residence, Heathfield House, Stourbridge outside office hours. The funeral procession covered a quarter of a mile before entering the church; police, fire fighters, council officials and many other dignitaries were there to show their respects and were followed by at least twenty-two carriages carrying relatives and friends. This funeral was fit for a V.I.P.

Mr Pargeter was a native of Wordsley and was born in the month of February 1826. His father, also called Philip, held a position at Shut End under the well- known firm of Messrs John Bradley and Co. His mother, Susannah, was of the Richardson family, so long and honorably known in the local glass trade industry.

In due time he went to school, and in the thirties of the last century was considered sufficient to enable boys to enter on the battle of life. While he was young, his mother and father migrated to Kingswinford with their large family. Kingswinford was not very far away, so they stayed close to all the connecting villages in the area and it was here that he spent most of his youth. On leaving school he entered the glass works of his uncle, Mr Benjamin Richardson, known then locally as the Old Glass Works. He was initiated into the art and mystery of the most beautiful of all industries of this neighbourhood. His uncle was for many years looked up to as the father of the glass trade. His taste and ingenuity, his experience and enterprise were acknowledged both by masters and workmen as giving him an unchallenged supremacy in the trade. Growing up under him, Philip Pargeter acquired a complete knowledge of the manufacture of glass in all its branches and ramifications. His special work, of course, was that of an engraver, at which he excelled.

In time, Philip Pargeter became a member of the firm Hodgetts, Richardson and Pargeter who carried on business at the Red House Glass Works, now the work of Stuart and Sons. Subsequently, the Red House Works came into Mr Pargeter's hands and were successfully carried on by him until the year 1882. This eventually was the place that was to make the grand coup which would bring credit to him and his cousin John Northwood and to the Stourbridge glass industry.

The Portland Vase

In this district attempts were made from time to time to imitate the ancient Portland Vase in glass. This was eventually accomplished at the Red House Glass Works. Mr Pargeter's cousin, John Northwood, had acquired a great name as a decorator of glass. "John," said Philip one day, "I believe I can make a copy of the Portland Vase if you can decorate it."

"I think I can," said Northwood. So they agreed that the work should begin at once. Philip Pargeter wasted no time to achieve his goal and started casting the glass which would become well known all over the world. The other copy of the Portland Vase was broken at the National Museum on 7th February 1845 by drunkard William Lloyd (real name William Mulcahy) when he smashed the glass case along with the Portland Vase into one hundred and eighty-nine pieces. He was found guilty of destroying the glass case, with a value of five pounds, but not of destroying the vase. He was fined three pounds, or alternatively he could go to prison for two months. He chose the prison sentence and while he was there an anonymous benefactor paid the fine by mail. The owner of the vase which was on loan did not press charges. At one stage my great uncle Philip Pargeter had fifty- five men, eighteen boys and five girls working for him at the Red House Glass Works. I've never seen the vase up close but it would be great to see it one day.

History of the Red House Glass Works from the beginning

1788 – Richard Bradley purchased the site

1788–94 – Red House built during this period

1796 – Richard Bradley died leaving Red House to his sister and niece

1826 – Lucy Ensell's daughter, Mary, inherited the site

1827 – Red House sold to Richard Bradley Ensell Junior

1827 – Particulars of sale valued at £1,147

1827 – Frederick Stuart, aged 11, started work at the Red House

1830 – Red House sold to firm of bankers Rufford and Co

1834 – Red House leased to Hodgetts and Davis

1845 – Glass excise abolished

1852 – Red House taken over by Edward Webb when Rufford and Co went bankrupt

1854 – Edward Webb leased Red House to Elizabeth and William Hodgetts until 1869

1869 – Red House leased to Philip Pargeter

1873 – Blank for John Northwood, Portland Vase blown at Red House

1876 – Stuarts bought J. Stonier and Co, Liverpool

1877 – Blank for John Northwood's Milton Vase blown at Red House

1881 – Philip Pargeter left Red House, lease taken over by Frederick Stuart

1885 – Frederick Stuart renewed lease on Red House

1900 – Frederick Stuart died, aged 83

1911 – Certificate of Incorporation as a Limited Company

1916 – Stuarts bought the White House Glass Works opposite the Red House

1920 – Stuarts purchased Red House from successors of Edward Webb

1924 – The name 'Stuart' registered as a trade mark

1927 – The name 'Stuart Crystal' first appeared

1927 – Stuart etched on every piece of glass

1936 – Red House closed and glass making transferred to a new site in Vine Street

1965 – New Factory opened in Gwent, Wales

1966 – Red House Cone listed as Grade II Building

1980 – Stuarts take over Strathearn Glass in Crieff, Scotland

1982 – Work commenced to save and restore the Red House Glass Cone

1984 – Stuarts open a decorating studio in Chepstow

1984 – Opening of the Red House Glass Works Museum

1987 – Stuart installs first Electric Continuous-Melt Tank Furnace in British lead crystal industry

1995 – Stuart Crystal bought by Waterford Wedgewood plc

1999 – Red House Cone re-listed as Grade II Star

1999 – Restoration begins on Red House adjoining buildings, restored as craft workshops

2001 – Closure of Stuart Crystal announced

2002 – Opening of Red House Glass Cone as a new visitor attraction

Apparently the items of glassware for the White Star liners, including the Titanic which sank on 15th April 1912, were made at the Red House Cone just a few years after my great uncle Philip Pargeter's death in 1906. Many years later, before the Internet caught on, I managed to track down the youngest survivor of the Titanic, Millvina Dean. My family and I visited her about five times over a ten year period. Every time I arranged to meet her she would bring out her expensive tea service for us to drink from along with biscuits and cake. I commissioned several paintings in oils and in watercolours and every time I went to see her in Southampton she would sign them for me along with reproduction menus. I asked many questions – she was a lovely lady and always willing to sit and talk. She never married and only found out that she was the youngest survivor of the Titanic tragedy late in life. I received many letters from her over the years and a Christmas card once that she signed for me. I sometimes took postcards when I went to see her and she would sign them for me to give to my friends. Some of the people that I gave them to didn't believe that they were genuinely signed by Millvina Dean and didn't keep them. On one occasion I told her that I thought there were many more people on the Titanic when it sailed than had been documented and she agreed. I don't think we will ever know the true figure.

Children of Philip Pargeter and Susannah Richardson continued:

Child 9: Mary Pargeter, born before 23rd September 1827 in Wordsley. Baptised at Holy Trinity Church, Wordsley. Died on 25th September 1910 at Number 10 Brewery Street, Wordsley at 83 years of age. Buried at Holy Trinity Church, Wordsley, Kingswinford.

Mary Pargeter married William Haden Richardson on 23rd September 1848 in Saint George the Martyr Church in Holborn, Middlesex, London. Witnesses at the wedding were James Elkington and Eleanor Lloyd. William Haden Richardson was born before 27th March 1787 in Kingswinford, Staffordshire and died on 21st December 1876. William's father's name was Joseph Richardson and his mother's name was Mary Richardson (nee Haden). Joseph Richardson was a furnace builder. William Haden Richardson's first marriage was to Sarah Pollard on 30th May 1808 at St Thomas's Church, Dudley.

Below is a drawing of Saint George the Martyr Church, Holborn, Middlesex, London. A nice church in the middle of the High Street.

ST GEORGE THE MARTYR CHURCH, HOLBORN.

The 1851 Census:

75 Lambs Conduit Street

William Haden Richardson – Head, age 66, Glass Manufacturer, Kingswinford, Staffordshire

Mary Richardson – Wife, age 26, Kingswinford, Staffordshire

William H. P. Richardson – Son, age 2

James Skinner – Servant, age 68, Porter, Durham

Elizabeth Skinner – Wife/Servant, age 69, Truro, Cornwall

The 1861 Census:

Wordsley, Kingswinford, Staffordshire

William Haden Richardson – Head, age 76, Proprietor of house, Kingswinford

Mary Richardson – Wife, age 34, Kingswinford

William H. P. Richardson – Son, age 12, Scholar, Middlesex, London

Alfred H. P. Richardson – Son, age 9, Kingswinford, Staffordshire

Thomas Richardson – Son, age 5, Kingswinford, Staffordshire

Martha Richardson – Daughter, age 3, Kingswinford, Staffordshire

Elizabeth Richardson – Sister, age 68, Spinster, Kingswinford, Staffordshire

The 1871 Census: Wordsley Gardens, Buckpool Road, Wordsley, Kingswinford

William Haden Richardson – Head, age 86, Former Glass Engraver, Kingswinford, Staffordshire

Mary Richardson – Wife, age 43, Kingswinford, Staffordshire

William H. P. Richardson – Son, age 22, Unmarried, Glass Engraver, Middlesex, London

Alfred P. Richardson – Son, age 19, Glass Fitter, Middlesex, London

Thomas P. Richardson – Son, age 15, Warehouse Boy, Kingswinford, Staffordshire

Elizabeth Richardson – Daughter, age 8, Scholar, Kingswinford, Staffordshire

Alexander J. H. Richardson – Son, age 6, Scholar, Kingswinford, Staffordshire

Mary P. Richardson – Daughter, age 2, Kingswinford, Staffordshire

William Haden Richardson is not mentioned on the 1881 Census. He died on 21st December 1876 in Wordsley, Kingswinford at 91 years of age.

The 1881 Census:

Brewery Street, Kingswinford, Staffordshire

Mary Richardson – Head, age 53, Wordsley

Thomas Pargeter Richardson – Son, age 25, Unmarried, Clerk at Works, Wordsley

Lizzie Richardson – Daughter, age 18, Unmarried, Wordsley

Alexander John Richardson – Son, age 16, Clerk at Works, Wordsley

The 1891 Census:

26 Brewery Street, Wordsley

Mary Richardson – Head/Widow, age 63, Living on own means, Wordsley

William H. P. Richardson – Son, age 42, Glass Engraver, Middlesex, London

William Worrall – Son-in-law, age 27, Glass Cutter, Brierley Hill

Elizabeth Worrall – Daughter, age 28, Wordsley

Ethel Worrall – Granddaughter, age 1, Wordsley

The 1901 Census:

Brewery Street, Wordsley

Mary Richardson – Head, age 73, Wordsley

Flora Morton – Granddaughter, age 18, Dressmaker, Wordsley [new born Daughter of Martha Haden Richardson and John Albert Morton]

Mary Richardson died on 25th September 1910 at Brewery Street, Wordsley. Buried on 29th September 1910 at Holy Trinity Church, Wordsley, Kingswinford. Mary Richardson (nee Pargeter) was 83 years of age.

Child 10: John Pargeter, born in baptism on 19th July 1829 in Wordsley. Died on 8th October 1891 in Market Street. John Pargeter married Sarah Palmer on 12th September 1852 at Saint Mark's Church, Pensnett. Witnesses at the wedding were John Richards and Martha Palmer. Sarah Palmer was born in baptism on 1st July 1827 in Wolverly, Worcestershire, and died on 21st May 1900 in Mount Pleasant, buried at Saint Mary's, Kingswinford. Sarah Pargeter (nee Palmer) was 71 years of age. Sarah's father's name was Frederick Palmer and her mother was Patience Palmer (nee East). Frederick Palmer and Patience East were married on 14th April 1822 in Wolverly, Worcestershire. Frederick Palmer was a forge man in Cookley.

Below is a photograph of the gothic-styled Saint Mark's Church, Pensnett. It was built in 1849 and is known in the area as the Cathedral of the Black Country. Saint Mark's stands five hundred feet above sea level and has eight bells in its tower, which have recently been restored and re-hung. In 2006 the church was completely refurbished and from the west end door you can see the Clee Hills.

ST MARKS CHURCH, PENSNETT.

The 1861 Census:

94 Town's End, Kingswinford

John Pargeter – Head, age 31, Stock Taker, Kingswinford

Sarah Pargeter – Wife, age 32, Cookley, Worcestershire

Frederick Pargeter – Son, age 5, Kingswinford

The 1871 Census:

28 Market Street [Market Hall Inn], Kingswinford

John Pargeter – Head, age 41, Stock Taker at Ironworks, Kingswinford

Sarah Pargeter – Wife, age 42, Cookley, Worcestershire

Frederick Pargeter – Son, age 15, Kingswinford

William Pargeter – Son, age 10, Kingswinford

Martha Pargeter – Daughter, age 5, Kingswinford

Sarah Pargeter – Daughter, age 2, Kingswinford

Maria Evans – General Servant, age 17, Unmarried, Kingswinford

The 1881 Census:

Market Street [Market Hall Inn], Kingswinford

John Pargeter – Head, age 51, Beer Seller, Kingswinford

Sarah Pargeter – Wife, age 52, Kingswinford

John Pargeter – Son, age 19, Saddlers Apprentice, Kingswinford

William Pargeter – Son, age 20, Shoe Manufacturer, Kingswinford

Martha Pargeter – Daughter, age 15, Kingswinford

Sarah Pargeter – Daughter, age 12, Kingswinford

(Son, John Pargeter, appears only in the 1881 Census – a lot of children lived with other families because there were too many children so this may have happened to him, or he may have been in a workhouse.)

The ages given on a Census were not always accurate, different people would report different ages for the residents of a house.

The 1891 Census:

22 Market Street, Kingswinford

John Pargeter – Head, age 61, Living on own means, Wordsley

Sarah Pargeter – Wife, age 61, Cookley, Worcestershire

William Pargeter – Son, age 30, Unmarried, Boat Dealer, Kingswinford

Martha Pargeter – Daughter, age 24, Unmarried, Boat Dealer, Kingswinford

Sarah Pargeter – Daughter, age 22, Unmarried, Dressmaker, Kingswinford

John Pargeter died on 8th October 1891 in Market Street, Kingswinford. John was about 61 years of age.

The 1901 Census:

Staffordshire Lunatic Asylum

Martha Pargeter – Patient, age 35, Unmarried, Kingswinford, Worcestershire

Sarah Pargeter is not mentioned on the 1901 Census. Sarah Pargeter (nee Palmer) died on 21st May 1900 at 4a Mount Pleasant, Wordsley, at 71 years of age.

Child 11: Richard Pargeter, born before 27th March 1831 in Wordsley, baptised at Holy Trinity Church, Wordsley. Richard died before 13th May 1832 in Wordsley and was buried at Holy Trinity Church. Richard Pargeter was only one year old.

Child 12: Elizabeth Pargeter, born before 4th August 1833 in Wordsley, baptised at Holy Trinity Church, Wordsley. Elizabeth died on 15th March 1904 and was buried on 19th March at Stourbridge Cemetery. Elizabeth was unmarried and remained a spinster all her life; she was housekeeper for her brother, Philip Pargeter, in later life until her death.

Child 13: Phyllis Pargeter, born before 2nd August 1835 in Stallings, Kingswinford, baptised at Saint Mary's Church. Phyllis died before 2nd March 1836 and was buried in Kingswinford.

Child 14: Caroline Pargeter, born on 5th March 1837 in Kingswinford, baptised at Saint Mary's Church, Kingswinford. Caroline married James John Russell on 20th April 1856 at Saint John's Church, Kate's Hill, Dudley. James John Russell was born in Brierley Hill, Staffordshire on 23rd November 1828. James' father was Edward Russell, a Forgeman, and his mother's name was Hannah. James died on 3rd April 1901 in the workhouse in Wordsley, Staffordshire, recorded as aged 66 on his Death Certificate. James was in fact 72 when he died, not 66. The reason for the inconsistency was that he was almost seven years older than Caroline and such a large age gap was frowned upon in those days, so people would lie about their age. Caroline Russell (nee Pargeter) died on 30th December 1904 in the workhouse in Wordsley at 67 years of age.

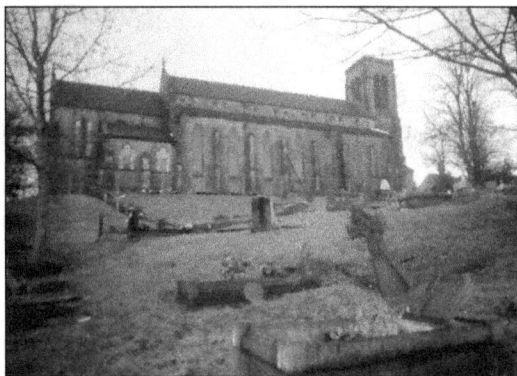

ST JOHN'S, KATE'S HILL, DUDLEY.

Above is a photograph of Saint John's, Kate's Hill, Dudley, showing the side view of the church. The graveyard looks unkempt and in need of maintenance. Many years ago when my father died, a headstone was erected and, like so many others, after a few years the soft ground beneath caused it to lean. I decided to put a concrete footing in the ground and the next day, when the concrete had set, I erected the headstone. The council said I needed permission to do this, and luckily this was granted to me a couple of weeks later even though I had already done the work. People laughed at me when I came up with the idea, but my father's headstone is still standing up straight after twenty five years!

The 1861 Census:

Dudley Street, Brierley Hill

James Russell – Head, age 27, Shingler at Iron Works, Kingswinford

Caroline Russell – Wife, age 24, Kingswinford

Susannah Russell – Daughter, age 3, Kingswinford

Phillis Evans – Daughter/Niece, age 14, General Servant, Kingswinford [new born Daughter of Susannah Pargeter and Edward Evans]

The 1871 Census:

Wistaston Road, Crewe, Cheshire

James Russell – Head, age 37, Shingler at Iron Works, Brierley Hill, Staffordshire

Caroline Russell – Wife, age 34, Iron Worker, Kingswinford, Staffordshire

Susannah E. Russell – Daughter, age 13, Scholar, Brierley Hill, Staffordshire

Mary A. Russell – Daughter, age 8, Scholar, Brierley Hill, Staffordshire

Caroline Russell – Daughter, age 6, Scholar, Brierley Hill, Staffordshire

Dianna Russell – Daughter, age 4, Scholar, Brierley Hill, Staffordshire

Edward Russell – Son, age 1, Crewe, Cheshire

The 1881 Census:

High Street, Kingswinford, Staffordshire

James Russell – Head, age 47, Shingler at Iron Works, Brierley Hill

Caroline Russell – Wife, age 44, Kingswinford, Staffordshire

Susannah E. Russell – Daughter, age 23, Dressmaker, Brierley Hill, Staffordshire

Mary Ann Russell – Daughter, age 18, Pianist, Brierley Hill, Staffordshire

Caroline Russell – Daughter, age 16, Pianist, Brierley Hill, Staffordshire

Edward Russell – Son, age 10, Scholar, Crewe, Cheshire

James Russell – Son, age 6, Scholar, Crewe, Cheshire

George Russell – Grandson, age 8 months, Newcastle-under-Lyme [new born Son of Susannah Elizabeth Russell]

The 1891 Census:

4 Unwin Passage, Wollaston, Stourbridge

James Russell – Head, age 57, Shingler at Iron Works, Brierley Hill

Edward Russell – Son, age 20, Iron Worker [Roller], Crewe, Cheshire

James Russell – Son, age 16, Iron Worker [Roller], Crewe, Cheshire

Continuation of 1891 Census, probably due to family split up:
The 1891 Census:

64 Brettell Lane, Amblecote, Kingswinford Holy Trinity Parish

Joseph Bullock – Head, age 29, Shingler at Iron Works/Innkeeper, Brierley Hill, Staffordshire

Mary Bullock – Wife, age 25, Publican, Brierley Hill, Staffordshire

Sydney Bullock – Son, age 5, Scholar, Wollaston, Worcestershire

Percy Bullock – Son, age 4, Scholar, Wollaston, Worcestershire

Henry Bullock – Son, age 2, Wollaston, Worcestershire

Amy Bullock – Daughter, age 1, Wollaston, Worcestershire

Caroline Russell – Mother-in-Law, age 54, Kingswinford, Staffordshire

Continuation of the 1891 Census:
The 1891 Census:

House 26, Court No. 5, Wolverhampton Street, Dudley

Sarah Knight – Head, age 36, Bedstead Painter, Dudley, Worcestershire

Louisa Knight – Daughter, age 8, Scholar, Dudley, Worcestershire

George Russell – Lodger, age 10, Scholar, Newcastle-under-Lyme

John Haines – Lodger, age 39, Labourer, Dudley, Worcestershire

The 1901 Census:

30 Mamble Road, Stourbridge

James Russell – Head, age 66, Shingler [Puddler], Brierley Hill, Staffordshire

Caroline Russell – Wife, age 64, Kingswinford, Staffordshire

Edward Russell – Son, age 30, Unmarried, Drain Sewerage Inspector, Crewe, Cheshire

George Russell – Son, age 20, with newborn Grandson, Unmarried, Roller at Iron Works, Newcastle-under-Lyme

Child 15: William Haden Richardson Pargeter, born on 2nd May 1839 in Kingswinford, baptised on 2nd June 1839 at Saint Mary's Church, Kingswinford. William married Mary Maria Pardoe on 24th April 1866 at Saint Mark's Church, Pensnett. Mary Maria Pardoe was born on 20th December 1845 in Kingswinford, her parents were John Pardoe and Christiana Pardoe (nee Hand). John Pardoe was a Glass Bottle Maker.

Pardoe family tree information
An inscription at the Holy Trinity Church, Section A, No. 33 reads:

In Memory of John Pardoe who died on 9th November 1853 aged 34 years

Also Christiana wife of the above who died on 23rd November 1852 aged 42 years

Also Edith Christiana Pargeter granddaughter of the above who died in 1883 aged 7 months

Also Mary Maria Pargiter who died on 25th March 1861 aged 45 years

Also William Haden Richardson who died in 1902 aged 67 years

The 1871 Census:

68 Camp Hill, Wordsley

William H. R. Pargeter – Head, age 31, Poor Rate Collector, Kingswinford

Mary M. Pargeter – Wife, age 25, Kingswinford

Philip J. Pargeter – Son, age 3, Kingswinford

William H. R. Pargeter – Son, age 2, Kingswinford

Christiana Pardoe – Mother-in-Law, age 60, Kingswinford

Mary E. Ball – Domestic Servant, age 16, Kingswinford

The 1881 Census:

Brook Street, Kingswinford

William H. R. Pargeter – Head, age 41, Commercial Clerk, Kingswinford

Mary M. Pargeter – Wife, age 35, Kingswinford

Philip J. Pargeter – Son, age 13, Scholar, Kingswinford

William H. R. Pargeter – Son, age 12, Scholar, Kingswinford

Christiana Pardoe – Mother-in-Law/Widow, age 70, Kingswinford

The 1891 Census:

15 Brook Street, Wordsley

William H.R. Pargeter – Head/Widower, age 51, Glass Factory Worker, Kingswinford

Philip J. Pargeter – Son, age 23, Unmarried, Commercial Traveller, Kingswinford

Mary A. Oldfield – Housekeeper, age 34, Unmarried, Wollaston

Mary Maria Pargeter (nee Pardoe) is not mentioned on the 1891 Census as she died on 14th March 1891 in Brook Street, Wordsley, at 45 years of age. (The Census was usually done around April to June.)

The 1901 Census:

7 Brook Street, Wordsley

William H. R. Pargeter – Head/Widower, age 61, Kingswinford

Mary A. Oldfield – Housekeeper, age 44, Wollaston

Hannah Whitehouse – General Domestic Servant/Widow, age 31, Coseley

William Haden Richardson Pargeter died on 2nd February 1907 in Brook Street, Wordsley at 67 years of age. He was a retired Glass Manufacturer.

Child 16: James Gould Pargeter, born in 1843 in Kingswinford.

Chapter Six
Moving to Wolverhampton

Generation No. 12

Joseph Pargeter, born in baptism on 4th May 1817 at Holy Trinity Church, Wordsley, died on 10th January 1869 at Level Street, Brierley Hill, Kingswinford at 51 years of age. Joseph married Ann Hillman on 16th May 1840 in Saint Martin's Church, Tipton. Joseph was a Boatman and an Iron Stocktaker. Ann Hillman was born about 1817 and baptised on 14th January 1821 in Kingswinford. Ann Pargeter (nee Hillman) died on 16th April 1888 in Stewkins, Wordsley at 71 years of age. Ann's father's name was George Hillman and he was a labourer in Kingswinford. Her mother was Anne Hillman, maiden name Pope. George and Anne married on 31st July 1808 in Oldswinford, Worcester.

HOLY TRINITY, HEATH TOWN.

Above is a drawing of Holy Trinity Church, Heath Town, Wolverhampton. This is where my three times great grandfather Alfred Thomas Pargeter married Margaret Ann Price (nee Quindleman) in 1864 and where he is also buried.

Children of Joseph Pargeter and Ann Hillman:

Child 1: Alfred Thomas Pargeter, born on 23rd November 1840 in Wall Heath, Kingswinford, baptised on 28th December 1840 at Saint Mary's Church, Kingswinford.

Child 2: Susannah Pargeter, born on 19th June 1842 in Himley Road, Kingswinford, baptised on 26th June 1842 at Saint Mary's Church, Kingswinford.

Susannah died on 24th September 1847 at Dawley Brook, Kingswinford at just five years of age.

Child 3: Mary Ann Pargeter, born on 3rd February 1844 in Dawley Brook, Kingswinford, baptised at Saint Mary's Church, Kingswinford. Mary Ann Pargeter married Edward Bragger on 23rd September 1872 in Saint Thomas's Church, Dudley. Witnesses at the wedding were Philip Pargeter and Mary Norris. Mary Ann Bragger (nee Pargeter) died on 13th April 1914 in Dudley at 70 years of age. Edward Bragger was born on 26th June 1852 in Brockmoor, Kingswinford. His father was William Bragger, a Miner, and his mother was Eliza Bragger (nee Westwood). Edward died on 11th October 1904 at Crown Street, Dudley. Edward was the brother-in-law of Mary's brother Alfred Thomas Pargeter.

The 1881 Census:

64 Springmire, Grocers Shop, Dudley, Worcestershire

Edward Bragger – Head, age 32, Engine Tender, Brierley Hill

Mary A. Bragger – Wife, age 32, Brierley Hill, Staffordshire

Joseph P. Bragger – Son, age 7, Scholar, Brierley Hill, Staffordshire

Flora Bragger – Daughter, age 5, Scholar, Brierley Hill, Staffordshire

Eliza Bragger – Daughter, age 3, Brierley Hill, Staffordshire

John E. Bragger – Son, aged 1, Dudley, Worcestershire

The 1901 Census:

43 Crown Street, Dudley, Worcestershire

Edward Bragger – Head, age 52, Colliery Engine Winder, Brierley Hill, Worcestershire

Mary Ann Bragger – Wife, age 52, Wallheath, Staffordshire

Annie Bragger – Daughter, age 23, Single, Dressmaker, Brierley Hill, Staffordshire

Mary Ann Bragger (nee Pargeter) was really 57 years of age at the time of the 1901 Census (she lied about her age).

Below is an article in the *Birmingham Daily Post* dated 20th February 1883 in Dudley:

The wounding case at Springs Mire, Dudley: Yesterday at the police court before the Mayor [Mr Job Garrett and Mr John Russell] Mr Edward Bragger [31] an engine tender of Springs Mire was again brought up on the charge of having murderously assaulted Alfred Pargeter, his brother-in-law, on Sunday the 11th instant. Police Sergeant Rudge stated that the man Pargeter was still unable to attend the court. Chief Superintendent Burton said there was a fear of death in the case for a clot had formed on Pargeter's brain and there was some difficulty in removing it. The Mayor said the prisoner's bail would be increased and the case was again adjourned for one week. (No further information found; the charges may have been dropped as they were related.)

Opposite is a drawing of St Mary's Church in its original form.

Child 4: Joseph Philip Pargeter, born on 2nd February 1846 in Dawley Brook, Kingswinford, baptised on 1st March 1846 at Saint Mary's Church, Kingswinford. Joseph died on 18th August 1846 at Dawley Brook at just six months old.

Child 5: John Pargeter, born on 28th February 1849 in Dawley Brook, Kingswinford, baptised on 25th March 1849 at Saint Mary's Church,

Kingswinford. No record found of who John married and he is not mentioned on the 1911 Census as he died on 18th January 1910 at Glenfield House, Wartell Bank, Kingswinford. He was 61 years of age.

Child 6: Joseph Pargeter, born on 4th November 1850 in Dawley Brook, Kingswinford, baptised at Saint Mary's Church, Kingswinford. Date of death unknown, last documentation found was (in Canada) 1894.

The 1871 Census:

78 Walsall Street, Wolverhampton

Sophia Jones – Head, age 36, Beerhouse Keeper

Joseph Pargeter – Lodger, age 19, Coke Grinder Burner, Brierley Hill, Staffordshire

Below is a drawing of Dawley Brook Cottages where Joseph and Ann Pargeter lived with their large family for many years. These solidly built cottages have weathered well – I saw them during my research when I was looking at the Census one day to find out more about my four times great grandfather. I noticed that the local police station was located in Dawley Brook Cottages, just a few doors away from my four times grandfather's home. However, despite searching further, I was unable to find any more information or photographs of the police station.

ST MARYS CHURCH.

DAWLEY BROOK COTTAGES

Child 7: Philip Pargeter, born on 4th November 1852 in Dawley Brook, Kingswinford, baptised at Saint Mary's Church, Kingswinford. Philip died on 9th March 1919 and was buried on the 16th at Queens Cross Cemetery. He married Maria Baggott on 25th September 1898 in Saint Luke's Church, Dudley. Witnesses at the wedding were Thomas Baggott and Florence Bragger. Maria Pargeter (nee Baggott) was born about 1858 in Dudley, died on 18th March 1931 and was also buried at Queens Cross Cemetery.

The 1891 Census:

104 Stourbridge Road, Woodside

Thomas Baggott – Head, age 23, Unmarried, Coal Dealer, Dudley, Worcestershire

Maria Baggott – Sister, age 32, Unmarried, Dudley, Worcestershire

Ellen Baggott – Sister, age 19, Dudley, Worcestershire

Philip Pargeter – Lodger, age 39, Unmarried, Labourer at Ironworks, Kingswinford, Staffordshire

The 1901 Census:

104 Stourbridge Road, Dudley

Philip Pargeter – Head, age 49, Labourer at Ironworks, Brierley Hill, Staffordshire

Maria Pargeter – Wife, age 43, Dudley, Worcestershire

Gladys Tetley – Niece, age 6, Birmingham, West Midlands

Child 8: Ann Pargeter, born on 14th February 1855 in Kingswinford, baptised at Saint Mary's Church, Kingswinford on 1st March 1855. Ann died on 8th April 1856 aged just one year.

Child 9: Ann Caroline Pargeter, born on 26th January 1857 in Kingswinford, baptised on 1st March 1857 at Saint Mary's Church, Kingswinford, died on 3rd March 1909, aged 51, in the workhouse in Heath Town, Staffordshire. Ann Caroline Pargeter married Sidney

Beckett Wakelam on 26th August 1889 in Holy Trinity Church, Wednesfield Heath, Staffordshire. Witnesses at the wedding were Philip Pargeter and Jane Turtin. Sidney Beckett Wakelam was born about 1840 and he was a padlock manufacturer and locksmith. Sidney died on 8th January 1905 at 38 Union Street, Willenhall, Staffordshire, at 65 years of age. His first marriage was to Emma Jones on 16th September 1867 at Holy Trinity Church, Willenhall, Staffordshire.

The 1891 Census:

1 Wall Street, Willenhall, Staffordshire

Sidney Wakelam – Head, age 50, Locksmith (Finisher), Willenhall, Staffordshire

Caroline Wakelam – Wife, age 35, Wordsley, Worcestershire

Albert Pargeter – Stepson, age 6, Scholar, Wolverhampton, Staffordshire

Chapter Seven
The Wolverhampton Connection

Generation No. 13

Alfred Thomas Pargeter was born on 20th November 1840 in Wall Heath, Kingswinford and baptised on 28th December 1840 in Saint Mary's Church, Kingswinford. He married Margaret Ann Price (a widow), formerly Quindleman, on 28th November 1864 in Holy Trinity Church, Wednesfield Heath, Staffordshire. Witnesses at the wedding were Henry Johnson and Eliza Johnson. Margaret Ann Quindleman was born about 1840, place of birth Tipperary, Ireland. Margaret Ann Pargeter or Mary Ann (nee Price) died on 17th August 1891 in Bradley Norton in the county of Stafford at the age of 50. Margaret's father was John Quindleman and he was a labourer (mother unknown).

Alfred Thomas Pargeter's second marriage was to Eliza Gething (a widow) (nee Walker). The wedding took place on 26th August 1907 at the Wolverhampton Register Office. Witnesses at the wedding were Sarah Connolly and Jane Woodcock. Eliza's father's name was John Walker and he was an engine worker at the ironworks. Eliza was born about 1839 in Staffordshire, and died after 1907.

Children of Alfred Thomas Pargeter and Margaret Ann Price:
Child 1: Joseph Pargeter, born on 26th April 1868 at No. 8 Moore Street, Wolverhampton, died on 16th January 1944.

On the facing page is a photograph of Moore Street in Wolverhampton taken during the winter. It strikes me as a calm picture and was taken in the late 1950s, early 1960s. You can see an old Ford Popular parked outside one of the houses. Joseph Pargeter, my great grandfather, was born there nearly one hundred years before this photograph was taken. I wonder what the conditions were like then. I cannot quite make out the house numbers, but can pinpoint my great-grandfather's home. If you look at the first house, half way up the wall you will see a metal cross. This was used to strengthen the house or to repair cracks that sometimes appeared in the brickwork. A long iron bar would have been inserted right through from one side to the other between the joists at first fixing level and then the metal cross plate, which is visible from the outside, was bolted on. Notice the arched brickwork above the old-fashioned sash windows.

MOORE STREET, WOLVERHAMPTON

Child 2: Alfred Pargeter, born on 5th September 1870 at Level Street, Brierley Hill, Kingswinford, died in the same place on 13th December 1870 at just three months old.

Child 3: Thomas Pargeter, born on 21st December 1871 at Level Street, Brierley Hill, Kingswinford, where he also died only one year later on 25th December 1872.

The 1871 Census:

Level Street, Kingswinford, Staffordshire

Alfred Pargeter – Head, age 30, Puddler, Kingswinford, Staffordshire

Margaret A. Pargeter – Wife, age 34, Ireland

Joseph Pargeter – Son, age 3, Scholar, Brierley Hill

The 1881 Census:

Tame Street, Bilston

Alfred T. Pargeter – Head, age 40, Puddler in Ironworks, Kingswinford

Magaret A Pargeter – Wife, age 44, Ireland

Joseph Pargeter – Son, age 12, Scholar, Wolverhampton

The 1891 Census:

13 Bradley Road, Smallthorne, Staffordshire

Alfred Pargeter – Head, age 51, Ironworker Puddler, Stafford

Margaret A Pargeter – Wife, age 53, Ireland

William Tacklawn – Lodger, age 48, Ironworker Puddler, Scotland

Generation No. 14

Joseph Pargeter, born on 26th April 1868 at No. 8 Moore Street, Wolverhampton, died on 16th January 1944 at No. 45 Holyhead Road, Coventry, Warwickshire, at 75 years of age. Joseph married Mary Alice Mullins on 2nd August 1890 at Saint Mark's Church, Shelton Hanley. Witnesses at the wedding were James Smith Bourne and Margaret Ann Pargiter. Joseph Pargeter was a jack of all trades doing many different types of building jobs. Mary Alice was born on 3rd October 1867 at Deanery Place, Wolverhampton and died on 27th March 1955 at Beake Avenue, Coventry, Warwickshire. Mary Alice Pargeter (nee Mullins) was 87 years of age.

A Patriotic Family

(Taken from the *Coventry Graphic* newspaper dated 26th July 1918)

Private J. Pargeter [my great grandfather] whose home is at no 9 Court 5, Well Street, Coventry, is serving in the army and his age is 51. His son, a rifleman, William Henry Pargeter [my great uncle] is a prisoner of war in Germany and another son, Private J. Pargeter [my grandfather], has also seen considerable active service.

JOSEPH AND MARY ALICE PARGETER

Above is a rare photograph of my great grandparents Joseph Pargeter and Mary Alice Pargeter (nee Mullins). They had 18 children, although I could only find documentation for eleven of them. This has been confirmed by my father and his brother and sisters and also by two of Joseph and Mary's grandchildren who are still alive and living in the Coventry area today. I am currently still looking for the other certificates for the remaining children. Joseph Pargeter was a jack of all trades and could turn his hand to anything. Some of the jobs that he had during his life were a scaffolder, a bricklayer, and he also worked on the rail tracks when he lived in Wolverhampton. He was also a labourer when he worked in Coventry and he helped to build the tall chimney at the back of Spon Street. Joseph also served in the First World War at the age of 51 along with two of his sons Joseph and William Henry.

The photograph was taken outside their home at No. 45, Holyhead Road, Coventry. Although some of these rare listed cottages are still there today, unfortunately No. 45 and several others in Holyhead Road were demolished around 1968–9 for the Ring Road project. How did the Council get away with that one? These buildings are part of Coventry's heritage.

My great grandparents were married in Saint Mark's Church in Shelton Hanley.

Saint Mark's Church is the largest church in the city and it stands at 120 feet high, 151 feet long and 75 feet wide. It was designed by J. Oates and erected in 1833 at a cost of £10,000. It opened on 19th June 1834 and can hold 2,100 people, 500 of which can be seated. In 1970 the church was cleaned to get rid of the grime which had accumulated over the past 136 years of pottery air.

Children of Joseph Pargeter and Mary Alice Mullins:

Child 1: Joseph Pargeter, born on 23rd October 1892 at Deanery Place, Wolverhampton, died on 17th November 1958 in Coventry. Joseph was a twin. He served in W.W.1 in France.

Child 2: Baby Pargeter, born on 23rd October 1892 at Deanery Place, Wolverhampton, but died less than an hour later. No record exists.

Child 3: William Henry Pargeter, born on 10th March 1894 at 18 Culwell Street, Wolverhampton, died on 19th December 1945 at Hertford Hill Sanatorium, Hatton Road, Warwick, at the age of 51. William Henry married Florence Annie Porter on 26th December 1919 at Saint Osberg's Church, Hill Street, Coventry. Witnesses at the wedding were William Badger and Mary Pargeter. Florence Annie Porter was born on 5th April 1896 at Higham Ferrers, Northamptonshire and died on 20th October 1975 at Whitley Hospital, Coventry. Florence was 79 years of age. Florence was a retired weaver. Her father was William Porter, a railway porter and later a labourer, and her mother's name was Mary, maiden name Jones. William Henry Pargeter was a scaffolder and he served in W.W.1 as a rifleman in France.

Opposite is a rare photograph and apparently the only one left of William Henry Pargeter and his wife Florence Annie Pargeter (nee Porter). There is no record to say where this photograph was taken. William Henry was a rifleman in the Royal Warwickshire Regiment and was taken prisoner by the Germans in W.W.1. It took me two years and hundreds of telephone calls to locate this photograph. I eventually found it in Northumberland with an uncle who is still alive and well and is almost ninety years of age. William Henry sent letters from the German prison but they have been either lost or destroyed. I was told many years ago that the family wasn't sure whether William Henry was dead or alive until he eventually came home. Sadly he and his father never got on and they never spoke to each other in later life.

WILLIAM AND FLORENCE PARGETER.

Overleaf is a lovely photograph of Saint Osberg's Church which is situated between Hill Street and Barras Lane near Coundon, Coventry. Several members of my grandfather's family were married there over the years including William Henry and Florence Annie. It's a lovely view of the church; notice the adjoining house – a rare sight. I visited the church several months ago and went inside – it's beautiful. The exterior still looks pretty much the same except there are now some additional statues. The original, smaller Saint Osberg's was built in 1807 and in 1843 further work began, making it the larger and more impressive structure that can be seen today. On the night of the

Coventry blitz, 14th November 1940, the church was badly damaged in the air raids. Half of the roof was blown off, windows blown out, the altar destroyed and a huge hole left in the side of the church. However, it has since been renovated and repaired and is once again a very impressive sight.

ST OSBERG'S CHURCH, COVENTRY.

Child 4: Hilda Margaret Pargeter, born on 25th August 1896 at 18 Culwell Street, Wolverhampton, died on 30th December 1974 at 78 years of age. Hilda Margaret married William Badger on 2nd April 1918 at Coventry Register Office. Witnesses at the wedding were Joseph Pargeter and Ada Badger. William Badger was born in

1894 in Smethwick and died on 4th December 1975 in Coventry at the age of 81, not 83 as stated on his Death Certificate. William's father was Frederick Badger and he was a packer at the cycle works. William's mother was Louisa Badger (nee Clayton).

Child 5 and 6: Twins, died soon after birth in June 1897.

Child 7: Mary Pargeter, born on 18th August 1899 at 13½ Southampton Street, Wolverhampton. Mary Pargeter married Claude Charles Billing on 25th September 1920 at Saint Osberg's Church, Hill Street, Coventry. Witnesses at the wedding were William Henry Pargeter and Elizabeth

Lucas. Mary Billing (nee Pargeter) died on 13th April 1977 at Walsgrave Hospital, Coventry at 78 years of age. Claude Charles Billing was born on 16th January 1898 at No. 91 Cannon Street, Bury St Edmunds, Suffolk and died in Coventry on 13th November 1952 at 54 years of

WOLVERHAMPTON GENERAL HOSPITAL.

age. Claude Charles Billing was a railway guard and later a storekeeper at the aircraft works. Claude Charles' father was William Harry Billing and he was a hay trusser and later in life a furnace charge hand. Claude Charles' mother was Emma Jane Billing, maiden name Dorling.

Child 8: John Pargeter, born on 14th December 1900 at 13½ Southampton Street, Wolverhampton, died on 24th February 1901 at the General Hospital in Wolverhampton at about ten weeks old. The inquest on John Pargeter took place on 25th February 1901. I have the inquest papers.

Above is a photograph of the Wolverhampton General Hospital.

Child 9: Margaret Pargeter, born on 14th March 1902 at No. 5 Cannock Road, Wolverhampton, died on 14th July 1902 at the same address. Margaret was just four months old.

Child 10: Alfred Pargeter, born on 22nd January 1904 at No. 5 Cannock Place, Wolverhampton, died on 29th October 1955 at No. 17, Court 5, Much Park Street, Coventry, at 51 years of age. Alfred, unmarried, was a general labourer. He was buried at London Road Cemetery, Square 354, No. 31. I was unable to trace any photographs.

Child 11: Baby Pargeter, born at Cannock Place, Wolverhampton, in 1905 and died soon after.

Child 12: James Pargeter, born on 25th June 1907 at No. 9, Court 5, Well Street, Coventry, died on 6th October 1965 at Gulson Road Hospital, Coventry, at 58 years of age. James, unmarried, was a builder's labourer. He was buried at London Road Cemetery, Square 354, No. 31 with his brother Alfred. Again there seem to be no photographs in existence.

Child 13, 14, 15 and 16: Four babies were stillborn between 1890 and 1911, although I could not trace the dates because stillbirths were not documented until 1st July 1927.

Child 17: Alice Pargeter, born on 5th October 1909 at No. 9, Court 5, Well Street, Coventry, died on 18th September 1910 at the same address when she was only 11 months old. No known photographs exist.

Child 18: Florence Margaret Pargeter, born on 23rd November 1911 at No. 9, Court 5, Well Street, Coventry. Florence married William Horton on 17th May 1930 at the Coventry Register Office. Witnesses at the wedding were Claude Charles Billing and Hilda Badger. Florence Margaret Horton (nee Pargeter) died on 19th April 1933 at Gulson Road Municipal Hospital, Coventry, at just 21 years of age. Florence was a radiator builder at the motor car works. William Horton was born on 31st July 1904 on the canal boat 'Rose' at Horton Bridge in Yiewsley, Hillingdon, Middlesex, and died on 12th February 1953 at Gulson Road Hospital, Coventry. William was a theatre scenery shifter, a cattle transport labourer and later on an assistant storekeeper for West Midlands Gas Board. William's father was George Horton, a canal boatman and contract labourer, and his mother's name was Sobiesky Horton (nee Bavington).

FLORENCE PARGETER

Above is a lovely photograph of my great aunt, Florence Margaret Pargeter. This photograph was probably taken sometime between 1928 and 1930 at her home No. 9, Court 5, Well Street, Coventry. Florence was buried at London Road Cemetery, Coventry and she was the last of 18 children born to my great grandparents, Joseph and Mary Alice Pargeter (nee Mullins).

Family tree of John Mullins

Not much is known about my grandfather, John Mullins, who came from Cork in Ireland but some records do exist. He is believed to have come to England during the disastrous Irish potato famine.

John Mullins was born about 1840 in County Antrim, Cork, Ireland. He married Caroline James on 15th April 1868 in Christchurch, Sandown, Isle of Wight. Their first child was born out of wedlock when John was at sea. They married promptly on his return. Witnesses at the wedding were C. Warder and Jane Streets. John Mullins died on 30th November 1923 at No. 11, Court 9, Well Street, Coventry, at

82 years of age. He was a cabman and an ostler. Caroline James, also known as Fanny James, was born about 1843 in Tettenhall, Staffordshire. Caroline Mullins (nee James) died on 18th March 1908 at No. 8, Clarence Street, Wolverhampton, at the age of 65.

Children of John Mullins and Caroline James:

Child 1: Mary Alice Mullins, born on 3rd October 1867, baptised at Saint Peter's Church, Wolverhampton, died on 27th March 1955 in Coventry.

Child 2: Elizabeth Mullins, born on 20th March 1873 in Wolverhampton, baptised at Saint Peter's Church, Wolverhampton, date of death unknown.

Child 3: John Thomas Mullins, born on 25th August 1874 in Wolverhampton, baptised at Saint Peter's Church, Wolverhampton, date of death unknown.

Additional information about the Mullins family

There is an interesting story which has been passed through the family. It is said that one of my great great grandfathers was Thomas Mullins and his wife was Nell Mullins (nee Lynch). Nell Lynch was a descendent of James Lynch of Galway, so it also follows that I am related to him as well. That may not mean a lot to anyone until you discover his history. The true story of James Lynch is that in 1493 in Galway, Ireland, while he was the mayor of Galway, one of his sons murdered a Spanish visitor. Since the crime was committed by the much respected mayor's son, nobody in Galway did anything about it. The people looked up to their mayor, and James felt honour-bound to put things right. So he decided to become the judge, jury and executioner within the community and found his son guilty of the murder of the Spaniard and consequently hung him. Everyone within the whole of Galway was completely shocked and news of this eventually spread throughout Ireland, bringing the same reaction from everyone who heard about it. The Galwegians have now established that the term 'lynching' originated from this course of events and the 'lynch mob' originates from James Lynch. James was originally named James Lynch Fitzstephen, but dropped the last part of his name. The Lynch family was the most prominent family for over three hundred years from the end of the fifteenth century and to this day there have been 64 members of the Lynch family who have served as mayors of Galway. The place where James Lynch hung his son all those years ago from the balcony of the building where he lived still exists today, although it is now a bank.

Chapter Eight
Moving to Coventry

Generation No. 15

Joseph Pargetter was born on 23rd October 1892 at Deanery Place, Wolverhampton. He was the first of 18 siblings. Joseph married Matilda Maud Collins on 5th August 1916 at Saint Osberg's Church, Hill Street, Coventry. Witnesses at the wedding were G. Tracey and Elizabeth Allibone. Joseph died on 17th November 1958 at No. 44 The Chantries, Hillfields, Coventry, at 65 years of age. Notice that the surname is now spelt with a double 't', although some of the children still spelt their names with a single 't' as listed later. Joseph was a superintendent for the Parks Department. Matilda Maud Collins was born on 17th March 1890 at No. 4, Court 1, Cow Lane, Coventry, and she died on 17th March 1975 at Whitley Hospital, Coventry, at the age of 85. (Unfortunately the hospital has now been replaced by a food superstore.) The parents of Matilda Maud Collins were Frederick Collins and Ellen Collins (nee Jones).

DEANERY PLACE, WOLVERHAMPTON.

Above is a photograph of Deanery Place, Wolverhampton, showing the harsh conditions in which they lived. These buildings were demolished during or after the war probably due to war damage or just that they were unfit to live in.

Children of Joseph Pargetter and Matilda Maud Collins:

Child 1: Ellen Collins (a.k.a. Nelly), born on 20th October 1912 in the workhouse at No. 11 London Road, Coventry, out of wedlock. Matilda gave birth to Ellen in 1912 – she was unmarried and never disclosed who Ellen's father was, she later married Joseph in 1916. Ellen Collins died on 14th August 1997 at Walsgrave Hospital, Coventry, at the age of 85. Ellen married Christopher Robinson on 2nd October 1936 at Saint Peter's Church, Hillfields, Coventry. Ellen was formerly a servant for a private family.

ELLEN ROBINSON

Christopher Robinson was born on 2nd November 1914 at No. 6, Court 6, Castle Street, Coventry, and died on 20th May 1961 at Coventry and Warwickshire Hospital. Christopher was just 47 when he died and an inquest into his death was held on 24th May 1961. Christopher's father was William Robinson, a labourer, and his mother's name was Alice Beatrice Robinson (nee Stafford).

Above is a photograph of my aunt, Ellen (a.k.a. Nelly) Robinson (nee Collins), when she was 15 years of age. The location of this picture is unknown, but it was probably in Leicester Street, Coventry. Nelly's father was unknown and she never did find out who her real father was during the whole of her life.

Workhouse foods and the truth about the workhouses

Food provided in workhouses is often thought to have been very plain and hardly enough to sustain people. However, this was often far from the truth. In Brighton in 1834 there were 336 workhouse inmates, as they were called, and they were given three meals a day – every day – and there were no limits on quantity. Men also received two pints of beer a day, children one pint a day, and women a pint of beer and a pint of tea. There were six meat dinners in the week and the inmates were served at the table usually with a governor carving for the men and boys, and the matron for the women and girls. A typical menu is shown below.

Below is a photograph of the workhouse at No. 11 London Road, Coventry, which opened in 1801, closing as a workhouse in the 1940s. It was a beautiful-looking place with lovely grounds in its day, although this belied the interior which was grim and the conditions harsh.

100 COVENTRY WORKHOUSE.PSD

The Menu

Breakfast

Women: One pint of tea with bread and butter

Men, Boys and Girls: Bread and gruel [of flour and oatmeal] (except for some old men who were allowed a pint of tea with bread and butter)

Dinner

Monday Pease soup and herbs with bread

Men and Women: A pint of table beer

Boys: About half a pint of table beer

Tuesday Beef and mutton pudding with vegetables

(With beer as per Monday)

Wednesday Boiled beef and mutton

(Sometimes there was pork too, hard puddings, bread, vegetables and beer as before)

Thursday Mutton and beef suet puddings and beer

Friday Beef and mutton puddings with vegetables and beer

Saturday Irish stew-meat, potatoes, herbs and beer

Sunday Boiled beef and mutton

(Sometimes pork with it)

Supper

Women: One pint of tea with bread and butter or cheese

Men and Boys: Bread and butter or cheese, with one pint of beer or tea for men and about half a pint for boys

Girls and small children: Bread and butter with milk and water

Most workhouses would make their own beer and most, if not all, of them had their own brew house located on the premises. You have no doubt heard the line: 'Please sir, can I have some more?' Well, from the evidence I have seen, I don't think that was said in the workhouses at that time, certainly not after 1836 when the new poor laws came in.

Children of Joseph Pargetter and Matilda Maud Collins continued:

Child 2: Hilda Pargeter, born on 8th May 1917 at No. 24, Court 1, Leicester Street, Coventry, died on 11th February 1919 at City Hospital, Coventry. Hilda was just 21 months old. No known photographs exist.

Child 3: Frederick Henry Pargeter, born on 7th September 1918 at No. 12 Leicester Street, Coventry, died on 18th September 1918 at the same place – he was only 11 days old. No known photographs exist.

Child 4: Gladys Pargeter, born on 16th February 1920 at No. 12 Leicester Street, Coventry. Gladys married George William Jones (a.k.a. Bill) on 4th August 1940 at Saint Peter's Church, Hillfields, Coventry. Witnesses at the wedding were Ethel Pargetter and Joseph Pargetter. Gladys died at the age of 68 on 24th January 1989 at Walsgrave Hospital, Coventry.

George William Jones was born on 18th April 1914 at No. 650 Scotswood Road, Elswick, Newcastle upon Tyne and died in Willenhall, Coventry, on 18th September 1969 at 55 years of age. George was a storekeeper and his father was John Henry Jones, a master hairdresser and his mother was Elizabeth Ann Jones (nee Hildreth).

Opposite is a photograph of George William Jones and Gladys Pargeter (centre of the picture) on their wedding day, taken at Saint Peter's Church, Hillfields, Coventry. The couple on the left are John Henry and Elizabeth Ann Jones with their daughter seated in front of them (name unknown). On the right of the picture are my grandparents Joseph and Matilda Maud Pargeter with their daughter Ethel (Gladys' sister) sitting in front of them.

Below is a very old photograph of Saint Peter's Church, dated 1866. During the 1900s a serious flood caused a great deal of damage to the graveyard, with headstones and people's remains being unearthed and destroyed. It was impossible to rectify it all and now most of the headstones that were recovered have been propped against the wall. Since 2010 the building has been used for living quarters for students or private dwellers. It was completely gutted and redeveloped for the new use, but I believe that the grounds are still owned by the Church.

ST PETERS CHURCH, COVENTRY.

GEORGE AND GLADYS PARGETER (CENTRE OF THE PICTURE)

The spelling of Pargetter with a double 't' was becoming more common and eventually most of the family would use this variation. However, in the Stourbridge area the spelling has remained with a single 't'.

Child 5: Philip Pargeter, born on 25th September 1921 at No. 12 Leicester Street, Coventry, died on 31st December 1986 at Walsgrave Hospital, Coventry. Philip served in the Royal Warwickshire Regiment for twelve years and was also an excellent boxer at the 1925 Boys' Club in Freehold Street, Coventry.

PHILIP PARGETER

Philip Pargeter was my father – he used the double 't' spelling of our surname late in life. Above is a photograph of him in his early twenties, taken when he was in the army. Until I began researching our family history, I had never seen this photograph – I found it with a member of the family in Wales. My father spent nearly 13 years in the army serving in the Royal Warwickshire Regiment, following in the footsteps of his predecessors. He enjoyed his time in the forces and often told me stories when I was young about the countries that he had seen. He had many jobs over the years after he was discharged from the army and eventually he finally settled down at the Roots Car Company which later became Chrysler and then Peugeot. (Before that time it had been the Humber Hillman.) After working for the company for almost 25 years, my father took his redundancy and retired. He told me that he enjoyed every day working there and I think he hardly took a single day off in all those years.

On several occasions I have tried to find out if there is anything that remains from the 1925 Boxing Club, but have been unsuccessful. The club has changed hands many times and I was told that the memorabilia was put into boxes and has now been lost.

When the fair came to Coventry, my father would go along and take part in the boxing matches for a small fee, which he used to win. When I was a toddler, he would take me and my brother Dennis to the fairground with him – it was the Pat Collins Fairground as I recall. My dad seemed to know everyone and I remember we were often invited into the caravans at the back of the fair for a cup of tea. He and my brother would then disappear for a while, leaving me at the caravans with our relatives. A large, mysterious-looking woman would look after me and I have since found out that she was a relation. I remember that she was a kind person and I think that she may have been the fairground's fortune teller. My brother later told me that our father took him to the tent in which the boxing ring was housed and he would watch him box against the local champions. Apparently he also used to take part in bare knuckle fights in many places from the mid thirties up until the mid sixties. He was very good at this kind of combat, although I believe it came to a sudden halt after he broke one of his thumbs in several places. He remained well known and well liked and kept in contact with the fairground people for many years. I don't know how much he would box for, but it would have been enough to pay the rent or buy his fags for the week. I remember my father talking about Alfred Thomas Pargeter (born 1840, died 1919) who was also a good bare knuckle fighter in his day; Alfred, my three times grandfather, is mentioned in Generation 13.

LEICESTER STREET, COVENTRY. 1931.

The photograph above was taken around Christmas time in 1931 in Leicester Street, Coventry. The top image is the restored version of the original photograph shown underneath. When my father was given this photograph he used to bend it in half to fit into his back pocket and carried it around with him everywhere to show his friends and relatives. As you can see, this eventually led to it having a pronounced crease across it and becoming very tatty and worn. I came to the decision to have it restored and, whilst quite an expensive process, I believe it was well worth it. The ten year old lad on the top row with the cheeky grin and flat cap is my father along with some of his sisters and brothers. Leicester Street no longer exists but I have an A4-sized picture of it in my collection which shows a very bleak view of how life was back then. It is a black and white image and even though it shows a rugged outlook of life, it does give a nostalgic view of the houses in the early thirties. When my father eventually lived in the Chantries, Hillfields, Coventry, he would walk alongside the canal which took him along Leicester Causeway, through Leicester Street right up to where his grandfather lived at the time by Saint Osberg's Church.

Child 6: Ethel Pargeter, born on 28th April 1923 at No. 18, Court 1, Leicester Street, Coventry. Ethel married Henry Merrilees on 29th April 1944 at Saint Luke's Church, Wallsend, Northumberland. Witnesses at the wedding were James Picarton and Winifred Merrilees. Ethel Merrilees (nee Pargeter) died on 27th June 1980 at Queen Elizabeth Hospital, Gateshead. Ethel was 57 years of age.

Henry Merrilees (a.k.a. Harry) was born on 27th December 1921 at Vine Street, Wallsend, Tynemouth, Northumberland and is currently still active. In fact, he is just about to celebrate his second 25th wedding anniversary with his second wife in Wallsend. Henry's father, Archibald Merrilees, was able seaman on board HMS Badmington R. N. and later became a shipwright. Henry's mother was Christina Merrilees (nee Carrick). Henry was also a shipwright.

Overleaf is a photograph of Ethel Merrilees (nee Pargeter) which was probably taken in Wallsend, Northumberland. The baby Ethel is holding in her arms is her son Michael who still lives in Northumberland and is now well into his sixties.

Child 7: Elsie Pargeter, born on 9th November 1924 at No. 18, Court 1, Leicester Street, Coventry and died there on 15th November at just six days old. An inquest was held on 17th November in Coventry. I was unable to trace any photographs.

ETHEL MERRILEES

Child 8: Walter Pargeter, born on 1st April 1926 at No. 18, Court 1, Leicester Street, Coventry, died on 2nd November 1928 at No. 18, Court 1, Leicester Street, Coventry. Walter Pargeter was just two years of age. No known photographs exist.

Child 9: Peter Pargeter, born on 11th October 1927 at no 18, court 1, Leicester Street, Coventry. Peter Pargeter or Pargetter, as the name is sometimes now spelt, married Ethel Margaret Pinfield on 1st January 1949 at the Register Office in Coventry.

Witnesses at the wedding were Joseph Pargetter and Elsie Pinfield. Peter is now 84 years old (at the time of writing) and still lives with his wife Ethel in Coventry. Peter served in the Royal Warwickshire Regiment and later on in life he worked for the Jaguar Motor Company in Coventry. They met when they were neighbours living in The Chantries, Hillfields, Coventry. The street is still there to this day.

Ethel Margaret Pinfield was born on 5th November 1930 at No. 10, Court 1, Swanswell Terrace, Coventry. Ethel was a capstan operator at an engineering works. Her father's name was Harold Fredrick Pinfield and he was a painter and decorator and her mother was Elsie Pinfield (nee Clarke). Ethel is still active today and living in the Coventry area.

ROYAL WARWICKS.

Above is a group photograph taken while Peter was serving in the Royal Warwickshire Regiment. Peter is in the top row, second from the right – as marked with a cross. I would very much like to identify the others in this photograph, but unfortunately, like many pictures taken at the time, they were not documented very well. I also have quite a few photographs of my father while he was serving in the forces, one of which was taken in Egypt. Another picture shows him with the football team he was with and he told me that in the three years that he played with his team they never lost a single game which is remarkable. During his time in the forces he also went to India and he has related many stories to me about his experiences there and the tattoos that he had done. On a few occasions my father and his brother Peter met up with each other in the forces abroad. Sadly though in later life they never bothered with each other much for some reason.

Child 10: Jean Pargeter (or Pargetter), born on 26th January 1929 at No. 18, Court 1, Leicester Street, Coventry. Jean married Harry Collier on 25th July 1949 at the Register Office in Coventry. Witnesses at the wedding were P. Pargetter and E. Merrilees. Jean died on 6th April 2007 at No. 49, The Rylands, Lawford Heath, Rugby. Jean was a wood worker at the motor works and later on in life she was a canteen manageress.

JEAN PARGETER (TOP LEFT)

Harry Collier was born on 12th September 1922 at Stone House, Newnham, Northants. Harry was a turner at the motor works. His father was James Collier, a labourer in the army ordnance stores, and his mother was Agnes Mariam Collier (nee Robinson). Harry died on 7th December 1991 at 49 The Ryelands, Lawford Heath, Rugby, Warwickshire.

Above is a photograph of Jean Pargeter (top left) with two of her sisters before she was married. On the right is Ellen Collins (a.k.a. Nelly) and sitting down is Gladys Pargeter.

Child 11: Bernard Pargeter, born on 6th October 1931 at No. 18, Court 1, Leicester Street, Coventry and died there on 25th October 1933 at just two years of age. An inquest was held on 26th October.

Below is a rare photograph of my uncle Bernard, taken at Leicester Street – probably the only photograph that was taken of him. It was thought to be lost or destroyed, but I eventually managed to track it down and take copies of it. It is a shame that people didn't take more photographs back then, and the few that were taken seem to get lost over the years. I am still searching for other photographs as I'm sure there are more pictures of my family somewhere. Apparently the first known photograph was taken as far back as 1820 and the earliest one which survives today dates back to 1825/1826, perhaps even earlier.

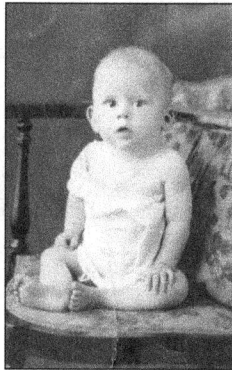

BERNARD PARGETER

Child 12: Barbara Pargetter, born on 25th February 1933 at No. 18, Court 1, Leicester Street, Coventry. Barbara married Christopher Thomas McFarlane on 29th March 1952 at the Coventry Register Office. Witnesses at the wedding were D. Lord and H. Stirling.

Christopher Thomas McFarlane was born on 23rd February 1930 at 41 Howard Street, Newcastle, and died on 26th March 2009 in Coventry at the age of 79. He was a porter at the hospital and his father, James McFarlane, was head porter. His mother's name was Agnes McFarlane (nee Thompson).

Barbara Pargetter's second marriage was to David Edward Mead on 22nd November 1958 at the Register Office in Lambeth, London. Witnesses at the wedding were A. and H. Mead. David Edward Mead was born in 1937 in Lambeth, London and died on 7th December 2012 in Swindon. David was a store man at the motor accessories. David's father was Horace Mead and he was a contract lorry driver. Barbara Mead (nee Pargetter) died on 9th December 1999 at the Princess Margaret Hospital, Swindon. Barbara was about 67 years of age.

Child 13: Sheila Francis Pargetter, born on 10th November 1934 at No. 18, Court 1, Leicester Street, Coventry. Sheila married Ernest Albert Parsons on 12th March 1955 at Saint Peter's Church, Hillfields, Coventry. Sheila died on 5th April 2004 at 36 Growmere Road, Walsgrave, Coventry, at 69 years of age. Ernest Albert Parsons was born on 17th June 1934 at Gulson Road Hospital, Coventry, and died on 19th October 1984 at Coventry and Warwickshire Hospital at 50 years old. Ernest Albert was a trimmer. His father was Albert Parsons and his mother's name was Margaret, maiden name Feasey. Albert was a grinder and they lived at Court 2, House 6, Spon Street, Coventry, and later at No. 66 Sackville Street, Coventry.

SHEILA PARGETTER (HOLDING THE SHIELD)

Above is a school photograph showing Sheila Pargetter. Sheila is the one holding the shield. I haven't yet discovered which school this picture was taken at, but I am still hopeful that I will be able to identify it one day. I would also really like to uncover the identities of the others in the photograph.

During the 1970s Sheila and her sisters Nelly and Gladys often used to go to the Barras Heath Club in Stoke on a Sunday evening. There was entertainment at the Club from about seven and I would sometimes join them for the evening. A good club in its day, but sadly no more.

Chapter Nine
Additional Information About
The Collins Family

James Collins was born about 1776 in Portsea, Hampshire. James married Elizabeth Hartley on 24th March 1800 at Saint Mary's Church on the Isle of Portsea.

Child of James and Elizabeth Collins was Henry Collins, born in baptism on 3rd October 1805 at Saint John the Evangelist Church at Portsea. Date of death 1869. Henry Collins married Eliza Purchess on 16th April 1835 in the parish of Alverstoke, Hampshire near Gosport.

Below is a very old copy of a print or sketch of Saint John the Evangelist Church at Portsea.

ST JOHN'S, PORTSEA

William Purchess was born about 1780 in Portsea, Hampshire. William Purchess married Hannah Stratton on 7th August 1803 at Saint Mary's Church on the Isle of Portsea. William was a stonemason.

Child of William and Hannah Purchess was Eliza Purchess, born in baptism on 19th February 1815 in Saint Mary's Church, Portsea.

Overleaf is a lovely old photograph of Saint Mary's Church in Alverstoke, Hampshire near Gosport.

ST MARY'S CHURCH, ALVERSTOKE

The 1851 Census:

33 Vauxhall Road, Birmingham Henry Collins – Head, aged 45, Railway Guard

Eliza Collins – Wife, age 34

William H. Collins – Son, age 13

Richard Collins – Son, age 8

Matilda Maud Collins – Daughter, age 5

Frederick Augustus Collins – Son, age 3

Kate Collins – Baby Daughter, age 3 months

Frederick Augustus Collins was born on 22nd June 1848 at No. 40, Garrison Lane, Aston, Birmingham. Frederick's first marriage was to Eliza Rigby on 10th September 1877 at St. Lukes Church, Bilston, Staffordshire. Witnesses at the wedding were William Rigby and Jane Rigby. Eliza was born in Birmingham in 1849 and died in 1883, also in Birmingham. Eliza was 34 years old. Her father's name was William Rigby and he was a time keeper; I could not trace her mother's name. Frederick Augustus Collins died on 17th December 1890 when he was only 42 years of age. Fred was a striker at the nailworks and later

GARRISON LANE, BIRMINGHAM

he worked at the cycle works in Coventry. I know that there was a photograph of my great grandfather, Frederick Collins, but it seems that unfortunately it has either been lost or destroyed. He gave the name Matilda Maud Collins to his daughter after his sister (third child named above).

Children of Frederick Augustus Collins and Eliza Rigby:

Child 1: Eliza J Collins, born 1877, Wolverhampton.

Child 2: Annie Maria Collins, born on 8th March 1880 at Court 10, Arthur Street, Aston, Birmingham.

Above is a drawing of Garrison Lane, Birmingham, looking rather grim. It doesn't look to be a great environment for children to grow up in, but I guess they wouldn't have known any different as their friends and family would have lived in the same conditions.

Frederick Augustus Collins' second marriage was to Ellen Jones on 24th July 1887 at Saint George's Church, Birmingham. There is a gypsy connection to one or both of my great grandparents mentioned above as my father used to tell me stories when he used to visit the

Pat Collins fairground in the sixties. I am currently researching this.

Children of Frederick Augustus Collins and Ellen Collins (nee Jones):

Child 1: Henry Frederick Collins, born on 26th May 1887 in Foleshill, Warwickshire, baptised on 30th May 1888 at Saint Michael's Church, Coventry, died on 1st October 1917 in France in W.W.1. Memorial to Henry Frederick Collins (a.k.a. Frederick Collins) is situated at Tyne Cot, Belgium. Frederick was just 30 years of age. Henry Frederick Collins was born in May of 1887, but his parents were not married until 24th July 1887.

On the facing page is a photograph of Henry Frederick Collins (a.k.a. Frederick Collins).

Location of this photograph is unknown, but it is a true reminder of how all the men who served in W.W.1 would have looked in their uniforms and they would have been so proud to wear them fighting for their country. Some would have welcomed the chance to go and fight abroad just to get away from their grim surroundings, they perhaps had no money or job and were probably part of a large family. Unfortunately for many soldiers of the Great War, including my great uncle Henry Frederick Collins, they never came back home. My great grandmother, Frederick's mother, was never told exactly how he died, and sadly she died never knowing as no one really told her the truth. We were told that a direct hit killed him outright and he had no chance. Truly never forgotten. Before researching my family tree I never knew what battalion Frederick was in and I was never told by any member of the family. However after nearly 100 years, I have tracked down Great Uncle Frederick's battalion. He was serving in the Second Battalion in the Royal Warwickshire Regiment and I also found out that there is some information about his death on that dreadful day. I was pleased to discover this, but sadly it came too late for others in the family. I have his army number as well as his medal card which doesn't tell me a lot but it is all interesting family history.

Overleaf is an extract from a transcript of the Second Battalion of the Royal Warwickshire Regiment which I located at the Royal Warwickshire Museum in Warwick. Frederick died on 1st October 1917,

FRED COLLINS.

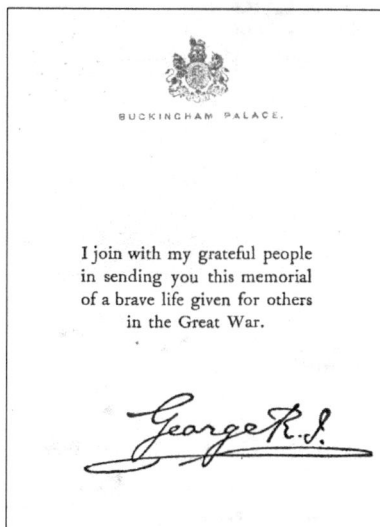

BUCKINGHAM PALACE.

I join with my grateful people in sending you this memorial of a brave life given for others in the Great War.

George R.J.

LETTER OF CONDOLENCE

TYNE COT COMMONWEALTH WAR GRAVES CEMETERY.

TRANSCRIPT, 3RD OCTOBER 1917.

but his death was not recorded until 3rd October as shown in the transcript. The men were carrying ammunition and supplies to the First Welsh Fusiliers. It is not noted whether Frederick was killed before mid-day on 1st October, but it seems that the Second Battalion moved up to a place called Hooge Crater at mid-day. They had their own names for trenches and craters.

On 3rd October 1917, the transcript clearly states that sometime from 1st to 3rd there were two soldiers killed, one of which was my Uncle Fred. Twenty-six wounded, six missing and eight shell-shocked. No names are given. I have a few of these transcripts in my possession from May to October 1917 and until I was able to track them down, no member of my family had ever seen them before.

The Transcript is a bit difficult to decipher, so I have transcribed it below ('Coy' stands for Company; 'Bn.' Stands for Battalion):

1917

Oct.   IN THE FIELD – DUGOUTS 1.17. c & d.
         HOOGE CRATER.

2nd.   The Bn. moved back to Dugouts, ZILLEBEKE LAKE
         at 12.0 noon and remained there until 4.40 p.m. when it
         moved back to camp at N.2.b.4.6.

         2 Lieut. G. B. Pountney joined.

         CAMP N.2.b.4.6.

3rd.   50 men working for 22nd Machine Gun Coy for carrying
         purposes.

         250 men carrying trench boards from HOOGE CRATER
         under supervision of 54th Coy R.E. The Bn marched to
         Dugouts on western bank of ZILLEBEKE LAKE with
         orders to remain and await further orders.

         2 Lieut. W. J. Benton joined.

         Casualties for period 1.10.17 to 3.10.17:- 2 Killed, 26
         Wounded, 6 Missing, 8 Shell Shock.

         ZILLEBEKE LAKE.

4th.   Battalion remained in reserve all day: 50 men working for 22nd M.O.Coy – Casualties

(party working with M.G. Coy) 2 Killed, 6 wounded, 8 missing.

5th.   50 men working as stretcher bearers at HOOGE CRATER. The Bn. marched back to

Camp at N.2.b.4.6. at 1.30 p.m.

CAMP N:2.b.4.6.

6th.   The Bn. remained in camp at N.2.b.4.6.

7th.   11.30 a.m. The Bn. moved up to ZILLEBEKE LAKE, had dinners on arrival.

3.30 p.m. Moved up to line East of POLYGONE WOOD. Battalion Head Quarters THE BUTTE. A. D & C Coys in front line, B Coy in Support.

Casualties:- 8 Wounded, 2 Missing

Children of Frederick Augustus Collins and Ellen Collins (nee Jones) continued:

Child 2: Elizabeth Collins, born on 12th March 1889 at No. 4, Court 1, Cow Lane, Coventry, baptised on 7th October 1889 at Saint Michael's, Coventry, quickly and privately, as stated on the baptism certificate, due to ill health. Elizabeth died on 16th October 1889 at just seven months old. No known photograph exists.

Following on is a beautiful interior photograph of the old Saint Michael's Church which was blitzed in the Second World War. My grandmother and aunts were baptised here. Saint Michael's was a church up until 1918 when it became a cathedral and the town therefore became a city once again.

Child 3: Matilda Maud Collins, born on 10th March 1890 at No. 4, Court 1, Cow Lane, Coventry, baptised on 12th March 1890 at Saint Michael's Church, Coventry, died on 17th March 1975 in Coventry.

ST MICHAELS CHURCH INTERIOR, COVENTRY.

Below is a photograph of Cow Lane, Coventry which no longer exists. Cow Lane was just by where New Union Street is today in Coventry.

My great grandfather, Frederick Collins, worked for the cycle works – the building is now a hotel at the bottom of Mile Lane. If you look up at the wall on the hotel you can see where they have kept

COW LANE, COVENTRY

the original cycle works sign, which has been restored. It is good to see this small historical remembrance has been preserved, although there is a lot in Coventry today that would benefit from some attention. For example, I know of at least five historical buildings which need to be restored to their natural beauty. The first is the White Friars, dating back to 1342, which became a workhouse. If it was restored, it could be opened to the public and not just stand there in a dilapidated state, forgotten. The second building is Drapers Hall, Bayley Lane; this dates back to 1831–2 and it is just rotting away. The third is the County Hall come prison in Cuckoo Lane, 1783–4, which had also fallen into disrepair, although I believe it has now been converted into a public house and restaurant. This building has a lot of history; probably the most talked about is the hanging of Mary Ball, the last woman to be publicly hanged in Warwickshire.

Mary Ball (nee Wright), an innkeeper, and her husband Thomas Ball lived in Back Lane, Nuneaton. Mary bought some arsenic, apparently to get rid of some bugs, which she kept on a shelf. Her husband Thomas returned from a fishing trip one day, feeling unwell. He looked for some salts to make him feel better and ended up drinking the arsenic, which killed him. Mary denied murder by poisoning, but later confessed after a zealous prison chaplain, trying to get her to repent, forced her hand over a lighted candle. Mary Ball was hanged in front of about 20,000 spectators at that very spot in Cuckoo Lane, Coventry by William Calcroft on 9th August 1849 at 10 a.m. Mary was 31 years old. Her death mask can still be seen at Little Park Police Museum just a few hundred yards away from the scene of the execution.

Then there is the Charterhouse, 1381, which is currently owned by the City College. The fifth building is where the Post Office has just become vacant as many other buildings have. The building is the old grammar school in Hales Street; a grammar school since 1557, it dates back to the 1100s and was originally the church of the hospital of St John's, which is a Grade 1 listed building. It's becoming like a ghost town round there once again. I believe that eventually there will be a massive shopping mall there one day. Some of the buildings are listed so cannot be knocked down, although quite a few have been destroyed by fire over the years. Developers will come and make changes to hopefully improve the area, but it is important to preserve our heritage wherever possible and restore the old buildings that are part of the true Coventry.

The old Grammar School which was founded in the 12th Century and the hospital of Saint John the Baptist on the corner of Hales Street are Grade I listed so developers will need to comply to regulations in

ST PAULS, COVENTRY.

order to develop this site. The signs that say 'Welcome to Historic Coventry' mislead people – where is this historic city? Something needs to be done to restore the old buildings and open them to the public so that people can see the real history of Coventry.

Ellen Collins' (nee Jones) second marriage was to John Allibone on 19th August 1893 in Saint Paul's Church, Foleshill, Coventry. Saint Paul's was built in 1841 and on its official opening day it was visited by George Eliot, the well known author from Nuneaton. George Eliot is the pen name of Mary Ann Evans and she is well known all around the world. Saint Paul's Church was badly damaged during the war and only the tower survived. It was rebuilt during the 1950s.

Above is a lovely picture of St Paul's Church, Foleshill Road, Coventry.

The Family Tree of John Allibone

John Allibone was born on 19th March 1860 at Jordan Well, Coventry and was baptised on 20th March 1860 at St Michael's Church, Coventry. John married Ellen Collins on 19th August 1893 in Saint Paul's Church, Foleshill, Coventry. Ellen Collins (nee Jones) was born on 10th May 1857 at Lionel Street, Birmingham. Ellen died on 23rd February 1941 at 84 years of age. On her death certificate, her age is shown as 82, but this is because her baptism date was used rather than her date of birth. This kind of inconsistency frequently happened in the records back then. John Allibone was a brickyard labourer and a soldier in WW1 and later a mechanic. He died between 1918 and 1919, location unknown. His father, George Allibone, was a labourer and bricklayer, and his mother's name was Elizabeth, maiden name Lacey.

Children of John Allibone and Ellen Collins (nee Jones):

Child 1: Ellen Elizabeth Allibone, born about 1893 possibly in the workhouse in Foleshill, Coventry. Ellen Allibone married Walter Charley on 20th March 1918 at Saint Mark's Church, Coventry. Witnesses at the wedding were Jack Allibone and Lucy Eva Fisher. Ellen Charley (nee Allibone) died on 5th November 1958 at No.33, Friars Road, Coventry. Ellen was 64 years of age. Walter Charley was born on 6th April 1894 at 33 New Street, Coventry and died on 15th June 1966 in Coventry. Walter was a master greengrocer in Hillfields, Coventry; his shop was just around the corner from Colchester Street. His father's name was William Charley, a labourer, and his mother's name was Mary, maiden name Bench.

Saint Mark's Church, where Ellen Allibone and Walter Charley were married, is located on the corner of Bird Street and Stoney Stanton Road. The foundation stone was laid on 5th June 1868 by Sir James Darling of Meriden Hall. It was consecrated the following year. The church, like so many others, was damaged by war time bombings in Easter 1941. The damage was repaired by 1946–47. Soon after, a new electronic organ was installed in Saint Mark's and the old one was transferred to Coventry and Warwickshire Hospital. The church was eventually closed to the public in 1972 and the electronic organ was then transferred to Saint Martin's Church, Green Lane, Coventry. Saint Mark's Church was soon after used, and still is, as an outpatients department for Coventry and Warwickshire Hospital.

Child 2: Jack Allibone, born on 2nd April 1896 in the workhouse in Foleshill, Coventry, died on 23rd March 1981 at Walsgrave Hospital, Coventry. Jack married Eva Ellen Legge on 12th June 1919 in Christchurch, Dorset. Eva Ellen Allibone (nee Legge) was born on 15th October 1900 in Dorset and died on 31st March 1988 at Green Park, Coventry.

Child 3: Emily Allibone, born on 29th January 1899 in the workhouse, Foleshill, Coventry, and died there on 15th April 1908 at just nine years of age. Emily lies in an unmarked grave at London Road, Coventry.

Overleaf is a photograph of Ellen Allibone (formerly Collins, nee Jones), taken around 1900. This is the photograph of my great grandmother who was the mother of Matilda Maud Collins, my direct grandmother on my father's side. I have also got a colour photograph of her taken in the back garden of No. 44, The Chantries, Hillfields, Coventry, where the Pargetter family lived for many years from about 1938 until 1974. Ellen lived for many years with my grandmother in her house and with Matilda's daughter, also named Ellen (a.k.a. Nelly). She had spent time in the Coventry workhouse many years earlier, which must have been a pretty grim experience. When her daughter, my grandmother, fell pregnant she was kicked out to fend for herself and spent a while in the workhouse at No. 11, London Road, while she gave birth to her daughter. After a while, she met my grandfather at a dance and was able to leave the workhouse.

The photograph is unfortunately very dark and in a fairly poor condition – it is only a copy of the original, which I have not been able to trace, but I will have the copy restored at a later date which should improve the quality of the image.

ELLEN COLLINS.

Chapter Ten
Willenhall, Coventry

Generation No. 16

Philip Pargetter (my father), born on 25th September 1921 at No. 12, Leicester Street, Coventry. Philip married Marjorie Fox Bennett Brown on 20th April 1946 at Saint Cuthbert's Church, Bedlington, Northumberland. Witnesses at the wedding were Thomas William McCauley and Gladys McCauley. Marjorie Fox Bennett Brown was born on 5th February 1928 at No 4, Telephone Row, Bedlington, Morpeth, Northumberland and died on 10th August 2005 in Northumberland at 77 years of age. Marjorie's father's name was John Brown and he was a colliery hewer and her mother's name was Margaret Jane Brown (nee McCauley).

Philip Pargetter's second marriage was to Helene Eugenia Ottens (nee Finger) and took place on 21st April 1951 at the Coventry Register Office. Witnesses at the wedding were Barbara Pargetter and Peter Pargetter; an interpreter, A. W. M. Hall, was also present to assist Helene who was German. Philip died on 31st December 1986 at Walsgrave Hospital, Coventry, at 65 years of age. Helene Eugenia Pargetter (my mother) (nee Ottens, formerly Finger) was born on 5th April 1916 in Dusseldorf Germany and died on 27th January 1995 at Walsgrave Hospital, Coventry at 78 years of age. My mother and my father are buried together at Canley Cemetery.

On the following page is a lovely photograph of my mother Helene and my half-sister Karin Luise. It was taken somewhere in Dusseldorf, Germany, probably Bomlitz, about 1944 or 1945. The picture was probably taken by Karin's father, Bernard Zeller, who was a captain in the German army. Or it may have been taken by Helene's father, my grandfather, Karl Finger. My father, Philip, met my mother, Helene, in Bomlitz in Germany where he was stationed at the time while serving in the army. Bomlitz was virtually blown off the map during the war, but it was later rebuilt in much the same style as it was before

MUM AND KARIN.

it was bombed. Notice the hairstyles in the photograph, which look old-fashioned to us now but were very trendy at the time. I remember as a child watching my mother deftly arrange her hair in minutes. She was also a brilliant cook and used to love making delicious German dishes for us, including cakes that were created in layers and looked fantastic. I used to watch my mother for hours cooking and baking and from an early age I learned to cook and bake as well. I still very much enjoy cooking for my family – although generally all they want these days is a curry!

Children of Philip Pargetter and Helene Eugenia Finger:

Child 1: Karin Luise Pargetter (formerly Zeller), born on 18th February 1940 in a place between Stuttgart and Ulm, Germany. Karin married Barry Sowter on 7th July 1962 at Saint George's Church, Coundon, Coventry. Witnesses at the wedding were Philip Pargetter and Charles Sowter. Barry Charles Sowter was born on 5th February 1938 at No 69, George Elliot Road, Foleshill, Coventry. Barry and Karin are now both retired and live in Coventry.

Child 2: Dennis Phillip Pargetter, born on 5th June 1952 at Gulson Road Hospital, Coventry, baptised on 20th July 1952 at Westwood St James Church, Coventry. Dennis married Vivienne Jeanette Lee on 21st October 1972 at Saint John's Church, Willenhall, Coventry. Dennis is a Master Builder. Vivienne Jeanette Lee was born on 22nd October 1955 at Tile Hill, Coventry. Vivienne's father was Stanley Joseph Lee, a fitter, and her mother was Christine Mary Lee (a.k.a. Molly) (nee Quinney). Dennis and Vivienne now live in the Rugby area just outside Coventry.

Child 3: Roy Pargetter, born on 28th March 1956 at No. 185, Monkswood Crescent, Henley Green, Coventry, baptised on 13th May 1956 at Saint Chad's Church, Wood End, Coventry. Saint Chad's was one of three identical churches built in Coventry which were designed by the architect Sir Basil Spence who also designed the new Coventry Cathedral. The other two matching churches are Saint John's in Willenhall and Saint Oswald's in Tile Hill, Coventry.

The German Family Tree:
My Mother, Helene Eugenia Finger and My Grandparents

Generation 1:

Johann Freidrich Fleischmann, was born in 1750 in Remscheld Rhineland, Prussia, Germany. Johann married Ellesabeth Mueller on 30th November 1775 in the Evangelist church in Remscheld Rhineland, Prussia, Germany.

Child of Johann Freidrich Fleischmann and Ellesabeth Mueller:
Child 1: Anna Dorothea Theresia Fleischmann, born on 6th November 1781 in Remscheld, Prussia, Germany

Generation 2:

Anna Dorothea Theresia Fleischmann, born on 6th November 1781 in Remscheld, Prussia, Germany. Anna married Johann Wilhelm Minck about 1808-9 in Remscheld, Prussia, Germany.

Child of Johann Wilhelm Minck and Anna Dorothea Theresia Fleischmann:
Child 1: Freidrich Minck, was born in 1810 in Remscheld, Prussia, Germany

Generation 3:

Freidrich Minck, was born in 1810 in Remscheld, Prussia, Germany. Freidrich married Sibilla Mieves on 12th January 1839 in Prussia, Germany. Freidrich was 29 and Sibilla was 17. Sibilla's parents are Wilhelm Mieves and Wilhelmina Schmitz.

Children of Freidrich Minck and Sibilla Mieves:

Child 1: Freidrich Minck, born in 1839 in Bergheim, Germany

Child 2: Wilhelmina Minck, born in 1840 in Bergheim, Germany

Child 3: Gertrudis Minck, born on 7th February 1841 in Bergheim, Germany; died on 15th April 1900 in Dusseldorf, Germany

Child 4: Hubertina Minck, born in 1842-3 in Bergheim, Germany

Child 5: Carl Minck, born in 1844 in Bergheim, Germany

Child 6: Francisck Minck, born unknown in Bergheim, Germany

Generation 4:

Gertrudis Minck, born on 7th February 1841 in Bergheim, Germany; died on 15th April 1900 in Dusseldorf, Germany. Gertrudis married Anton Heinrich Finger on 17th November 1865 in Dusseldorf, Germany. Anton Heinrich Finger was born in 1840 in Heddinghausen, Germany; died on 15th November 1909 in Dusseldorf, Germany. Place of residence at the time of marriage was Heddinghausen, Westfalen, Prussia, Germany. Parents of Anton Heinrich Finger: Joseph Finger, a metal worker, and Maria Finger [nee Thiele] Anton, was a Postal worker.

Children of Anton Heinrich Finger and Gertrudis Minck:

Child 1: Gertrude Finger, born on 17th March 1866 in Dusseldorf, Germany

Child 2: Freidrich Finger, born on 12th October 1868 in Dusseldorf, Germany

Child 3: Hubertine Finger, born on 17th January 1872 in Dusseldorf, Germany

Child 4: Helene Finger, born on 4th July 1874 in Düsseldorf, Germany

Child 5: Karl Finger, born on 13th April 1878 in Dusseldorf, Germany

Generation 5:

Karl Finger, born on 13th April 1878 in Dusseldorf, Germany; died on 4th August 1961. His last address was Ellerstrabe 96, Germany.

Below is a photograph of Ellerstrabe 96, the last home of my grandfather, Karl Finger. Some of his siblings were born there, as was my mother. He was a goldsmith and a silversmith. The property is very large and it seems that they were quite wealthy; however, my mother never experienced wealth in her life.

ELLERSTRABE 96

Karl Finger's first marriage was to Adele Esser on 20th June 1902 in Dusseldorf, Germany. Adele Finger [née Esser] died on 20th May 1905 in Dusseldorf Germany witnessed by the matron of St Mary's hospital. Witnesses at the wedding were Heinrich Weber and Heinrich Schmitz. Adele Finger [née Esser] was a catholic and was born at 9.30 in the morning on 4th August 1884 in Dusseldorf Germany. Parents of Adele Esser are Heinrich Esser and Maria Esser [nee Weber]

Children of Karl Finger and Adele Esser:

Child 1: Maria Gertrude Finger, AKA Gertrude born on 22nd September 1902 in Dusseldorf, Germany died unknown.

Child 2: Adele Helene Finger, born on 2nd October 1903 in Dusseldorf, Germany, died on 3rd October 1905 when she less than two years old.

Child 3: Karl Heinrich Finger, born on 14th February 1905 in Dusseldorf, Germany. Died on 16th October 1905 in Dusseldorf Germany

Karl Finger's second marriage was to Johanette Katharina Elisabeth Vopel on 17th November 1908 in Dusseldorf, Germany. Johanette born on 15th October 1887 in Gellerhausen Waldec died on 6th August 1918 in Dusseldorf Germany. Johanette was just 30 years of age. Parents are Heinrich Vopel and Freda Vopel [nee Gruss]

Children of Karl Finger and Johanette Katharina Elisabeth Vopel:

Child 1: Katharina Maria Finger, Aka Miessa born on 18th July 1909 at Kronenstrabe 47 in Dusseldorf, Germany, date of death unknown. Katharina was named after her mother. Katharina Maria Finger married Gustav surname unknown in the late 1920s early 1930s. They had one daughter together called Gisela; date of birth marriage and death are unknown but it is believed they were all in Dusseldorf Germany

Overleaf are photographs of Kronenstrabe 47 and my grandmother, Johanette Katharina Elisabeth Finger (née Vopel) which I understand was taken by my grandfather Karl. Johanette was Karl's second wife and my mother's mother, my grandmother. She was a very hard woman but very fair to her children and looked after them well; my mother was her fourth child. Unfortunately, Johanette died when my mother was only about 18 months old. The exact location of this photograph is unknown but it was taken in Germany, probably Dusseldorf.

KRONENSTRABE 47

JOHANETTE KATHARINA ELISABETH FINGER.

Children of Karl Finger and Johanette Katharina Elisabeth Vopel continued

Child 2: Karl Adolf Finger, born on 9th November 1911 in Dusseldorf, Germany, date of death unknown. Karl Finger Married Alma [surname unknown]

Child 3: Franziska Louise Finger, born on 1st October 1913 at Palmenstrabe 21 in Dusseldorf, Germany. Franziska is my mother's sister and she is now (at the time of writing) 97 years of age and still lives in Germany. I've never met her, but she sends my sister a letter every now and then.

Franziska writes in really old German and her letters are very hard to understand so it takes a while for my sister to decipher them. My mother was able to read and write the old style well. She once wrote a letter for me to take to school (Whitley Abbey School) when I was off sick for a week after being knocked down by a car in the fog after a school detention back in 1969. I explained to the school that my mother's English was not that good though it was readable. My teacher, who taught German, said that my mother could write the letter in old German if it was easier for her and he would be able to read it. I passed this message back to my mother who then happily wrote her note in her own language. I took the letter to school and gave it to my House Head who then took it to the German teacher, who was regarded as one of the best. He started to read the letter but after a while he told me, and all the other teachers, that it was nonsense and not German at all. Other teachers who also knew German tried to decipher the letter but not one of them was able to. Eventually, my mother had to write another letter as best she could, in English, for the school records to explain why I had been off school. They never asked for a letter to be written in old German again.

The last time I heard, my Auntie Franziska was still doing well. Her husband was a very rich man and they lived a good life. I'm not sure whether she is now living with friends or in a care home in Dusseldorf.

Below is a photograph of Franziska Finger before she was married. When my mother lived in Germany, she was the closest to Franziska out of all the members of her family.

FRANZISKA FINGER

Child 4: Helene Eugenia Finger, born on 4th May 1916 in Dusseldorf, Germany, died on 27th January 1995 at Walsgrave hospital, Coventry

Below is a lovely picture of my mother which was taken in Bomlitz, Germany, in 1945.

HELENE EUGENIA FINGER

It was taken in the woods in farmland where my mother was sent by her family. I recently found this photograph in an album at my sister's home. My mother and father met in Bomlitz when he was stationed there towards the end and after the war. My father decided to bring her back to England to get married along with my sister, but they had to first complete a lot of paperwork and naturalization documents before they were eligible to travel. Eventually they were allowed to make the journey and subsequently arrived in Coventry. My father's family was not very hospitable to my mother and sister and only one or two family members helped them. Eventually one of my aunts asked them to move in with her not very far away in Colchester Street Hillfields. They stayed there for a while before being offered their own council house at No. 32, Hawthorn Lane, Tile Hill, Coventry. My father worked as a baler at the time before working through several other jobs until he eventually settled down at the Roots Motor Works in Stoke Aldermore, Coventry. He would stay there for 23 years before taking his redundancy in the mid-seventies.

Karl Finger's third marriage was to Thekla Korkuc on 2nd January 1920 in Düsseldorf, Germany. Thekla Korkuc born on 23rd September 1897 in Russia, died on 24th January 1984 in Dusseldorf Germany.

Below is an old photograph of Karl and his third wife Thekla taken somewhere in Düsseldorf.

KARL FINGER AND THEKLA KORKUC

I was told a story by my mother and sister of the time when the Germans were rounding up all the Jews. One night, my grandfather's friend who lived next door to him was taken away with his wife and their children. Karl immediately approached the local authorities to find out where they had been taken, but with no success. He was persistent, but was eventually warned by someone in authority to mind his own business and never to ask about his friend and family again or he may disappear one night with his own family as well. My grandfather knew that they had been taken to one of the concentration camps and were no doubt going to be executed. Despite his attempts, he never saw his friend again.

My sister told me another story about when she and my mother lived in Bomlitz. Food was scarce and people had to get by as best they could. On one occasion, a group of people were waiting with the intention of stealing from the food dump which was heavily guarded by soldiers with dogs. A local policeman, who was part of the group, knew that the penalty for stealing food was to be shot on sight, but he was prepared to risk his life to get food for his family. My sister hid and watched from the bushes in the freezing cold, snowy night in fear, as my mother, the policeman and the rest of the group quietly looted from the dump. The soldiers on guard shone their torches around the dump trying to spot any activity in case there were any looters around that night. Luckily no one was caught on this occasion and they managed to get away without being seen.

Child of Karl Finger and Thekla Korkuc:
Child 1: Thekla Wanda Finger, born on 12th October 1919 in Düsseldorf, Germany died unknown. Karl and Thekla had just the one child together.

Generation No. 17

Roy Pargetter (me), born on 28th March 1956 at 185 Monkswood Crescent, Henley Green a.k.a. Wood End, Coventry. I married Susan Patricia Bishop on 21st September 1974 at Saint John's Church, Willenhall, Coventry. Witnesses at the wedding were Barry C. Sowter and P. E. Bishop. Susan was born on 28th October 1956 at Gulson Road Hospital in Coventry. Her father's name is Walter Geoffrey Bishop and he now lives in Wales. Susan's mother, now deceased, was Pauline Elizabeth Bishop (nee Jones). I have had many jobs over the years including being a machinist, working in an abattoir, a roofer, and a driver. I am also a published author of several books, a four times champion gardener winning 16 awards in total, and founder of the Special Needs Card. Susan Pargetter (nee Bishop) was a supermarket shelf stacker and a machinist at the G.E.C. in Coventry.

During the period 1956 to 1960 I was put into a care home on a few occasions while my mother received electric shock treatments due to her suffering several breakdowns. During her time growing up in Germany she had witnessed the terrible horrors of both World Wars, especially WW2. She told me some of what occurred, but not everything as it was too upsetting. As for the electric shock treatment that she received at Hatton Hospital, Warwick, it's a fact that the treatment, along with other methods that they tried, did not work and actually caused more harm than good.

Below is a photograph of Roy and Susan Pargetter (nee Bishop)

ROY AND SUSAN PARGETTER (NEE BISHOP)

Children of Roy Pargetter and Susan Bishop:

Child 1: Ricky Roy Philip Pargetter, born on 18th March 1978 at Walsgrave Hospital, Coventry.

Child 2: Lisa Dawn Pargetter, born on 6th May 1982 at Walsgrave Hospital, Coventry. Lisa Pargetter's partner was David Marsh, a car seat maker, and they have a child, Shania Star Marsh who was born on 5th December 2000 at Walsgrave Hospital, Coventry. Shania is currently a scholar.

Child 3: Luke Michael Joseph Pargetter, born on 10th February 1991 at Walsgrave Hospital, Coventry. Luke was in fact a twin, but sadly we lost his brother.

Generation No. 18

Ricky Roy Philip Pargetter was born on 18th March 1978 at Walsgrave Hospital, Coventry. Ricky married Claire Marie Pargetter, formerly Gleeson (nee Alcock), on 9th August 2003 at the Register Office in Coventry. Witnesses at the wedding were Martin Crayton and M. Madeley. Claire was born on 31st March 1978 in Coventry. Ricky was a gardener, painter and decorator, and also a boxer and is now a full-time father. Claire was a burger bar assistant and a supervisor at a rest home and is now a home help supervisor.

Children of Ricky Roy Philip and Claire Pargetter:

Child 1: Shannon Nicole Pargetter, born on 25th February 1996 at Walsgrave Hospital, Coventry. Shannon is currently a scholar and is from a different relationship.

Child 2: Shane Ricky Roy Pargetter, born on 20th December 1997 at Walsgrave Hospital, Coventry. Shane is currently a scholar.

Child 3: Ronan Andrew Pargetter, born on 9th November 1999 at Walsgrave Hospital, Coventry. Ronan is currently a scholar.

Child 4: Katie Claire Pargetter, born on 25th October 2006 at Walsgrave Hospital, Coventry. Katie is currently a scholar.

Chapter Eleven

The History of the Richardson Family and their Successors 1810–1928

History of the Glassworks:
Dudley Flint Glassworks to Hawkes' Glassworks,

1776–1843

Benjamin Richardson was born about 1698 probably in Walsall, Staffordshire. Benjamin married Susannah Lester on 22nd September 1723 in Kingswinford, Staffordshire. Susannah was born on 22nd December 1704 in Sherbourne, Dorset. Susannah's parents were Daniel and Susannah Lester, maiden name unknown. The date of death of Benjamin and Susannah is unknown.

Children of Benjamin Richardson and Susannah Lester:
Child 1: John Richardson, born in baptism on 4th August 1724 at Saint Matthew's Church in Walsall, Staffordshire, died in 1818.
Child 2: Anne Richardson, born in 1726, date of death unknown.
Child 3: Benjamin Richardson, born in 1730, date of death unknown.
Child 4: Hannah Richardson, born in 1732, date of death unknown.

John Richardson married Mary Haden on 25th August 1746 at Saint Mary's Church, Kingswinford. Mary Haden was born in 1724 and died in 1814. John Richardson was a bricklayer.

Overleaf is a photograph of Saint Matthew's Church in Walsall where John Richardson was baptised. The crypt can be dated back as early as 1150. The actual church was built in the 14th Century and has some lovely features. The ancient internal pillars were eventually replaced in Georgian times in about 1821 by cast iron ones which are still in place to this very day. The original parish records are still

ST MATTHEWS, WALSALL

kept at the church rather than in the archives where most records are now kept for safety reasons. During my research I asked for a copy of one of my great grandfather's baptism records at Walsall archives, but was told that they only had rewritten copies. Wanting a copy of the original, I contacted the church itself and they sent me a copy, although with a rather hefty bill for nearly twenty pounds! Walsall is a very old town with a lot of history, there are still some old buildings, but sadly many are disappearing. While I was there for an afternoon, I visited Pargeter Street where Philip Pargeter, the glass manufacturer and engraver, built many houses as he owned a very large tract of land.

Children of John Richardson and Mary Haden:

Child 1: Elizabeth Richardson, born in 1747, date of death unknown.

Child 2: Benjamin Richardson, born in 1749, date of death unknown.

Child 3: John Richardson, born in 1754, date of death unknown.

Child 4: Mary Richardson, born in 1757, date of death unknown.

Child 5: Joseph Richardson, born in baptism on 23rd December 1759, died in 1841 and buried on 7th June 1841. Joseph was a furnace builder and a yeoman farmer. Joseph Richardson married Martha Haden on 23rd August 1784 in Kingswinford, Staffordshire. Martha was baptised on 31st March 1765 and died in 1841 in Kingswinford, Staffordshire. Martha was the daughter of John and Elizabeth Haden. Mary Haden and Martha Haden were related.

Child 6: William Richardson, born in 1762, date of death unknown. William married Elizabeth Beddard about 1885.

Children of Joseph Richardson and Martha Haden:

Child 1: William Haden Richardson, born before 27th March 1785, died on 21st December 1876. William's first marriage was to Sarah Pollard on 30th May 1808 and his second was to Mary Pargeter on 23rd September 1848.

Child 2: John Richardson, born before 31st December 1786 in Kingswinsford, Staffordshire.

Child 3: Mary Richardson, born before 11th January 1789 in Kingswinsford, Staffordshire.

Child 4: Thomas Richardson, born before 23rd January 1791 in Kingswinford, Staffordshire. Unable to trace the name of the woman who Thomas married.

Child 5: Elizabeth Richardson, born before 14th October 1792 in Kingswinford, Staffordshire.

Child 6: Susannah Richardson, born before 3rd August 1794 in Kingswinford, Staffordshire, died on 26th December 1868. Susannah married Philip Pargeter on 3rd January 1814.

Child 7: Joseph Richardson, born before 11th December 1796 in Kingswinsford, Staffordshire.

Child 8: Martha Richardson, born before 30th June 1799 in Kingswinford, Staffordshire.

Child 9: Benjamin Richardson, born before 9th March 1802 in Kingswinford, Staffordshire, died on 30th October 1887. Benjamin married Ann Gething on 4th October 1824 in Saint Peter's Church in Wolverhampton. Ann's date of birth is unknown, she died before 1851.

Child 10: Maria Richardson, born before 1st April 1804 in Kingswinford, Staffordshire. Maria married Frederick Northwood about 1838.

Child 11: Jonathon Richardson, born before 24th August 1806 in Kingswinford, Staffordshire, died before 1861. Jonathon married Sarah Lloyd on 29th October 1826 in Trysull, Staffordshire.

The Richardsons: An insight into the family

In 1810 William Haden Richardson joined Dudley Flint Glassworks at the age of 25. He became the firm's traveller. William's own notebook indicates that they began glass making in Bilston as early as 1802. He then moved to Grafton's Brierley Glassworks and later on to Hawkes', where he worked from 1810 to 1828.

William's younger brother Benjamin joined the firm later and worked his way up to the position of manager.

Wordsley Flint Glassworks

Wordsley Flint Glassworks was built by John Hill. He hired local furnace builder Joseph Richardson to build a new ten pot furnace, but he ran into financial problems and had to sell the works to Richard Bradley, a wealthy local industrialist. Bradley and his brother-in-law George Ensall had experience in glassworks, namely the Harlestone Glasshouse in Coalbournbrook. On 23rd February 1796, Richard Bradley died and control of his properties was passed on to his heirs. The Wordsley Flint Glassworks continued to be controlled by the Ensall family until 1810 when all operations were discontinued. Soon after, a legal dispute took place for the ownership of the company. Eventually the whole property was divided up into six lots and sold in 1827. The old glassworks had been converted into a steel house when it was bought by George William Wainwright who eventually turned it back into an operational glasshouse. George employed his brother Charles to work in the business and they decided to hire Benjamin Richardson, who was at the time the manager of Thomas Hawkes, to manage their new firm. In July in the year 1828 the furnace was lit.

After about a year the Wainwright brothers decided to sell the business. Benjamin Richardson and his brother William Haden Richardson jumped at the chance to own it and for the first time they operated their own business. William was 44 years old at the time and he was the eldest of 11 children. His brother Benjamin was 27 years of age and he was the ninth child. William was very knowledgeable about glass making because he had gained a lot of experience by working for several Midlands factories. He had also worked as a furnace builder with his father Joseph, who was a master glasshouse furnace builder and had built the original glasshouse in 1781. Their grandfather John Richardson was a bricklayer and was well known in the area.

Benjamin Richardson learned the trade at Thomas Hawkes'. He was a fast learner and soon made his way to the top, becoming manager of the company. Not long after, a man called Thomas Webb, who was 25 years old, decided to join the company as a partner with an investment of £3,000 – a fortune back then. This money was possibly supplied by his father John Webb. Thomas Webb would hold a 50 per cent ownership in the newly formed company and the Richardson brothers would each own 25 per cent. The Richardson brothers invested £1,200 between them and the total input of funds was enough to make the partnership work. The new firm was called Webb and Richardson's. In the year 1832 Webb and Richardson's were by now doing pioneering work. They introduced a machine for reproducing pressed glass. This was practically a new invention, but was apparently first developed in the United States of America. There are records showing that the Webb and Richardson's firm paid an excise duty of around £745 in 1883. This would prove that the company was doing very well and that they had become the largest of Stourbridge and Dudley glassmakers. The Webb and Richardson firm had only been operating for about three years.

Meanwhile, in 1833, John Webb, who ran his own business called Webb and Shepherd, died and everything that he had invested in the company was left to his only son Thomas Webb. Not long after Thomas decided to resign from his partnership at Webb and Richardson's and he received over £7,000 for his interests. A year later another brother, Jonathan Richardson, took over Thomas Webb's place in the partnership. The firm was renamed W.H.B. and J. Richardson, although this would not become official until the year 1842. Even though this was the case the partnership was effective as soon as Jonathan took over from Thomas Webb. In 1839 Richardson's firm was being described as a manufacturer of plain and rich glass of every colour. This was noted from the letters which Benjamin had written with joy about the experiments with new colours which were called canary yellow and cornelian white.

In 1842 the glass trade suffered due to the deep depression that hit the country. The Richardson brothers wrote many letters to each other as one was in London trying to secure deals while the others were doing their best to keep the business afloat. During my research I was lucky enough to find 80 of those letters and I have retained copies in my documents. I have read every single letter and I found the contents fascinating as I discovered what was happening all those years ago. There are pieces talking of underhand dealings and also how the Richardsons had been ripped off by certain solicitors. These hastily written letters are sometimes difficult to read and it seems that the post was sorted and delivered really quickly as they were travelling between the brothers virtually every day. One of the letters also mentions the death of a member of the Richardson family which I was able to trace after looking for it for a while. Eventually, in 1845, the glass industry received some relief as the dreaded glass excise duty was lifted. The Richardsons were understandably very relieved and the business was soon back to normal. In 1849

W.H.B. and J. Richardson exhibited coloured and opaline glass at the Birmingham exhibition. During the same year the Richardson firm was awarded the Royal Society of Art's Silver Isis Medal for their combination of cutting with Venetian ornamentation. At the exhibitions of British manufactures held by the R.S.A. in 1847, 1848 and 1849 the Richardson firm displayed a wide selection of cut, frosted, engraved, enamel, gilded, stained and coloured glass. This was a large display which included every type of glass ranging from tableware to the centre pieces. In 1851 at their great exhibition which was held at Crystal Palace in Hyde Park, London, the Richardson firm won a Bronze Medal for crystal and coloured glass and also secured an order for glass from Queen Victoria herself.

However, the business declined and sadly, on 14th February 1852, W.H.B. and J. Richardson was declared insolvent. Some of the Richardson papers, references, tools and assets were put in hiding from the bankruptcy commissioner. As a result of the bankruptcy, the workforce was laid off and had to look for new jobs elsewhere. For example, Philip Pargeter, a nephew of the Richardson brothers, was serving an apprenticeship with the company as an engraver. When he left, he soon set up his own engraving shop. John Northwood, who was also related to the Richardsons and the Pargeters went to work for his brother William as a builder.

JOHN NORTHWOOD.

Above is a photograph of my great uncle John Northwood. John was born in baptism in 1836 and died in 1902. There is a statue of him at the Merry Hill Shopping Centre in Brierley Hill near Dudley, West Midlands.

The site where Merry Hill now stands is where the former steel works, Round House Steel Works, was located. This is where many of my relatives worked as steel makers and puddlers. One of my great grandfathers, Alfred Thomas Pargeter, worked there at one time. He started out as a puddler at a very young age in the 1850s. When I looked on the 1911 Census he was listed at the age of 71. He stated on the Census form that he was still a puddler and was living in what I have now established was a workhouse in the Wolverhampton area. He stated that he was still married; this would have been to his second wife. It works out that Alfred was a puddler for around 50 years or longer. I was lucky enough to find an old picture which dates back to 1875 of the Round House Steel Works, it was an enormous factory. There are also several paintings of it and the surrounding area showing the many glass cones. One that I particularly liked showed the steel works at night with the large openings in the roof wide open showing the sky above all lit up from the white hot metal; this would have been visible for miles and miles around. The work was hard and dirty with very long hours and I would imagine that there were many horrible accidents which occurred within the factory relating to hot metal. A puddler was the person who thrust the long ladle into the furnace to remove the scum from the top of the metal – a very dangerous and skilled job.

Alfred Thomas Pargeter was also related to John Northwood, as he was his uncle. Just as I have today, Alfred had many well known uncles around at the time and over the years they have become more famous, like John Northwood, Philip Pargeter, William Haden Richardson, and his brother Benjamin Richardson, as they were the great pioneers of the glass trade in their day and they were to change the whole industry for the better and for many generations to come and that still goes on to this very day. I'm not sure how old John Northwood is in the picture, but I think it was taken not long before his death when he was 65 years old.

The Round House Steel Works:

In 1853 the Richardson firm reopened under the management of Benjamin Richardson and soon many of the craftsmen started to return to their old jobs. These craftsmen included John Northwood, Thomas Bott, William Jabez Muckley and his brother, L. Locke, Philip Pargeter, E. Guest and many others. The firm very quickly re-established itself in the market and business prospered once more. They held an exhibition in Dublin during the same year. Benjamin Richardson's older brother William Haden Richardson was to leave the company not long after.

On 14th September 1863 the two nephews formed a new partnership of Hodgetts, Richardson and Pargeter with their Richardson uncles. The most surprising thing about the new partnership was that it was not responsible for any new designs or masterpieces of glass. However, the company would continue to operate a steady output of commercial glass. The partnership would last for six years altogether and eventually it was dissolved in 1869. Philip Pargeter remained however for two more years as the manager of the firm.

In 1871 Philip Pargeter left to take over the Red House Glass Works. Benjamin Richardson eventually talked his son, Henry Gething Richardson, into coming back to the firm. From then on the new firm was called Hodgetts and Richardson and Son. In 1876 they were known to manufacture Flint ruby and Venetian glass, cut, engraved and etched as ornamental glass of every description. During the same year, 1876, William James Hodgetts patented the first machine for applying threading. This machine allowed for the easier application of threading which led to hundreds of designs using this process. Richardson had a definitive edge at this point in time.

Also in 1876, William Haden Richardson, the co-founder, died. William, who was married to Mary Pargeter, was 91 years of age. His brother Benjamin was 75, but despite his age he still managed to run the firm. Benjamin eventually retired in 1881 and he died in 1883. William James Hodgetts also retired from the firm around this time and he died in 1884.

THE ROUND HOUSE STEEL WORKS

In 1892 the firm was trading under Henry G. Richardson and he registered a design for miniature fir cones in opalescent glass with rustic crystal branches. In 1898 they followed with Campanula with opalescent bluebell flowers arranged on straw or light amber rustic feet. The design was in a naturalistic style remembering bamboo and flowers or tree trunks and is similar to John Walsh's work.

In 1916, H. G. Richardson died. The business was carried on by his two sons Benjamin and William Haden Arthur Richardson. The First World War forced production to scale down significantly.

In about 1924, the firm stopped manufacturing glass but it did continue to trade as Henry G. Richardson and Sons, Flint Glass Manufacturers. They paid the lease on the glassworks until the year 1928. In 1930, Webb's Crystal Glass Company Ltd of Dennis Glassworks bought the firm.

Opposite are prints of paintings of William Haden Richardson and Benjamin Richardson which were either given to, or loaned to, the Broadfield House Glass Museum in Stourbridge by the Richardson family. Many of the Richardson's and Pargeter's pieces of glass can be seen at this museum along with the history of glass making. Early in 2011 the Stourbridge Council tried to move the whole contents of Broadfield House a few miles away to the Red House Glass Cone as a permanent fixture for everyone to see all the glass, but eventually,

WILLIAM RICHARDSON   BENJAMIN RICHARDSON

after a long debate, it was decided to leave things at Broadfield House. Just as a matter of interest, you can go to the Red House Glass Cone for a day out as it is now a museum and you can watch them making glass in the original surroundings where my great uncle Philip Pargeter worked and owned the Glass Cone almost 140 years ago.

There is one name that hasn't been mentioned in all the information which I have collected during the years of my research. His name is Bonnie Nicklin; I'm not sure if he is related to Sarah Nicklin who married Thomas Pargiter on 21st August 1726, but it would be nice if he was. Bonnie Nicklin was totally deaf from childhood and he began his work as a glassmaker in Dudley in the early 1890s at the young age of eleven. Most of his working life was spent at Stuarts where eventually he was to become one of their top glassmakers. He retired in 1954 but continued to work part time until he was over the age of 80. He was awarded the British Empire Medal in 1948 for his achievements as a craftsman. Bonnie Nicklin died in 1980 when he was over 100 years old.

An insight into tracing my family tree

When I first decided to research my family tree and create a book of all the information, I have to say that I wasn't really committed to it – after all, who would benefit from it? My family thought it was a waste of time, money and effort. However, I decided to go ahead with it and the more I researched, the more involved with it I became. I have always been interested in history and it was my favourite subject at school. I hadn't anticipated that it would cost so much though! Writing this now, I have spent over seven thousand five hundred pounds and expect the final figure will be higher than this.

A lot of people probably wouldn't go to this expense nor have the time or interest to dedicate to such a task, but it is in the very challenge that I have gained the most satisfaction. My research has taken me all over the country and put me in touch with a whole host of different people who I never would have met if I hadn't decided to find out about the history of my family.

I have documented everything – all the places I have been to during the course of my research, all the churches I have visited and all the people who I have met. It has been such a rewarding exercise – this and writing several other books is the best thing I have ever done. My children and grandchildren will always have this record and hopefully someone from a future generation will take it upon themselves to add to it.

Visiting the churches came to be a great joy for me – such beautiful buildings, they are awe-inspiring. Modern day places of worship are generally quite plain in comparison.

And now, after almost seven years, I am bringing it to a close although it seems I could go on forever unearthing new snippets of information – it's incredible! My ancestors have taken me all over England, from cities to villages and sometimes to the middle of nowhere trying to locate a church or something. At the last count, I have collected more than two thousand pieces of A4 paper full of information about my family and have been told that I could expect to find a great deal more – probably even twice as much more.

For instance, my father told me that one of my great grandfathers on the Pargeter side was a judge and executioner and the story has remained in my mind for years. Unfortunately my father couldn't read or write because he had so much time off school due to illness when he was growing up in the twenties, but he would relate many stories about the past to me. I am saddened that he will never get to read this book – he would have been amazed that I managed to find out so much.

I have also made about two thousand telephone calls over the last three years in my efforts to trace the Pargetters and piece it all together. Some that I spoke to were frustrated at not being able to remember specific details, such as where a wedding took place or a long-ago name, but on more than one occasion I was able to provide the information to piece together a missing link and that prompted them to remember more from further back in time. I have helped others with their family trees too, although some then tried to take advantage of me to shortcut their own research!

Archives are great for obtaining information. Online research is good too although care must be taken to do it properly or it can easily lead you in the wrong direction and before you know it you are researching the wrong side of the family, which has happened to many people. It takes a great deal of time and dedication to research a family tree properly – not something you can do in a couple of days! You need to look at all the censuses and documents that you can – it can be frustrating at times, but also incredibly interesting and rewarding.

I have had my share of problems and sometimes needed to get away from it for a while, before going back with a clear head and a fresh mind to the same issue that seemed impossible to solve. However, some records are no longer in existence and you may need to follow a different route to find alternative information and documentation.

Photographs are great when you can get hold of them and on some occasions I have swapped information for rare old photographs of my family going back as far as the 1850s. I love old photos and I have compiled albums to keep them safe and am still looking for more as I know that they exist somewhere.

Newspaper stories and clippings also provide a wealth of information and can go back centuries, some even containing photographs. Prison records may also prove useful and generally have photographs of people from as far back as the 1840s. In London, prisons were known as 'clinks' and are registered as far back as 1151 and there is proven documentation of their existence. The documentation for the court system in London for the Old Bailey courts dates back to 1584. I haven't seen these documents myself, but they do exist. Also, juries back then in court rooms were just extra people brought in by the judge or judges to deliver a guilty verdict on the people charged. This corrupt system was all to change in 1668 in the reign of Charles 2nd as jurors were no longer told to find people guilty, but had to listen to the evidence and make their own judgements, and this system as you know is in operation to this day to find the truth and give people a fair trial.

My Family Wills

The wills of the Pargitor, Pargiter, Pargeter, and Pargetter family throughout the centuries, including those of their relatives by marriage, are listed below. Wills are an invaluable source of information and insight into the lives and wealth of a family.

It is very interesting to read the wills and discover how rich some of them were in their day and how much they left their sons, daughters and other relatives. They are also dated and enabled me to fill in some information that I was unable to find elsewhere in my research.

There are several places to look for wills. The best places in my opinion are Litchfield wills and York wills. Not everyone made a will though so it can sometimes be frustrating. Wills can be found that go as far back as Roman times, and those of kings and queens or other well known people can go back even further.

London is another very good place to trace wills. I am currently obtaining wills all the time and hope to have a collection of about two hundred in the next couple of years or so. To keep all the document dust-free and safe, I have separated them into plastic A4 pockets and have filed them into binders for easy reading. Unfortunately, some of my relatives didn't make a will and they were the ones I wanted so that I could find certain dates, so it meant delving into the archives even deeper to find the information that I needed. To date, I also have in excess of eight hundred and fifty birth, marriage and death certificates in my collection. The documents differ over the various countries and places, for instance, in this country, birth certificates don't state the time of birth only the day, but on the German birth certificates they do. Also, Scottish documents contain more information than English ones.

The Wills of the Pargetter Families and their Relatives

Alice Pargeter of Upper Boddington, 1656

Ann Pargiter of Thenford, Northamptonshire [Wife of John]

Anna Pargeter of Dudley, 1725

Benjamin Pargeter of Stourbridge, Solicitor, 1863

Caroline Elizabeth Pargeter of Foxcote, Worcestershire, Spinster, 1862

Caroline Pargeter of Stourbridge, Widow, 1803

Cassandra Pargeter, 1698

Christopher Pargiter of Sulgrave, 1640

Cresent Buttery of Marston Lawrence, Northamptonshire, 1612

Cresent Pargiter of Greatworth, 1627

Dame Elianor Pargiter of Greatworth, 1685

Edith Mary Pargeter of Oak Villa Norton, Stourbridge, Spinster, 1917

Edmund Pargiter of Astroppe, 1567

Elizabeth Dix of Cradley, 1746

Elizabeth Pargeter of No. 9 Bourne Street, Dudley, Widow, 1904

Elizabeth Pargeter of Heathfield House, Stourbridge, Spinster, 1904

Ezekiel Pargiter of Greatworth, 1684

Francis Pargiter of London, 1685

Francis Pargiter of Thenford, 1696

George Pargeter of Halesowen Road, Netherton, 1908

George Pargiter of Thenford, 1565

Granada Pargiter of Wolverhampton, 1726

John Pargeter, 1748

John Pargeter of Althop, Northamptonshire, 1706

John Pargeter of Rowley Regis, 1730

John Pargiter of Thenford, Northamptonshire, 1657

John William Pargeter of Manor House, Chaddesley Corbett, 1900

Joseph Pargeter of Careless Green, Oldswinford, Ironmonger, 1849

Joseph Pargetter of Hillfields, Coventry, Park-keeper, 1958

Katherine Pargeter of Farthinghoe, Northamptonshire, Widow, 1726

Mary Pargeter of Rowley Regis, Widow, 1716

Matilda Maud Pargetter of Hillfields, Coventry, Widow, 1966

Mary Pargeter of Careless Green, Oldswinford, Spinster, 1771

Nicholas Hancock Pargeter of Careless Green, Oldswinford, Ironmonger, 1797

Philip Pargeter of Heathfield House, Bachelor, 1895

Philippi Pargeter of the City of Litchfield, 1699

Richard Pargeter of Rowley Regis, Nailer, 1729

Richard Pargeter of Ryton, 1649

Robert Pargeter of Thorpe Mandeville, Northamptonshire, 1717

Robert Pargiter of Greatworth, 1558

Robert Pargiter of Greatworth, 1595

Theodore Pargiter of Greatworth, 1656

Thomas Henry-Braye Pargeter, Bachelor, 1922

Thomas Henry Pargeter [Junior] of Norton, Oldswinford, 1881

Thomas Henry Pargeter [Senior] of Norton, 1880

Thomas Pargeter of Cradley Heath [Park Lane presb], 1827

Thomas Pargeter of Cradley Heath, parish of Halesowen, Yeoman, 1729

Thomas Pargeter of Foxcote, 1847

Thomas Pargeter of Halesowen, 1781

Thomas Pargeter of the Delph, Kingswinford, 1828

Thomas Pargeter Richardson, Widower, 1923

William Haden Pargeter, son of William W. R. Pargeter [younger], 1923

William Haden Richardson [the younger] of Birmingham, 1920

William Haden Richardson Pargeter of Brook Street, Wordsley, 1898

William Hancox Pargeter of Dunley, near Stourport, 1948

William Pargeter of Dudley, Nailor, 1715

William Pargeter of Oldswinford, Yeoman, 1776

William Pargeter of the Delph, Nail Factor, 1839

William Pargiter of Greatworth, 1584

William Pargiter of Sulgrave, 1675

William Pargiter of Sulgrave, 1617

Yate Pargiter of Thenford, 1693

The information in this book has been thoroughly researched to the best of my ability and I therefore believe it to be correct and true. I would like to thank all the people in all the archives that I have visited in different parts of the country for their time and their help, especially those at Coventry and Dudley archives where I have spent an enormous amount of time. I also thank all the people who have assisted me in obtaining the photographs shown within this book and their kind permission to use them and the people who I met at the various churches for showing me around and supplying me with information about my relatives. Special thanks also to my relatives in England and in America for the photographs that they gave me. I hope that whoever reads this work will be inspired to research their own family tree as the journey of finding my relatives all over the country and abroad was an incredible experience.

Roy Pargetter

Organisations I would like to thank:

The Herbert Art Gallery and Museum, Coventry

Coventry Heritage and Arts Trust

Birmingham Register Office and Archives

Northamptonshire Register Office and Archives

Suffolk Register Office

North Tyneside Register Office

Worcestershire Register Office and Archives

Warwickshire Register Office and Archives

Staffordshire Register Office

Derbyshire Register Office and Archives

Lincolnshire Register Office and Archives

Stoke-on-Trent Register Office

Wolverhampton Register Office and Archives

Dorset Register Office

Sandwell Register Office and Archives

Dudley Register Office and Archives

Walsall Register Office and Archives

The Red House Glass Cone staff

London Register Offices and Archives

The Express and Star newspaper

The Black Country Archives

Oxford Register Office and Archives

Coventry Register Office and Archives

Dusseldorf Register Office and Archives

Northumberland Register Office

Morpeth Register Office

The Bugle, Cradley Heath

Updates

The Pargeter/Pargetter family causes of death on Chapter 5 Generation 11. The cause of death was first registered on a death certificate in England and Wales in July 1837.

Below is the nearest cause of death entry within the book to that date.

Philip Pargeter died on 31st May 1851 c.o.d [Liver disease] aged 58, husband of Susannah Richardson [5x Great Grandfather].

Susannah Pargeter [nee Richardson] died on 18th December 1868 c.o.d [Heart disease and Bronchitis] aged 74, wife of Philip Pargeter [5x Great Grandmother].

Children of Philip Pargeter and Susannah Richardson:

Child 1: Thomas Pargeter died on 23rd November 1867 c.o.d [Bronchitis] aged 52, husband of Mary Ann Beddard.

Mary Ann Pargeter [nee Beddard] died about 1888-90 c.o.d [unknown] aged about 72-74, wife of Thomas Pargeter.

Child 2: Ann Jones [nee Pargeter] died on 29th July 1849 c.o.d [Puerperal fever aka infection during childbirth] aged 33, wife of John Jones.

John Jones died on 31st March 1859 c.o.d [Coma] aged 47, husband of Ann Pargeter.

Child 3: Joseph Pargeter died on 10th January 1869. Information on wife and children on Chapter 6 Generation 12.

Child 4: Martha Unitt [nee Pargeter] died on 10th July 1904 c.o.d [Senile decay aka Dementia] aged 85, wife of Henry Unitt.

Henry Unitt died on 23rd December 1885 c.o.d [unknown] aged 63, husband of Martha Pargeter.

Child 5: Susannah Evans [nee Pargeter] died on 26th February 1856 c.o.d [Typhoid fever] aged 35, wife of Edward Evans.

Edward Evans died on 5th June 1865 c.o.d [Heart disease] aged 46, husband of Susannah Pargeter.

Child 6: Sarah Whitehouse [nee Pargeter] died on 13th July 1907 c.o.d [Senile decay] aged 79, wife of Isaac Whitehouse.

Isaac Whitehouse died on 17th March 1873 c.o.d [Bright's disease aka severe inflammation of the kidneys] aged 64, husband of Sarah Pargeter.

Child 7: Maria Elcock [nee Pargeter] died on 28th August 1901 c.o.d [Cerebral paralysis] aged 76, wife of William Elcock.

William Elcock died on 5th November 1861 c.o.d [Epilepsy] aged 39, husband of Maria Pargeter.

Child 8: Philip Pargeter died on 19th December 1906 c.o.d [Heart failure] aged 80. [No issue]

Child 9: Mary Richardson [nee Pargeter] died on 25th September 1910 c.o.d [Senile decay] aged 83, wife of William Haden Richardson.

William Haden Richardson died on 21st December 1876 c.o.d [Old age] aged 91, husband of Mary Pargeter.

Child 10: John Pargeter died on 8th October 1891 c.o.d [Heart disease] aged 61, husband of Sarah Palmer.

Sarah Pargeter [nee Palmer] died on 21st May 1900 c.o.d [Heart failure and Bronchitis] aged 71, wife of John Pargeter.

Child 11: Richard Pargeter died between 11th 13th May 1832 c.o.d [unknown] aged 1.

Child 12: Elizabeth Pargeter died on 15th March 1904 c.o.d [Heart disease] aged 66. [No issue]

Child 13: Phyllis Pargeter died on 27th February 1836 c.o.d [unknown] aged 8 months.

Child 14: Caroline Russell [nee Pargeter] died on 30th December 1904 c.o.d [Asthenia and Vascular disease] aged 67, wife of John James Russell.

John James Russell died on 3rd April 1901 c.o.d [Hemiplegia aka Paralysis] aged 66, husband of Caroline Pargeter.

Child 15: William Haden Richardson Pargeter died on 2nd February 1907 c.o.d [Locomotor ataxia aka symptoms of advanced syphilis] aged 67, husband of Mary Maria Pardoe.

Mary Maria Pargeter [nee Pardoe] died on 14th March 1891 c.o.d [Acute bronchitis] aged 45, wife of William Haden Richardson Pargeter.

Child 16: James Gould Pargeter died unknown c.o.d [unknown], husband of Sarah Ann Westwood.

Sarah Ann Pargeter [nee Westwood] died unknown c.o.d [unknown], wife of James Gould Pargeter.

The Pargeter/Pargetter family causes of death on Chapter 6 Generation 12:

Joseph Pargeter died on 10th January 1869 c.o.d [Apoplexy aka Heart failure] aged 51, husband of Ann Hillman. [4x Great Grandfather]

Ann Pargeter [nee Hillman] died on 16th April 1888 c.o.d [Paralysis] aged 71, wife of Joseph Pargeter. [4x Great Grandmother]

Children of Joseph Pargeter and Ann Hillman:

Child 1: Alfred Thomas Pargeter died on 20th February 1919. Information on wife and children on Chapter 7 Generation 13.

Child 2: Susannah Pargeter died on 24th September 1847 c.o.d [Scarlatina anginosa aka Scarlet fever] aged 5.

Child 3: Mary Ann Bragger [nee Pargeter] died on 13th April 1914 c.o.d [Influenza and Pneumonia] aged 70, wife of Edward Bragger.

Edward Bragger died on 11th October 1904 c.o.d [Morbus cordis aka Heart disease] aged 55, husband of Mary Ann Pargeter.

Child 4: Joseph Philip Pargeter died on 18th August 1846 c.o.d [laryngitis] aged 6 months.

Child 5: John Pargeter died on 18th January 1910 c.o.d [Pertussis aka Whooping cough] aged 61. [No issue]

Child 6: Joseph Pargeter [died unknown, believed to be in Canada]

Child 7: Philip Pargeter died on 9th March 1919 c.o.d [Acute bronchitis] aged 68, husband of Maria Baggott.

Maria Pargeter [nee Baggott] died on 18th March 1931 c.o.d [Heart failure and Senile decay] aged 73, wife of Philip Pargeter.

Child 8: Ann Pargeter died on 8th April 1855 c.o.d [Convulsions] aged 1.

Child 9: Ann Caroline Wakelam [nee Pargeter] died on 3rd March 1909 c.o.d [Carcinoma of the uterus aka Cancer of the womb] aged 51, wife of Sidney Beckett Wakelam.

Sidney Beckett Wakelam died on 8th January 1905 c.o.d [Gamma in pharynx] aged 65, husband of Ann Caroline Pargeter.

The Pargeter/Pargetter family causes of death on Chapter 7 Generation 13:

Alfred Thomas Pargeter died on 20th February 1919 c.o.d [Pneumonia] aged 79, husband of Margaret Ann Quindleman and Eliza Gething. [3x Great Grandfather]

Margaret Ann Pargeter [formally Price nee Quindleman] died on 17th August 1891 c.o.d [Liver cancer] aged 51,1st wife of Alfred Thomas Pargeter. [3x Great Grandmother]

Eliza Pargeter [formally Gething nee Walker] died believed to be in Wolverhampton Staffordshire after 1911 c.o.d [unknown], 2nd wife of Alfred Thomas Pargeter.

Children of Alfred Thomas Pargeter and Margaret Ann Quindleman:

Child 1: Joseph Pargeter died on 16th January 1944. Information on wife and children on Chapter 7 Generation 14.

Child 2: Alfred Pargeter died on 13th December 1870 c.o.d [Tabes mesenteric aka Tuberculosis] aged 3 months.

Child 3: Thomas Pargeter died on 25th December 1872 c.o.d [Scarlatina anginosa] aged 1.

The Pargeter/Pargetter family causes of death on Chapter 7 Generation 14:

Joseph Pargeter died on 16th January 1944 c.o.d [Cerebral arteriosclerosis aka hardening of the arteries of the brain] aged 75, husband of Mary Alice Mullins.   [2x Great Grandfather]

Mary Alice Pargeter [nee Mullins] died on 27 March 1955 c.o.d [Carcinoma of the uterus] aged 87, wife of Joseph Pargeter. [2x Great Grandmother]

Children of Joseph Pargeter and Mary Alice Mullins:

Child 1: Joseph Pargeter died on 17th November 1958. Information on wife and children on Chapter 8 Generation 15.

Child 2: Baby Pargeter a twin of Joseph Pargeter above died on 23rd October 1892 c.o.d [unknown] aged 45 minutes.

Child 3: William Henry Pargeter died on 19th December 1945 c.o.d [Tuberculosis aka T.B] aged 51, husband of Florence Annie Porter.

Florence Annie Pargeter [nee Porter] died on 20th October 1975 c.o.d [Bronchopneumonia] aged 79, wife of William Henry Pargeter.

Child 4: Hilda Margaret Badger [nee Pargeter] died on 30th December 1974 c.o.d [Heart failure] aged 78, wife of William Badger.

William Badger died on 4th December 1971 c.o.d [Emphysema and Bronchitis] aged 81, husband of Hilda Margaret Pargeter.

Child 5: Baby Pargeter died in June 1897 c.o.d [unknown] aged 0

Child 6: Baby Pargeter a twin of child 5 died in June 1897 c.o.d [unknown] aged 0

Child 7: Mary Billing [nee Pargeter] died on 13th April 1977 c.o.d [Heart failure] aged 78, wife of Claud Charles Billing.

Claud Charles Billing died on 13th November 1952 c.o.d [Tuberculosis and Asthma] aged 54, husband of Mary Pargeter.

Child 8: John Pargeter died on 24th February 1901 c.o.d [Shock due to severe burns on the hands and face] aged 10 weeks.

Child 9: Margaret Pargeter died on 14th July 1902 c.o.d [Cellulitis of face and convulsions] aged 4 months.

Child 10: Alfred Pargeter died on 29th October 1955 c.o.d [Pulmonary tuberculosis] aged 51. [No issue]

Child 11: Baby Pargeter died in 1905 shortly after birth c.o.d [Unknown]. Aged 0.

Child 12: James Pargeter died on 6th October 1965 c.o.d [Heart failure] aged 58. [No issue].

Pargeter Babies 13,14,15, and 16 were all stillborn between [1890-1911]. There are some records available, but stillbirth documents were not recorded until about 1927.

Child 17: Alice Pargeter died on 18th September 1910 c.o.d [Marasmus aka reduced body weight] aged 11 months.

Child 18: Florence Margaret Horton [nee Pargeter] died on 19th April 1933 c.o.d [Tuberculosis] aged 21, wife of William Horton.

William Horton died on 12th February 1953 c.o.d [Lung carcinoma aka Cancer and Pneumonia] aged 49, husband of Florence Margaret Pargeter.

The Pargeter/Pargetter family causes of death on Chapter 8 Generation 15:

Joseph Pargeter died on 17th November 1958 c.o.d [Pulmonary disease and Emphysema] aged 65, husband of Matilda Maud Collins. [Grandfather]

Matilda Maud Pargeter [nee Collins] died on 17th March 1975 c.o.d [Bronchopneumonia and Cerebrovascular disease] aged 85, wife of Joseph Pargeter. [Grandmother]

Children of Joseph Pargeter/Pargetter and Matilda Maud Collins:

Child 1: Ellen Robinson [nee Collins] died on 14th August 1997 c.o.d [Bronchopneumonia and Vascular disease] aged 85, wife of Christopher Robinson.

Christopher Robinson died on 20th May 1961 c.o.d [Head injuries after falling from a bus] aged 47, husband of Ellen Collins.

Child 2: Hilda Pargetter died on 11th February 1919 c.o.d [Laryngeal diphtheria] aged 21 months.

Child 3: Frederick Henry Pargetter died on 18th September 1918 c.o.d [Acute diarrhoea] aged 11 days.

Child 4: Gladys Jones [nee Pargetter] died on 24th January 1989 c.o.d [Bronchopneumonia] aged 68, wife of George William Jones.

George William Jones died on 18th September 1969 c.o.d [Cancer of liver and kidneys] aged 55, husband of Gladys Pargetter.

Child 5: Philip Pargetter died on 31st December 1986. Information on wife and children on Chapter 10 Generation 16.

Child 6: Ethel Merrilees [nee Pargetter] died on 27th June 1980 c.o.d [Cervical cancer] aged 57, wife of Henry Merrilees.

Henry Merrilees died on 3rd August 2016 c.o.d [Dementia] aged 96, husband of Ethel Pargetter.

Child 7: Elsie Pargetter died on 15th November 1924 c.o.d [Accidental asphyxiation aka Suffocation] aged 6 days.

Child 8: Walter Pargetter died on 2nd November 1928 c.o.d [Bronchopneumonia] aged 2.

Child 9: Peter Pargetter died on 28th May 2016 c.o.d [Encephalitis aka Inflammation of the brain and Pneumonia] aged 88, husband of Ethel Margaret Pinfield.

Ethel Margaret Pargetter [nee Pinfield] died on 27th October 2015 c.o.d [Old age] aged 84, wife of Peter Pargetter.

Child 10: Jean Collier [nee Pargetter] died on 6th April 2007 c.o.d [Myocardial aka Heart failure and Thrombosis] aged 78, wife of Harry Collier.

Harry Collier died on 7th December 1991 c.o.d [Bronchial carcinoma aka Lung cancer] aged 59, husband of Jean Pargetter.

Child 11: Bernard Pargetter died on 25th October 1933 c.o.d [Toxaemia and Asphyxia] aged 2.

Child 12: Barbara Mead formally McFarlane [nee Pargetter] died on 9th December 1999 c.o.d [Acute lymphatic leukaemia] aged 67, wife of Christopher Thomas McFarlane and David Edward Mead.

Christopher Thomas McFarlane died on 26th March 2009 c.o.d [Chest infection] aged 79, 1st husband of Barbara Pargetter.

David Edward Mead died on 7th December 2012 c.o.d [Abdominal haemorrhage] aged 75, 2nd husband of Barbara Pargetter.

Child 13: Sheila Frances Parsons [nee Pargetter] died on 5th April 2004 c.o.d [Bronchopneumonia and Pulmonary infarction] aged 69, wife of Ernest Albert Parsons.

Ernest Albert Parsons died on 19th October 1984 c.o.d [Bronchopneumonia carcinoma] aged 50, husband of Sheila Frances Pargetter.

The Pargeter/Pargetter family causes of death on Chapter 10 Generation 16:

Philip Pargetter died on 31st December 1986 c.o.d [Heart failure] aged 65, husband of Marjorie Fox Bennett Brown and Helene Eugenia Finger. [Father]

Marjorie Fox Bennett Pargetter [nee Brown] died on 10th August 2005 c.o.d [Pulmonary oedema] aged 77, 1st wife of Philip Pargetter.

Helene Eugenia Pargetter [nee Finger] died on 22nd January 1995 c.o.d [Pneumonia] aged 78, 2nd wife of Philip Pargetter. [Mother]

The Finger family Causes of Death on Chapter 10

Karl Finger died on 4th August 1961 c.o.d [Cancer] aged 83, husband of Johanette Katharina Elisabeth Vopel. [Grandfather]

Johanette Katharina Elisabeth Finger [nee Vopel] died on 6th August 1918 [c.o.d Tuberculosis] aged 30, wife of Karl Finger. [Grandmother]

The Collins family causes of death on Chapter 9

Henry Collins died on 27th May 1869 c.o.d [died suddenly probably due to drink and put down on his death certificate as a Visitation of God] aged 64, husband of Eliza Purchess. [3x Great Grandfather]

Eliza Collins [nee Purchess] died about 1905 c.o.d [unknown] aged 89, wife of Henry Collins. [3x Great Grandmother]

Child of Henry Collins and Eliza Purchess:

Child 1: Frederick Augustus Collins died on 17th December 1890 c.o.d [Tuberculosis] aged 42, husband of Ellen Elizabeth Jones. [2x Great Grandfather]

Ellen Elizabeth Allibone formally Collins [nee Jones] died on 23rd February 1941 c.o.d [Chronic myocarditis aka Disease of the heart muscle] aged 84, wife of Frederick Augustus Collins and John Allibone. [2x Great Grandmother]

John Allibone died 1918 in mysterious surroundings c.o.d [unknown], wife of Ellen Elizabeth Collins [nee Jones].

Children of Frederick Augustus Collins and Ellen Elizabeth Jones:

Child 1: Frederick Collins died on 1st October 1917 c.o.d casualty of WW1 [No issue] aged 30.

Child 2: Elizabeth Collins died on 16th October 1889 c.o.d [Tubercular meningitis] aged 7 months.

Child 3: Matilda Maud Collins married Joseph Pargeter and is connected from Chapter 8 Generation 15:

Children of John Allibone and Ellen Elizabeth Collins [nee Jones]:

Child 1: Ellen Elizabeth Charley [nee Allibone] died on 5th November 1958 c.o.d [Mitral stenosis aka Heart failure] aged 64, wife of Walter Charley.

Walter Charley died on 15th June 1966 c.o.d [Acute cardiac failure] aged 72, husband of Ellen Elizabeth Allibone.

Child 2: Jack Allibone died on 23rd March 1981 c.o.d [Bronchopneumonia and Renal failure] aged 84, husband of Eva Ellen Legge.

Child 3: Eva Ellen Allibone [nee Legge] died on 31st March 1988 c.o.d [Cardiac failure and Depression] aged 87, wife of Jack Allibone.

Child 4: Emily Allibone died on 15th April 1908 c.o.d [Peritonitis aka Infection of the stomach lining] aged 9.

Workhouse Births List

MOTHER'S NAME	M/F	D.O.B.	ADDRESS	CHILD'S NAME
No name entered	m	16.8.1922	9h 3ct Sherbourne Street	Joseph Edward
Adams Florence	m	16.9.1904	Coventry	William
Adams Isabel Annie		1.4.1917	18 Spon Street	Not registered
Adams Isabel Annie		14.7.1921	18 Spon Street	Not registered
Adams Mabel	f	2.8.1918	107 King Edward Road	Queenie
Adcock Dora Louisa Martha	m	18.1.1921	89 Gorton Road	John
Adkins Ellen	f	1.12.1882	St. Michael	Not registered
Adler Frances Florence		28.5.1914	2h 14ct Far Gosford Street	Not registered
Adler Frances Florence		28.5.1914	2h 14ct Far Gosford Street	Not registered
Adler Sarah	f	11.1.1894	Holy Trinity	Florence Maud
Ainge Lilian Mary Ann Doris May	f	8.3.1913	Coventry	Doris May
Ainge Lilian May	m	28.1.1915	25 All Saints Lane	Arthur
Akers Elsie	m	1.12.1919	28 Bishop Street	John
Akers Elsie	m	22.5.1921	28 Bishop Street	George
Albert Mary		29.8.1866	N. F. A	Not registered
Alford Annie	m	29.6.1914	432 Foleshill Road	Frederick
Allcock Ida Miriam	m	19.11.1929	60 Spon Street	Victor
Allcock Selina		24.10.1929	151 Cambridge Street	Not registered
Allen Ann and Edward Thomas	m	8.5.1889	Casual pauper	Alfred
Allen Annie	f	29.7.1909	Coventry	Florence May
Allen Annie	m	5.2.1911	Coventry	Joseph
Allen Maria	f	11.2.1898	St. Michael	Maud
Allenson Mary	m	18.2.1889	St. Michael	Walter
Alliban Esther	f	21.1.1894	St. Michael	Elsie Lydia
Allibane Esther	m	27. 12.1885 N. F. A		William Henry
Allibone Eva	m	28.8.1929	79 Gilbert Street	John
Allsopp Edith	f	12.6.1918	104 Little Park Street	Joan
Alton Alice Mary	m	29.3.1925	19 Bucks Hill, Nuneaton	Joseph Lawrence
Ambrose Hilda	m	1.2.1920	9 Middlesbrough Road	Leonard
Amos Edith	m	26.1.1898	St. Michael	William
Anderton Rose	m	2.7.1929	14 Clements Street	Bertram
Ansell Sarah	f	19.5.1891	Holy Trinity	Ada
Anstee Matilda	f	26.4.1927	39 Pinley Gardens	Edna May
Anstiss Amelia	f	6.1.1921	Caravan in Rood Lane	Amelia

Anthony Lilian	f	6.9.1918	7 Grosvenor Road	Elsie
Aorbury Mary Ann	m	23.11.1876	St. Michael	Not registered
Appleton Margaret	f	15.04.1878	St. Michael	Not registered
Archer Eliza	m	11.3.1926	7 Gilbert Place, Brook Street	Frederick
Archer Elizabeth	m	19.2.1929	7 Gilbert Place, Brook Street	Albin John
Archer Emma	m	03.03.1876	Holy Trinity	William Henry
Archer Emma	m	9.12.1880	St. Michael	Amos Henry
Arnold Ann		23.8.1861	N. F. A	Not registered
Arnold Caroline	f	19.1.1881	St. Michael	Alice
Arrowsmith Annie	f	24.8.1899	St. Michael	Annie
Arthurs Alice Mary	f	4.2.1927	St. Faiths Shelter	Nellie
Ash Ethel	m	16.8.1921	Gloucester House", Barras Lane	Herbert William
Ashby Fanny	m	10.7.1894	Holy Trinity	William Frederick
Ashby Jane	m	8.4.1906	Coventry	William
Ashby Jane	m	8.4.1906	Coventry	Sidney
Ashfield Annie	m	20.5.1928	40 Swanswell Terrace	Frederick Arthur
Ashly Lilian May	f	15.3.1930	33 Greyfriars Lane	Doreen
Ashmore Elsie May	f	25.1.1927	Coton Union	Vera May
Askew Mary	m	16.2.1921	46 Bright Street	Bernard
Askill Ada	f	11.4.1925	Bermuda Road, Chilvers Coton, Nuneaton	Irene
Aston Mabel	f	14.6.1922	46 South Street	Elsie
Aston Mary Ann	f	20.11.1898	St. Michael	Elizabeth
Athersuch Emma	m	12.3.1881	Holy Trinity	Eli
Atkins Elizabeth Ann	f	7.12.1898	St. Michael	Nellie
Atkins Ellen	f	24.12.1884	St. Michael	Ellen Mary
Atkins Martha	m	1.5.1855	N. F. A	Samuel
Austin Emma	f	12.3.1880	Holy Trinity	Jane
Austin Emma		22.8.1862	N. F. A	Not registered
Austin Sarah		26.12.1862	N. F. A	Not registered
Ayres Isabella	m	1.8.1903	Coventry	Arthur

MOTHER'S NAME	M.F	D.O.B.	ADDRESS	CHILD'S NAME
Bacon Ellen Maud	m	21.5.1928	112 Spon Street	Cyril William
Bagley Theresa	m	8.11.1917	128 Harnall Lane East	Edward Gilda
Bailey Clara		16.2.1912	Coventry	Not registered
Bailey Elizabeth Annie	f	24.4.1910	Coventry	Gladys May
Bailey Nellie	m	2.10.1915	30 Hertford Place	Ernest Ambrose
Baker Ada Mary and Wm Joseph	m	28.11.1909	Coventry	William Lawrence
Baker Annie May	f	8.2.1913	Coventry	Annie
Baker Doris	f	9.9.1928	7 Barrack Place	Jean
Baker Emma	f	5.9.1880	St. Michael	Emily
Baker Sarah		26.2.1866	N. F. A	Not registered
Baker Selina	f	16.10.1893	Holy Trinity	Lily Jane
Bale Selina	m	25.3.1898	Holy Trinity	Edwin
Ball Hetty	m	23.2.1899	St. Michael	William
Ball Jane Louisa	f	05.07.1876	Holy Trinity	Not registered
Ball Phoebe	f	2.10.1898	St. Michael	Lily
Baller Florence May	f	12.2.1928	19 Chauntry Place	Edith Mary
Bambrick Elizabeth	m	8.4.1912	Coventry	Victor Starr
Banford Mabel	f	15.1.1919	38ct 2h Spon Street	Ivy
Bantley Winifred	f	23.11.1908	Coventry	Winifred
Barnacle Ann	m	12.3.1892	Holy Trinity	Harry Noah
Barnacle Ann and John	f	30.9.1886	N. F. A	Florence
Barnacle Sarah Ann	f	20.7.1888	St. Michael	Sarah Ann
Barnet Mary Ann Eliza	f	11.8.1899	St. Michael	Annie
Barnett Beatrice	f	13.6.1919	11 Kingsway	Margaret
Barnett Beatrice Winifred	f	28.12.1921	Burnley Union	Doris
Barnett Mary Ann	m	31.8.1879	Holy Trinity	Alfred
Barnett Nellie	m	11.7.1929	36 Ford Street	George
Barnsley Nellie		14.4.1915	240 Leicester Causeway	Not registered
Barratt Rebecca	f	29.9.1899	St. Michael	Doris
Barrett Clarice	f	23.1.1922	78 Cambridge Street	Clarice Nellie
Barrett Hilda	m	22.9.1929	57 Bramble Street	Roy
Barton Edith Florence	m	25.1.1918	8h 7ct Chantry Place	Percy

Barton Elizabeth	f	12.3.1887	N. F. A	Elizabeth
Barton Lilian E	m	8.8.1922	62a Much Park Street	Reginald George
Bascott Maria	m	6.12.1853	N. F. A	Maria
Baskerville Edith	f	15.11.1918	32 Maycock Road	Violet May
Basnett Amelia	m	17.1.1913	Coventry	Edward
Bassett Mary	f	9.6.1926	Meriden Union	Kathleen May
Bassett or Sanders Rosalina	m	23.12.1901	Coventry	William Charles
Basson Edith	f	4.5.1910	Coventry	Edith Emma
Bastock Harriett	f	30.12.1911	Coventry	Hilda
Bates Alice	f	31.3.1916	173 Hearsall Lane	Sylvia Alice
Bates Alice Maud	f'	20.4.1912	Coventry	Lucy
Bates Ann	m	23.7.1854	N. F. A	James
Bates Caroline and John	m	27.6.1888	Holy Trinity	John
Bates Ethel	m	11.3.1924	29 Lockhurst Lane	Bernard
Bates Ethel	m	15.4.1926	29 Lockhurst Lane	Ronald
Batson Mabel	f	22.5.1926	228 St. Georges Road	Jessie Eileen
Baum Harriett	f	25.09.1875	St. Michael	Not registered
Baxter Gertrude Annie	f	8.3.1928	St. Faiths Shelter	Margaret
Bayliss Harriet	f	11.3.1890	St. Michael	Annie
Bayliss Hilda	f	26.5.1929	26 Marsworth Street	May Audrey
Bazely Fanny	m	29.8.1929	117 The Chantries	John
Beadles Ada Elizabeth	m	13.7.1911	Coventry	Ivor
Beasley Elizabeth	f	29.1.1927	3 Warwick Lane	Elizabeth
Beaumont Millicent	f	25.4.1909	Coventry	Phyllis Emma
Beck Ann	m	22.10.1884	St. Michael	Lawrence
Beeby Lydia Maria	f	5.2.1921	248 Munition Cottages	Evelyn Alice
Beecham Ida Elizabeth	m	2.2.1928	St. Faiths Shelter, Holyhead Road	Colin
Beesley Elsie	m	16.7.1922	93 Narrow Lane	William
Bell Mary Ann	f	11.6.1903	Coventry	Mary Elizabeth
Bellamy Mary	f	16.6.1890	Holy Trinity	Mary Agnes
Bennet Nellie	m	9.11.1917	189 Leicester Causeway	Raymond Eric
Bennett Alice E	m	4.8.1922	37 East Street	Cyril
Bennett Florence	m	25.6.1919	36 Trafalgar Street	Arthur
Bentley Evelyn	f	12.11.1926	16 Upper Well Street	Millicent

Bentley Millicent Annie	m	18.1.1928	61 Vernon Street	William
Benton Ivy Lavina		20.2.1924	64 Brook Street	Not registered
Benton Sarah Ann	f	24.11.1919	Foleshill Union	Sarah Ann
Beresford Minnie	f	11.3.1929	301 Corporation Cottages	Betty
Berry Alice		20.6.1917	9 Silver Street	Not registered
Berryman Maggie	f	10.6.1920	5 Willow Place, Burton on Trent	Kathleen Margaret
Betts Sarah Elizabeth	f	5.10.1917	15 Earlsdon Avenue	Gladys May
Bickley Alice May	m	3.8.1927	46 Castle Square	Raymond
Bickley Maud	f	9.5.1918	49 Henrietta Street	Marjorie
Bicknell Harriett Hetty	f	5.1.1908	Coventry	Ivy
Biddle Nellie	f	12.9.1928	24 Ash Grove, Stoney Stanton Road	Joan
Bidwell Mabel Ellen	m	28.7.1915	39 Croft Road	Ronald
Binder Violet	m	26.7.1928	5 Dane Road, Stoke	Alan
Binning Amy	f	2.10.1921	Y.M.C.A The Quadrant	Gladys
Birch Annie Elizabeth	f	18.2.1926	Nuneaton Union	Doris
Birch Annie Elizabeth	m	8.5.1929	18 Canal Road, Longford	Cyril
Birchall Ann	m	22.10.1883	St. Michael	Joseph Henry
Birchall Elsie		23.2.1917	bk 36 Primrose hill Street	Harold George
Bird Elizabeth		3.10.1860	N. F. A	Not registered
Bird Jane		14.11.1859	N. F. A	Not registered
Bird Rose	m	23.7.1910	Coventry	John
Bisbon Sarah Ann	f	9.6.1891	Holy Trinity	Annie
Black Mary Ann	f	27.02.1878	Holy Trinity	Elizabeth
Blackford Elizabeth	f	06.04.1876	St. Michael	Not registered
Blackman Florence	m	18.2.1917	34 Collingwood Road	Edgar
Blackwell Alice L	f	17.2.1905	Coventry	Louisa
Blackwell Alice L	f	18.3.1903	Coventry	Alice
Blackwell Florence	f	11.2.1917	31 Hertford Place	Gladys
Blackwell Florence	f	3.4.1913	Coventry	Winifred
Blackwell Florence	m	3.4.1913	Coventry	John
Blackwell Florence		5.6.1911	Coventry	Not registered
Blakeman Ada	f	4.8.1929	3ct 9h Smithford Street	Mary Doreen

Bland Elizabeth		18.11.1858	N. F. A	Not registered
Blood Emily		5.9.1929	6 Heath Crescent	Jessie
Blundell Amy	m	27.7.1883	St. Michael	Not registered
Bone Mary Ann	m	9.5.1855	N. F. A	Alfred
Boneham Gertrude Lilian	m	12.12.1924	49 Cope Street	William Michael
Booton Rose	m	12.9.1927	The Mount, Davenport Road	Douglas Henry
Borrett Clarice May	m	11.3.1925	11 Mulliner Street	Reginald Gordon
Boss Beatrice May	f	24.1.1929	29 Lower Ford Street	Frances
Boss Beatrice May	f	26.3.1930	9 Whitrfriars Street	Mary Doreen
Bott Edith Eleanor	m	31.5.1913	Coventry	William Thomas
Bott Florence May	m	9.12.1913	Coventry	Leonard
Bottrill Lucy	m	8.12.1865	N. F. A	William
Bottrill Minnie Alice	m	20.1.1926	73 Church Road, Stockingford	Bertram
Bottrill Minnie Alice	m	25.1.1925	73 Church Road, Stockingford	Tom
Boulton Selina	m	17.2.1930	247 Munition Cottages, Foleshill	Derek
Boun Mary Ellen	m	10.3.1929	51 Raglan Street	John
Bown Elsie	f	7.9.1929	167 Munition Cottages	Iris Marjorie
Bown Mary		19.8.1916	4 Chauntry Place	Not registered
Bowson Mary	m	20.11.1891	St. Michael	Arthur
Boyce Bertha	m	12.12.1924	32 Stanley Street	Stanley
Boyce Bertha		12.12.1924	32 Stanley Street	Not registered
Boyce Minnie	f	12.3.1920	17h 19ct Little Park Street	Kathleen Mary
Boyers Elizabeth		6.5.1887	Holy Trinity	Not registered
Boyers Rose Ann		28.1.1883	St. Michael	Not registered
Boyles Evelyn May	m	18.8.1920	21 Wyley Road	John
Bradbury Frances Amy	f	12.2.1926	49 Clay Lane	Joyce
Bradley Doris		5.12.1929	N. F. A	Not registered
Bradley Hilda	f	11.5.1929	18 Thawley Road	Hilda
Bradnick Mary Ann	m	11.12.1878	St. Michael	Basil Ernest
Bramstone Elizabeth	f	13.2.1894	St. Michael	Annie Burden
Bramstone Mary Ann	f	6.6.1918	35 Well Street	Elizabeth May Mary

Bramwell Emma		1.12.1905	Coventry	Not registered
Bray Elizabeth Rosina	m	8.2.1921	15ct 3h Gosford Street	Raymond
Brentnall Lucy	m	20.10.1928	117 Richmond Street	Ralph
Brewer Maud	f	29.6.1910	Coventry	Lilian May
Briggs Lucy	f	24.10.1927	Meriden Union	Marguerite
Bright Kate	f	29.11.1919	Foleshill Union	Violet
Brockhouse Elsie May	f	4.1.1927	Nuneaton Union	Doreen
Brogden Elizabeth	m	17.3.1897	St. Michael	George William
Bromfield Emily	f	9.9.1892	St. Michael	Mabel
Brookes Martha	f	12.5.1867	N. F. A	Lily
Brookes Mary Ellen	m	6.1.1907	Coventry	Maurice
Brooks Annie	m	28.2.1895	St. Michael	Thomas
Brooks Mary Ann		12.8.1921	17 Whitefriars Street	Not registered
Brooks Winifred	f	7.7.1911	Coventry	Pauline
Brown Adelaide	m	3.5.1920	6 Hill Cross	William James
Brown Alice		1.2.1917	126 Melbourne Road	Not registered
Brown Doris Rose	f	12.4.1927	17 Cromwell Street	Grace Margery
Brown Emily	f	14.9.1898	St. Michael	Ethel
Brown Emily	m	31.12.1899	St. Michael	Charles
Brown Ethel	m	3.3.1927	Nuneaton Poor Law Institution	Kenneth
Brown Florence	f	25.12.1911	Coventry	Florence
Brown Jessie	m	30.10.1917	N. F. A	Jack
Brown Mary	f	16.10.1911	Coventry	Ivy
Brown Sarah		2.12.1860	N. F. A	Not registered
Brown Sarah Elizabeth	f	23.11.1892	St. Michael	Florrie
Bryant Alice and John	m	9.11.1904	Coventry	Leonard
Buch Elsie May	f	1.11.1917	58 Whitefriars Lane	Alice
Bulcock Catherine	m	3.1.1882	St. Michael	Frederick
Bull Annie and James	f	1.8.1898	St. Michael	Gladys
Bull Laura Elizabeth	m	6.11.1896	St. Michael	John
Bull Mary	m	5.2.1912	Coventry	William Henry
Bull Mary Ann	m	2.6.1894	Holy Trinity	William
Bull Sarah Ann	m	8.3.1897	Holy Trinity	Thomas

Bull Sarah Ann		12.11.1891	St. Michael	Not registered
Bull Sarah Ann		8.11.1890	Holy Trinity	Not registered
Bullock Leah	m	21.5.1925	5 Abbey Cottages, Binley	Arthur Lionel
Bunker Ada	m	22.6.1911	Coventry	Herbert George
Burden Phyllis	f	1.12.1929	101 Hastings Road	Audrey
Burdett Mary Jane	m	8.12.1912	Coventry	Henry
Burgess Florence	f	7.10.1916	104 Little Park Street	Margaret Lois
Burke Gertrude	m	27.12.1921	5 Freeth Street	Norman
Burke Gertrude	f	7.12.1922	23 New Street	Elsie
Burke Louisa	m	01.05.1878	Holy Trinity	Edmund
Burr Edna	m	3.2.1930	32 Henry Street	Horace
Burrows Dorothy	f	23.3.1926	22 Churchill Avenue	Bessie
Burrows Henrietta	f	13.8.1881	St. Michael	Jessie Caroline
Burton Emily Violet	f	2.2.1929	49 Stockton Road	Hazel Doreen
Burton Harriet	m	31.8.1887	St. Michael	Bertie
Burton Lilian E	m	11.1.1918	Leopold Road	Ronald Edward
Busby Alice	f	1.4.1886	N. F. A	Ada Annie
Butler Ivy Eliza	m	12.10.1929	8 Adelaide Street	Frank
Butt Roberta	f	02.05.1877	Casual Pauper	Not registered
Byatt Alice	m	13.3.1904	Coventry	Thomas

MOTHER'S NAME	M/F	D.O.B.	ADDRESS	CHILD'S NAME
Cady Elizabeth Alice	f	29.9.1928	46 Gas Street	Eileen Florence
Cahill Alice Veronica	m	16.10.1916	1 West Street	Harold Leonard
Caldecott Doris	m	26.12.1928	137 Humber Road	Raymond
Callow Eliza	f	8.6.1914	4 Cow Lane	Gladys
Callow Minnie and Arthur	f	30.7.1911	Coventry	Mary
Calloway Fanny	f	14.2.1925	23 Yardley Street	Gladys May
Calloway Fanny	m	21.6.1921	23 Yardley Street	Leslie
Campbell Annie and Cornelius	f	1.4.1896	casual pauper	Priscilla
Campton Alice Frances	f	15.1.1924	13 Steam Yard, East Street	Elsie
Carlins Sarah Ann	m	20.10.1917	26 Hostel, Holbrooks Lane	Jack
Carnall Beatrice May	f	15.2.1930	1ct 11h Whitefriars Street	Annie
Carnall Beatrice May	f	18.9.1927	1ct 11h Whitefriars Lane	Gladys
Carpenter Amy	m	22.7.1912	Coventry	Frank
Carpenter Martha	f	28.3.1899	St. Michael	Alice Kate
Carter Katie	f	18.4.1929	24 Castle Street	Kathleen
Carter Leah	f	24.2.1899	St. Michael	Ethel
Cartwright Emily Alice	f	7.9.1884	St. Michael	Emily Alice
Cartwright Maud	f	17.6.1917	1ct 2h Chauntry Place	Rose Mary
Carvell Emma	f	7.6.1896	St. Michael	Florence
Cashmore Florence Gertrude	f	8.9.1927	88 North Street	Sheila May
Cashmore Hannah	f	17.4.1854	N. F. A	Elizabeth
Castle Bessie and Cyril	f	16.4.1915	122 Avon Street	Constance May
Caufield Margaret	f	9.8.1925	3 Little Fields, Stoke Heath	Sheila
Caulfield Margaret	f	4.3.1930	70 Sackville Street	Eileen
Caulfield Violet	m	25.6.1927	38 Castle Street	George Leslie
Causer Matilda	m	10.9.1894	St. Michael	Francis John
Cave Mary Jane (nee Sidwell)	m	5.11.1884	St. Michael	Horace
Challis Beatrice	f	19.10.1918	7 Allesley Old Road	Betty

Challis Nellie	f	26.6.1925	50 Holyhead Road	Margaret Mary
Chamberlain Elizabeth	f	14.6.1897	St. Michael	Gladys May
Chaplin Rose Emma	m	16.5.1912	Coventry	James
Chapman Jane Elizabeth	m	22.2.1929	213 Munition Cottages	Albert Edward
Charley Ellen	f	12.2.1894	St. Michael	Florence
Chatwin Agnes Elizabeth	m	9.7.1926	St. Faiths Shelter, Holyhead Road	Norman
Chew Ellen and Joseph	f	3.1.1892	Casual pauper	Frances
Chinn Maria	m	2.4.1889	St. Michael	Arthur
Chittam Maria	f	6.3.867	N. F. A	Ann
Chittem Elizabeth	f	21.1.1914	Coventry	Kathleen
Chittem Elizabeth	f	7.11.1910	Coventry	Lily
Chittem Henry & Emily	m	15.9.1880	St. Michael	William
Chittem Matilda	f	2.7.1900	Coventry	Georgina Lines
Clamping Emma	f	13.3.1919	11 London Road	Irene
Clancy Ellen	f	9.10.1926	6 Swan Street	Maud
Clark Norah	f	11.6.1920	24 May Street	Eleanor Mary
Clark Rose Elizabeth	f	23.11.1920	14 Satchwell Street, Leamington	Beatrice Mary
Clark Sarah	m	30.4.1881	St. Michael	Septimus
Clarke Alice Kate	m	17.4.1917	104 Little Park Street	Eric Wilfred
Clarke Catherine	f	2.1.1930	8ct 7h Cox Street	Kathleen
Clarke Clara	m	13.4.1929	332 Corporation Cottages	John Augustus
Clarke Eliza		6.5.1883	St. Michael	Not registered
Clarke Elizabeth and William	m	12.12.1888	St. Michael	Henry Frederick
Clarke Elsie	m	14.4.1914	2a Coombe Street, Stoke	John
Clarke Esther	f	25.12.1855	N. F. A	Esther
Clarke Ethel Emily		4.11.1927	19 Winchester Street	Not registered
Clarke Harriet	m	10.10.1919	County Club, Stoneleigh Terrace	George Walter
Clarke Mabel	m	15.7.1929	45 Whitefriars Street	Frank
Clarke Mabel	m	27.10.1925	8 Whitefriars Lane	Charles Edward
Clarke Mabel		3.6.1927	8 Whitefriars Lane	Not registered
Clarke Marjorie W	m	3.1.1930	St. Faiths Shelter, Holyhead Road	Hugh

Clarke Mary	m	15.2.1921	69 Severn Road	Joseph
Clarke Mary Ann		24.12.1928	31 Highfield Road	Not registered
Clarke Sarah Ann		30.6.1929	Foleshill Union	Not registered
Clay Annie	m	28.7.1890	Holy Trinity	David
Clay Ellen	f	10.10.1885	N. F. A	Mary
Clay Ellen	f	10.10.1885	N. F. A	Martha
Claydon Harriet	f	26.9.1893	Holy Trinity	Violet May
Clayton Lilian	m	29.10.1912	Coventry	Albert
Clayton Mabel Annie	m	20.11.1924	15 Henley Road, Bell Green	George Henry
Cleaver Ann	f	11.3.1889	St. Michael	Elizabeth Caroline
Cleaver Annie	m	12.1.1912	Coventry	Lewis Arthur
Cleaver Annie Elizabeth	m	1.2.1921	b/o 18 Silver Street	Leslie
Cleaver Elizabeth		20.12.1894	Holy Trinity	Not registered
Cleaver Kate	m	19.11.1911	Coventry	Arthur
Cleaver Kate	m	19.11.1913	Coventry	James
Cleverley Florence	f	2.2.1930	42 Red Lane	Gwendoline
Cleverley Sarah Elizabeth	m	9.6.1929	19 bk 53 Queen Victoria Road	Ronald
Clews Eva	f	1.9.1926	5 Summer Row, Spon Street	Elsie May
Clifford Annie	m	28.8.1910	Coventry	Frederick Henry
Clifford Annie	m	8.12.1928	31 Cook Street	Michael Joseph
Clitherow Kathleen	m	23.4.1929	12 Minster Road	Eric Charles
Coates Esther	f	5.4.1901	Coventry	Florence
Coates Esther and Joseph	m	21.2.1909	Coventry	Leslie
Coates Esther H and Joseph	m	19.11.1907	Coventry	Henry
Cocking Annie	m	23.4.1928	19 Colony Cottages, Holbrooks Lane	John
Cockrill Clara	f	3.12.1891	St. Michael	Louisa
Cole		12.2.1862	N. F. A	Not registered
Cole Alice Emily	f	24.6.1915	6 Blythe Road	Norah
Cole Ann	m	16.5.1885	St. Michael	Charles Edwin
Cole Ann		24.11.1887	Holy Trinity	Not registered
Cole Louisa Ann	m	25.9.1917	19 St. Agnes Lane	William
Cole Margaret	f	4.6.1929	St. Faiths Shelter	Catherine Margaret

Cole Mary Josephine	f	14.12.1919	104 Little Park Street	Patricia Mary
Colledge Esther	m	12.6.1900	Coventry	Herbert Henry
Collett Jane	f	1.11.1886	St. Michael	Jane Elizabeth
Collett Jane	f	5.1.1889	St. Michael	Ellen
Colley Emma		13.1.1868	N. F. A	Not registered
Colley Sarah Ann	f	29.04.1878	St. Michael	Emma
Collins Ellen	f	11.1.1918	Transferred from Brentford Union	Kathleen Ellen
Collins Ellen	m	6.11.1921	Warwick Union	Ernest George
Collins Mabel	m	3.3.1929	12 Bedford Street	Edward
Collins Matilda Maud	f	21.10.1912	Coventry	Ellen
Collyer Annie	m	22.4.1917	13ct 3h Sherbourne Street	John Henry
Collyer Annie	f	3.1.1910	Coventry	Constance
Colman Winifred Elizabeth	m	26.10.1926	29 Villiers Street	Robert
Congrave Annie and Albert	f	1.12.1908	Coventry	Margaret
Connell Elizabeth and James	f	28.5.1893	Casual pauper	Rose Ann
Connelly Catherine	m	23.12.1918	The Hut, Park Road	John
Cook Gladys	m	12.2.1929	27 Adelaide Street	John Arthur
Cooke Daisy Joyce	m	14.9.1929	60 Leicester Causeway	Geoffrey
Cooke Louisa	f	30.9.1897	St. Michael	Margaret Louisa
Cooke Mary	f	2.3.1913	Coventry	Gladys
Cooknell Marion Ada	f	16.3.1927	Nuneaton Poor Law Institution	Mary
Cooknell Marion Ada	f	24.10.1925	244 Westbury Road, Stockingford	Gladys
Coome Agnes		19.11.1918	104 Little Park Street	Not registered
Cooper Elsie Ivy	f	21.4.1929	37 Clayfield Cottages, Kenilworth	Joan Annie
Cooper Gladys	m	16.9.1927	Nuneaton Union	William
Cooper Hannah	f	28.2.1890	St. Michael	Alice
Cooper Lily	m	20.5.1912	Coventry	Herbert Henry
Cooper Minnie		24.11.1893	St. Michael	Not registered
Cooper Miriam	m	23.6.1918	12 Spriggs Row, Hales Street	Ernest
Cooper Violet Agnes	m	8.2.1929	66 Hastings Road	Frederick Bernard

Cope Nettie	f	20.5.1929	31 Whitmore Park	Joan
Copson Amelia	f	16.10.1866	N. F. A	Amelia
Copson Ann	f	16.5.1880	St. Michael	Elizabeth Davis
Corby Olive May	f	11.12.1927	St. Faiths Shelter	Patricia
Cotterill Rose	f	1.4.1919	3ct 20h Much Park Street	Beryl Joan
Cottle Edith Lilian	f	5.1.1927	122 Colony Cottages	Moyra Winifred
Court Elsie	f	25.2.1918	6ct 13h Chauntry Place	Lucy May
Cowley Sarah Ann	m	15.9.1894	St. Michael	Harry Wheeler
Cowley Sarah Ann	m	3.3.1892	Holy Trinity	William Henry
Cox Ellen and John	m	19.10.1897	Holy Trinity	John
Cox Ellen and John	f	8.7.1895	Holy Trinity	Elizabeth Ellen
Cox Eva Clara		17.4.1927	12ct 8h Well Street	Not registered
Crabtree Marjorie	f	18.3.1929	24 Dane Road	Joyce
Cramp Annie	m	22.12.1922	4 Coronation Road	Leslie
Cramp Edith Alice	f	25.10.1928	St. Faiths Shelter	Joyce Mary
Cramp Ellen	m	9.5.1926	99 Whitmore Park Cottages	Dennis
Cramp Emily	f	11.9.1894	Holy Trinity	Elizabeth
Cramp Olive	m	23.1.1910	Coventry	Albert William
Cribdon Susannah	f	30.12.1886	Holy Trinity	Emma
Crofts Ada Elizabeth	m	26.2.1907	Coventry	Leonard
Crofts Caroline	f	21.8.1893	St. Michael	Annie Eliza
Crofts Jane	m	21.4.1908	Coventry	Frederick
Crofts Jane	f	30.7.1913	Coventry	Ada Gladys
Crofts Selina	m	17.12.1879	Holy Trinity	Not registered
Cronan Sarah Ann	m	21.8.1929	5 Swan Street	Stephen
Crosby Ann		25.7.1866	N. F. A	Not registered
Cross Alice	m	24.6.1926	151 Whitmore Park Cottages	Harold Granville
Cross Louisa		17.3.1889	Holy Trinity	Not registered
Crump Mary Ann	f	1.12.1883	St. Michael	Fanny
Crump Mary Ann	m	19.6.1886	N. F. A	Ernest
Crump Mary Ann	m	4.12.1881	N. F. A	Not registered
Crump Priscilla	f	21.1.1891	St. Michael	Nellie
Cuckson Ethel	f	5.3.1916	58 Huntingdon Road	Irene
Cullen Dorothy	f	30.12.1927	39 Gas Street	Dorothy
Culliford Kathleen Matilda	m	16.1.1928	57 Spring Road, Little Heath	Donald George

Cunningham Annie	f	23.5.1918	55 Arthur Street	Elizabeth
Cunningham Eileen	m	5.10.1927	28 Howard Street	Philip
Cureton Mary Jane	m	7.7.1909	Coventry	Frank
Cureton Mary Jane and Charles	f	1.6.1912	Coventry	Lily
Curtis Elizabeth		16.7.1924	b/o 412 Stoney Stanton Road	Not registered
Curtis Matilda		3.12.1911	Coventry	Not registered
Curtlin Mary	m	8.11.1929	168 Corporation Cottages	Robert William
Cutter Nellie May	f	2.7.1927	St. Faiths Shelter	Sheila
Cuttiford Kathleen Matilda	m	31.1.1929	57 Spring Road	Noel

MOTHER'S NAME	M/F	D.O.B.	ADDRESS	CHILD'S NAME
Dadley Amelia	f	11.7.1907	Coventry	Gwendoline
Daffern Ethel	m	26.8.1919	101 London Road	Wilfred
Daffern Gladys Lavinia	m	19.12.1921	The Bungalow, Whitley	William Arthur
Daffern Gladys Lavinia	f	3.1.1925	7 The Quadrant	Edith
Daft Lilian	m	28.3.1926	Meriden Union	Edward Albert
Dale Alice	m	29.9.1927	Nuneaton Union	Kenneth
Dallas Annie	m	3.1.1918	1 Paynes Lane	Harold
Dalton Ethel		30.9.1915	21 Silverton Road	Not registered
Dalrymple Isabella	m	28.12.1888	Casual pauper	Archibald
Daniels Ellen		25.1.1901	Coventry	Not registered
Danks Helen	f	21.1.1929	15 Gresham Street	Gwyneth
Darker Mary Ann	m	2.5.1927	Nuneaton Poor Law Institution	Cyril
Darlison Frances May	f	6.12.1922	85 Spon Street	Frances
Dashwood Nellie Mary	f	11.2.1927	321 Corporation Cottages	Daisy Dorothy
Davidson Emily Mary	m	14.10.1928	35 Somerset Road	David
Davies Emma		10.3.1868	N. F. A	Not registered
Davis Alice	f	20.12.1909	Coventry	Alice
Davis Alice	f	24.1.1913	Coventry	Gladys
Davis Alice Mary	m	5.8.1908	Coventry	Horace
Davis Ellen May	f	13.7.1928	30 Yardley Street	Rosalind May
Davis Emma	f	17.2.1860	N. F. A	Eliza
Davis Florence	m	5.6.1929	31 Oxford Street	Arthur
Davis Hilda May	f	9.3.1929	65 Little Park Street	Jean
Davis Jane and James	f	28.8.1891	St. Michael	Jane Elizabeth
Davis Jane and James	f	30.5.1895	Holy Trinity	Catherine Ann
Davis Jane and James	m	7.8.1897	Holy Trinity	Joseph James
Davis Lily	m	4.6.1918	Middlesbrough Hostel, Radford Street	Frank
Davis Lucy	f	18.11.1927	St. Faiths Shelter	Violet
Davis Maria	m	5.3.1888	St. Michael	Ernest Henry Glover

Dawson Edith Selina	m	19.5.1921	91 Highland Road	Roy
Dawson Selina	f	30.9.1910	Coventry	Sylvia
Dawson Selina and John Edward	m	23.12.1907	Coventry	Alexander
Dean Ellen Jerry	m	11.12.1925	8h 2ct Gosford Street	George
Dean Florence Ethel	f	20.10.1917	Ordnance Hostel, Swan Lane	Ethel May
Deeley Amy Louisa	m	1.6.1922	2h 1ct Swanswell Terrace	Albert Hendry Victor
Deeming Ann		9.5.1866	N. F. A	Not registered
Delaney Ethel	m	7.8.1929	117 Corporation Cottages	Bernard
Delaney Ethel Patricia	f	10.1.1928	117 Corporation Cottages	Eileen
Delaney Ethel Patricia	f	10.1.1928	117 Corporation Cottages	Patricia
Delaney Ethel Priscilla	m	24.5.1926	20 Guild Road	Lawrence Patrick
Delaney Rose	m	7.12.1929	29 Pinley Gardens	James Henry
Dempsey Beatrice May	f	5.10.1929	16 Northfield Road	Nora
Dennis Annie Mary	f	27.7.1912	Coventry	Evelyn Annie
Denny Jane	m	28.4.1883	St. Michael	John
Desborough Elizabeth	f	12.6.1918	60 Mulliner Street	Lily
Desborough Kate	f	7.12.1919	60 Mulliner Street	Kitty
Devaney Mary and William	f	7.5.1895	St. Michael	Ellen
Devonport Ethel May	m	7.10.1919	15 Chapel Street	Reginald
Dewey Charlotte Plummer	m	17.4.1904	Coventry	George
Dexter Winifred Susan	m	2.9.1928	28 Coronation Road	Bernard
Dillon Elizabeth	f	31.10.1877	St. Michael	Matilda
Dixon Florence Irene	m	2.7.1921	Bakers Restaurant, Fleet Street	Ronald
Dobbins Daisy	f	15.10.1927	29 Alma Street	Freda
Docker Esther		13.11.1866	N. F. A	Not registered
Donnellan Kathleen	m	22.3.1918	132 Colony Cottages, Holbrook Lane	Richard

Doody Madge Kathleen	f	22.8.1927	14 Corporation Cottages	Margaret
Dooney Margaret	m	18.4.1926	6 West Avenue, Stoke Park	Gerald
Dore Agnes Lilian. Born 1899	m	13.10.1920	Y.W.C.A, Park Road	Arthur Charles
Downing Dorothy Ida	m	21.9.1917	30 Cambridge Street	George Frederick
Dowswell Sarah	m	16.11.1928	54 The Butts	Dennis Roland
Doyle Ann	f	02.02.1877	St. Michael	Not registered
Doyle Bertha Bellamy	f	23.8.1892	St. Michael	Bertha
Doyle Clara Beatrice	f	31.1.1929	16 Upper Well Street	Florence May
Doyle Clara Beatrice	f	8.9.1927	3ct 7h Greyfriars Lane	Beatrice Mary
Doyle Emily	f	19.6.1916	3 Leicester Street	Eva
Doyle Jane	m	4.8.1891	St. Michael	Joseph
Doyle Lizzie		23.4.1894	St. Michael	Not registered
Dry Sarah	m	28.4.1922	264 Foleshill Road	Colin William
Duckett Daisy	m	28.5.1913	Coventry	Douglas
Duggins Eliza (nee Sparkes)	m	12.4.1885	St. Michael	Harry
Duggins Elizabeth and George	f	14.11.1891	St. Michael	Elizabeth
Duggins Jane	m	12.8.1897	St. Michael	Joseph Henry
Duncan Maria	m	13.08.1876	St. Michael	Not registered
Dungley Margaret Maud Amelia	m	31.5.1928	77 Holyhead Road	Lawrence
Dunkley Lydia	m	3.3.1891	St. Michael	George
Dunn Sarah Ellen	f	14.3.1928	b/o 39 Gas Street	Rhoda May
Dunt Ida Lobelia	f	21.11.1912	Coventry	Violet
Dunton Ann	f	27.03.1877	Holy Trinity	Not registered
Dunton Ann	m	9.9.1879	St. Michael	William Richard
Dunton Ellen	f	13.8.1879	Holy Trinity	Jessie Eveline
Dunton Rose	m	19.6.1914	11 Leicester Street	Albert
Dunton Rose	m	5.6.1916	11 Leicester Street	Alfred
Dyke Edith	f	22.11.1918	84 Grafton Street	Betty
Dyke Gladys	f	11.6.1929	37 Cope Street	Eileen Margaret
Dyson Beatrice Agnes	f	9.8.1929	4 Yardley Street	Beatrice
Dyson Minnie	m	2.12.1925	4 Yardley Street	Joseph Leonard

MOTHER'S NAME	M/F	D.O.B.	ADDRESS	CHILD'S NAME
Eagleton Mary Jane	f	5.6.1912	Coventry	Mary Jane
Earl Alice	f	18.3.1923	36 Well Street	Edna
Eaton Amy	f	16.6.1929	21 Leopold Road	May
Eavaley Beatrice	f	31.5.1929	6 Whitefriars Street	Barbara
Eaves Elsie	f	2.7.1928	12 Fynford Road	Eileen
Eaves Elsie	f	8.11.1929	17 Allesley Old Road	Sheila
Eaves Hannah		23.10.1861	N. F. A	Not registered
Eburne Rhoda Ellen	f	6.1.1917	21 Swan Street	Rhoda
Edmunds Clara	f	28.2.1892	St. Michael	Gertrude W
Edmunds Mary	f	26.2.1901	Coventry	Ivy
Edwards Annie	m	1.5.1893	Holy Trinity	Ernest
Edwards Elizabeth		10.2.1860	N. F. A	Not registered
Edwards Elizabeth (nee Reaves)	f	4.3.1887	St. Michael	Frances
Edwards Evelyn Murial	m	14.9.1927	18 Sparkbrook Street	Lewis William
Edwards Lettice	m	26.12.1921	1ct 6h Smithford Street	Eric
Edwards Rose Ellen	m	15.3.1928	44 Lower Ford Street	Eric Philip
Egan Kathleen May	m	15.7.1927	11 London Road	George
Eggleton Rose	f	1.3.1927	19 Queen Street	Phyllis Nancy
Eld Alice Elizabeth	f	8.12.1907	Coventry	Florence
Eld Elizabeth	m	12.5.1893	Holy Trinity	George
Elks Elizabeth Fanny	f	4.6.1918	11 Foleshill Road	Minnie
Elks Lilian E		8.7.1929	106 Cross Road	Not registered
Ellerthorne Florence	f	7.9.1884	St. Michael	Florence Mary
Ellis Daisy	m	7.7.1927	The Elms, Walsgrave	John
Embra Lucy Louisa	m	14.2.1921	Belmont St. Patricks Road	Anthony
England Hannah	f	23.9.1860	N. F. A	Esther
Ernbury Ellen Louisa	m	7.7.1918	407 Stoney Stanton Road	John Edward
Evans Clara May	f	6.1.1927	4h 9ct Chauntry Place	Florence Emily
Evans Gertrude	m	16.3.1930	Meriden Union	John
Evans Grace	m	16.1.1918	104 Little Park Street	William Henry
Evans Jessie	m	29.7.1916	24 Whitefriars Lane	John Thomas Donovan
Evans Mary Ellen	m	31.7.1918	104 Little Park Street	Clifford
Evans Nellie	m	13.1.1920	175 George Street	Lewis

Evans Winifred	m	15.9.1929	149 Cambridge Street	Maurice
Evans Winifred	f	18.1.1905	Coventry	Ethel Winifred
Evans Winifred Jessie	m	9.10.1910	Coventry	Albert
Evatt Gertrude Alice	f	6.6.1928	92 Spon Street	Brenda
Evatt Gertrude Alice	f	6.9.1926	91 Spon Street	Eileen
Eyre Harriett	m	30.12.1915	4ct 15h Well Street	Frederick Arthur

MOTHER'S NAME	M/F	D.O.B.	ADDRESS	CHILD'S NAME
Farrar Jane Elizabeth	m	31.5.1921	95 Narrow Lane	Alfred Oliver
Farren Beatrice Ada	m	29.4.1928	119 Lower Ford Street	William Edward
Farren Beatrice Ada	m	5.1.1927	119 Lower Ford Street	George
Farren Elizabeth	m	23.07.1877	St. Michael	Not registered
Farrer Jane Elizabeth	m	31.3.1917	32 Leicester Street	Eric Charles
Farrow Eva	f	28.5.1929	2ct 5h Warwick Lane	Alma
Faulkner Ellen	f	21.2.1928	5 b/o 49 Station Street West	Gladys
Faulkner Ellen Agnes	m	4.6.1899	St. Michael	Walter
Fearn Alice Eliza Lilian	f	30.10.1927	41 Ash Grove, Stoney Stanton Road	Lilian
Feeley Mary	f	17.4.1854	N. F. A	Ann
Fell Mary Ann	m	19.3.1892	Holy Trinity	Edward
Fell Mary Ann		29.3.1897	N. F. A	Not registered
Fenn Alice	f	19.10.1918	6 Weldale Street, Reading	Mildred Mary
Fenn Elsie May	f	30.3.1918	32 Victoria Road	Clara Winifred
Fenn Emma	f	30.9.1915	Three Tuns Hotel, Hertford Street	Mabel
Fennell Clara	m	19.03.1877	Holy Trinity	Not registered
Fennell Margaret	m	24.11.1929	Greenway", Broad Lane	Douglas Gordon
Fife Elsie		30.10.1928	b/o 100 Clay Lane	Not registered
Finch Ellen Susan	m	10.2.1914	Coventry	Albert George
Finch Rachel	m	7.4.1879	Holy Trinity	Not registered
Fincher Ellen	m	20.8.1927	6 Cook Street	Edward
Fisher Daisy M	m	24.11.1919	104 Little Park Street	Claude
Fisher Jane		29.2.1924	3ct 38h Gosford Street	Not registered
Fitzgerald Gertrude	f	15.6.1926	Regent House", Humber Road	Joyce Edith
Flanagan Elsie	m	11.8.1911	Coventry	James
Fleming Harriet	f	16.1.1888	Holy Trinity	Annie Elizabeth
Fletcher Annie L	m	30.4.1905	Coventry	Horace
Fletcher Isabel	f	11.3.1897	Holy Trinity	Isabel
Fletcher Isabel	m	28.7.1899	Holy Trinity	George
Fletcher May	f	22.4.1918	Hostel 24, Colony 1, Holbrook Lane	Beatrice Doreen

Flint Harriett and Charles Joseph	m	18.9.1904	Coventry	Charles Joseph
Flowers Ada	f	8.7.1904	Coventry	Gladys
Flowers Ada	m	9.2.1900	St. Michael	Henry
Flowers Alice	m	29.9.1928	11ct 3h St. John's Street	John
Flowers Alice Mary Elizabeth	m	22.9.1926	11ct 13 St. John Street	Joseph Bernard
Flowers Florence	m	5.4.1929	12h 14ct Little Park Street	Walter
Flowers Hannah	f	25.12.1854	N. F. A	Sophia
Floyd Emily	f	26.11.1923	3 Brunswick Road	Audrey Violet
Flynn Elizabeth	m	27.10.1904	Coventry	Ernest Samuel
Ford Maria (nee Malelin)	f	11.2.1885	St. Michael	Ellen
Forster Constance Evelyn	f	5.2.1930	bk 5 Fleet Street	Edna Mairs
Foster Eleanor Frances	m	8.2.1917	580 Foleshill Road	Francis Rupert
Foster Margaret L	m	27.10.1911	Coventry	Ernest
Fraley Annie	m	8.5.1889	Casual pauper	John
Fraley Annie	m	8.5.1889	Casual pauper	Thomas
Franklin Agnes	f	19.7.1928	St. Faiths Shelter	Gwendoline
Franklin Lucy	m	16.4.1921	18 Compton Street, Leamington	Cecil
Freeman Elizabeth		7.6.1862	N. F. A	Not registered
Freeman Florence	m	6.8.1929	24 Peel Street	John
Freestone Violet	f	28.5.1929	47 Collingwood Road	Violet
Freeth Ellen	f	20.11.1928	6 Rood Lane	Gladys Ellen
Freeth Ellen	f	9.6.1926	3ct 6h Fleet Street	Doris
Freeman Sarah and William	f	7.6.1885	N. F. A	Laura
French Ann	m	16.7.1854	N. F. A	William
French Ethel Murial	f	1.6.1928	Foleshill Union	Thelma Doreen
Frith Ada	f	6.7.1917	15 Coniston Road, Earlsdon	Phyllis May
Frost Ellen	f	5.9.1929	139 Stoney Stanton Road	Ellen
Frost Lillian	f	3.4.1906	Coventry	Dulcie Lillian
Frost Lillian	m	3.4.1906	Coventry	Louis Edward
Fulcher Sarah	f	6.9.1855	N. F. A	Maria
Fulwell Caroline	f	3.5.1912	Coventry	May

MOTHER'S NAME	M/F	D.O.B.	ADDRESS	CHILD'S NAME
Gadd Ellen	f	5.3.1930	26 Wellington Street	Doreen
Gadsby Matilda	m	6.9.1881	St. Michael	Harry
Garby Florence	m	13.10.1927	7 Villiers Street	Frank
Gardner Ada	m	19.6.1917	23 Cambridge Street	William
Gardner Ann Maria	m	26.4.1888	St. Michael	William Robert
Gardner Ann Maria	m	9.5.1887	St. Michael	William Mark
Gardner Annie	f	10.11898	St. Michael	Annie
Gardner Bessie	f	24.9.1929	42 Humber Road	Marjorie
Gardner Bessie	m	6.8.1928	66 Stoney Stanton Road	Edward
Gardner Constance	m	22.9.1918	104 Little Park Street	Eric Gordon White
Gardner Dora Alice	m	25.10.1929	14 Hawkins Road	Armand
Gardner Dorothy	f	14.9.1910	Coventry	Dorothy
Gardner Hilda	m	4.10.1927	28 Union Street	Raymond
Gardner Lucy	f	28.6.1892	St. Michael	Alice May
Gardner Lucy		5.3.1897	N. F. A	Not registered
Gardner Mary	m	6.2.1907	Coventry	John
Gardner Mary Ann	f	14.11.1904	Coventry	Alice
Gardner Mary Ann		21.8.1903	Coventry	Not registered
Gardner Theresa	f	23.3.1928	152 Whitmore Park Cottages	Patricia
Garfield Winifred	f	28.5.1928	5 Wyken Way, Stoke Heath	Thelma
Garner Charlotte	m	11.5.1923	Round House, Fillongley	John Henry
Garrett Annie or Hannah	m	8.12.1917	N. F. A	Alfred William
Gascoigne Alice	m	11.4.1929	4h 13ct St. John's Street	Albert Edward
Geaves Alice	m	5.11.1928	288 Munition Cottages	John
Geelan Mary Ann	m	3.1.1929	261 Harnall Lane East	Michael James
Gentry Alice May	f	31.5.1920	76 Avon Street, Upper Stoke	Kathleen
George Ann	f	15.2.1883	St. Michael	Henrietta Maud
Gerrard Ada	m	27.7.1929	25 Gilbert Street	James
Gerrard Gladys May	m	23.8.1922	b/o 99 Queen Victoria Road	Kenneth John
Gerrard Gladys May	f	7.4.1925	b/o 99 Queen Victoria Road	Mary Elizabeth
Gerrard Gladys May	f	8.1.1928	b/o 99 Queen Victoria Road	Irene

Gething Alice	f	10.1.1925	4ct 4h Sherbourne Street	Sarah Jane
Gibbard Violet	m	17.3.1920	174 Station Street East	Eric
Gibbard Violet	m	7.2.1918	174 Station Street East	Clement
Gibbons Dora	f	22.8.1927	43 Clay Lane	Margaret
Gibbs Violet May	f	24.7.1922	1ct 1h Gulson Road	Lilian Gertrude
Gifford Martha	m	4.9.1903	Coventry	Alfred
Gilbertson Mary Ann		8.3.1860	N. F. A	Not registered
Giles Mabel Annie	f	21.7.1917	5ct 4h Little Park Street	Margaret
Gilkes Florence	m	30.5.1905	Coventry	Arthur
Glenn Mary G	m	28.4.1922	Mansfield Villa", Binley Road	Jerrod Ernest
Glover Ada	f	21.5.1905	Coventry	May
Glover Flora Evelyn	f	10.3.1926	9ct 3h Sherbourne Street	Flora Evelyn
Glover Flora Evelyn	m	17.3.1925	9ct 3h Sherbourne Street	Samuel
Godderidge Emma J	f	2.8.1925	92 Sutton Hill, Nuneaton	Ruby Elizabeth
Godfrey Florence T (nee Lane)	f	27.12.1884	St. Michael	James
Godwin Bertha Mary	m	25.3.1909	Coventry	Reginald Harry
Golby Rachael	m	16.6.1928	Chapel Road, Foleshill	John Cyril
Golder Clara	f	27.6.1927	6 Queen Victoria Road	Edith
Golder Elizabeth	f	17.2.1927	20 Adelaide Street	Elizabeth Joan
Goodman Marian	m	22.10.1901	Coventry	Thomas Edward
Goodwin Dorothy	m	2.8.1919	31 Cook Street	George Frederick
Goodwin Lizzie	f	27.3.1914	Coventry	Ethel May
Goodyear Elizabeth	f	28.6.1909	Coventry	Phyllis Gwendoline
Goodyear Elizabeth	f	6.6.1927	29 Station Street East	Margaret
Goodyear Elizabeth Rose Annie	m	23.4.1922	b/o 4 Cherry Street	Norman
Goodyer Elizabeth Rosanna	f	15.5.1904	Coventry	Gladys Rose May
Goss Jane Elizabeth	m	16.10.1929	87 Highfield Road	George Stanley
Gough Ann Maria	m	2.4.1886	N. F. A	James Henry
Gough Harriet	f	10.5.1888	St. Michael	Alice Maud
Gould Dorothy Evelyn	m	19.11.1926	Meriden Union	Robert William
Gould Evelyn	f	6.7.1929	34 Lawrence Saunders Road	Mavis

Gould Maud	f	4.7.1914	6 Trafalgar Street	Irene Gardner
Goulding Ida	m	25.8.1916	28 Narrow Lane	Edward
Gow Adelaide	f	16.3.1921	Bishops Itchington, nr Leamington	Gladys
Grant Elsie May	m	18.11.1927	8ct Jordan Well	Horace
Grant Elsie May	f	31.7.1929	11 London Road	Mabel
Grant Keziah		18.7.1903	Coventry	Not registered
Grant Miriam Maud	f	26.1.1930	1 Ivy Terrace, Leigh Street	Joan
Greaves Lena	m	24.3.1930	Foleshill	John
Green Ada and James	m	8.10.1898	St. Michael	Arthur
Green Annie	m	21.02.1878	Holy Trinity	Charles
Green Caroline	f	4.4.1904	Coventry	Florence
Green Edith	f	15.12.1929	8 Common Way	Kathleen
Green Elsie Rose	f	11.2.1930	17ct 12h Little Park Street	Mary
Green Gladys	f	28.3.1930	17 Allesley Old Road	Vera
Green Hannah R	f	03.11.1877	St. Michael	Not registered
Green Maisie	f	19.8.1921	25 Hope Street	Maisie Gertrude Maud
Greenall Lily	m	20.9.1910	Coventry	John
Greenall Lily	m	24.12.1908	Coventry	Leonard
Greenall Lily		24.12.1908	Coventry	Not registered
Greenall Lily	m	24.7.1913	Coventry	Frederick
Greenall Rose	m	30.7.1910	Coventry	Thomas
Greenway Ann	f	14.12.1855	N. F. A	Mary Elizabeth
Greenway Annie Amelia	f	7.5.1929	St. Faiths Shelter	Patricia Mary
Gregory Hannah	f	16.1.1882	Holy Trinity	Not registered
Gregory Hannah	f	16.1.1882	Holy Trinity	Not registered
Griffin Gladys	m	14.12.1929	3 Bath Street	Eric Thomas
Griffin Lilian Amy	m	9.4.1928	10ct 2h Bishop Street	Bernard
Griffiths Alice	f	14.5.1893	St. Michael	Maud Beatrice
Griffiths Beatrice	f	12.12.1905	Coventry	Florence
Griffiths Beatrice	f	12.4.1909	Coventry	Clara
Griffiths Doris May	m	16.8.1926	90 Humber Avenue	Douglas Albert
Griffiths Hannah	m	26.12.1879	St. Michael	Henry
Grimsley Elizabeth	f	6.10.1916	7 Ironmonger Row	Louisa May
Grindley Kate	m	3.11.1888	Holy Trinity	William John
Grinsell Amelia	m	6.11.1926	4 Caravan, Rood Lane	George

Groom Alice Gertrude	m	24.8.1929	16 Centaur Road	John
Guest Elizabeth	m	18.8.1927	1ct 12h Thomas Street	Harry
Guest Ivy May		11.10.1923	2ct 12h Much Park Street	Not registered
Guest Ivy May		25.9.1925	N. F. A	Not registered
Guest Ivy May		5.1.1918	12h 12ct Much Park Street	Not registered
Guest Ivy May	f	5.4.1927	11 London Road	Kathleen Mary
Gummow May. Born 1898	f	24.11.1918	Whitemore Park Hostels	Margaret
Gunn Amy Beryl	m	2.4.1926	St. Faiths Shelter, Holyhead Road	Sydney Robert
Gunn Ellen	f	22.9.1900	Coventry	Emma
Gunn Ellen	f	26.2.1905	Coventry	Amy
Gunning Louisa Maria & Charles	m	6.2.1892	Casual pauper	Charles
Gutteridge Catherine	m	25.12.1892	St. Michael	John Henry
Gutteridge Fanny	f	30.6.1887	St. Michael	Fanny Gibbs
Gwilham Mary and Richard	m	18.10.1903	Coventry	Richard

MOTHER'S NAME	M/F	D.O.B.	ADDRESS	CHILD'S NAME
Hagarty Mary	m	20.4.1917	104 Little Park Street	Arthur Cyril
Hale Perle	m	23.12.1926	111 Gosford Street	Keith
Haley Eliza	m	28.05.1878	St. Michael	Ambrose
Haley Kate	m	1.11.1912	Coventry	Joseph
Haley Kate	m	10.11.1917	12h 12ct Whitefriars Lane	Arthur
Halfacre Gertrude J	f	1.8.1929	St. Faiths Shelter	Gertrude
Halford Elizabeth	m	8.8.1920	2 Paynes Row, Station Street West	Reginald Desmond
Hall A Maria	f	26.09.1877	St. Michael	Mary Jane
Hall Ada Jane	f	27.10.1925	11 London Road	Joyce
Hall Alice and Arthur	f	2.2.1908	Coventry	Winifred
Hall Annie	m	12.1.1899	Holy Trinity	Charles
Hall Edith Annie	m	31.12.1928	16 Meadow Street	Barrie James
Hall Emma		18.1.1863	N. F. A	Not registered
Hall Harriet	m	13.1.1897	Holy Trinity	John
Hall Harriet	m	5.6.1895	Holy Trinity	Frank
Hall Margaret	f	22.10.1918	141 Spon Street	Maria Blanche
Hallam Eliza	f	1.7.1880	Holy Trinity	Mary Ann
Hallam Eliza		13.2.1889	N. F. A	Not registered
Hallett Ellen	m	30.12.1919	30 Berkley Road	Kenneth William
Hallam Elizabeth	f	17.10.1875	St. Michael	Ann Maria
Hamblin Lilian	f	20.3.1929	32 King Richard Street	Sheila Louise
Hammersley Emily Gertrude	f	18.2.1911	Coventry	Nora Emily
Hammersley Gertrude	m	16.11.1928	St. Faiths Shelter	Bernard
Hammett Helena	m	24.7.1927	St. Faiths Shelter	Norman Edward
Hampson Ellen May	m	29.3.1927	1ct 3h Sherbourne Street	Charles
Hancox Emma	f	9.2.1887	St. Michael	Alice
Hancox Lilian M	f	17.7.1929	21 Hillside, Stoke Heath	Joyce
Hancox Lilian May	m	12.6.1928	21 Hillside, Stoke Heath	John Cyril
Hancox Minnie	f	8.12.1929	1ct 3h Paynes Lane	Eva Margaret
Handland Ann S	m	2.8.1907	Coventry	Albert W
Hands Maria		21.8.1866	N. F. A	Not registered
Hankerson Eliza	f	7.2.1884	St. Michael	Louisa

Hankerson Eliza	m	9.1.1887	St. Michael	Charles Henry
Hanks Emma Elizabeth	f	9.9.1928	32 King Richard Street	Beatrice Lilian
Hannagan Ellen	m	10.2.1907	Coventry	Robert
Hannagan Ellen	m	10.2.1907	Coventry	Edward
Hannaghan Ellen	f	17.7.1902	Coventry	Alice Maud
Hannaghan Ellen	m	5.4.1905	Coventry	Leonard
Hanson Mabel Mary & Harry Vict	m	9.11.1909	Coventry	Hubert
Hantwill Annie	m	4.5.1918	48 Lower Wellington Street	Ronald
Hardy Emma		21.2.1909	Coventry	Not registered
Harper Amy	f	6.9.1895	St. Michael	Ada
Harper Ellen	f	28.12.1877	St. Michael	Not registered
Harper Winifred Florence	f	28.3.1929	St. Faiths Shelter	Joyce Beatrice
Harrington Mary Ann J	m	3.9.1917	27 Bk, 6 Ordnance Hostel, Swan Lane	Laurence
Harris Charlotte	m	7.8.1917	Government Colony, Holbrooks Lane	Selwyn
Harris Doris Nellie	f	24.11.1929	120 Albany Road	Margaret Jean
Harris Elizabeth	m	21.11.1891	St. Michael	Frank
Harris Elizabeth	m	6.6.1885	N. F. A	Richard Henry
Harris Elizabeth		9.1.1888	Holy Trinity	Not registered
Harris Ethel	f	17.7.1905	Coventry	Ethel
Harris Ethel	f	28.3.1901	Coventry	Florence
Harris Ethel B	f	16.4.1903	Coventry	Florence May
Harris Louisa	m	15.1.1916	30 Spriggs Yard, Bedworth	Albert Edward
Harrison Jennie	m	6.3.1918	11 Hill Cross	Gilbert
Harrison Mary	m	23.05.1878	Holy Trinity	William
Harrison Mary	f	30.4.1882	St. Michael	Alice
Harrison Nellie	m	17.7.1923	12 Bulls Head Lane, Stoke	William
Harrison Nellie	m	6.1.1921	56 Winchester Street	Frank
Harrod Ada	f	4.3.1895	St. Michael	Elizabeth
Harrod Ann Maria	f	29.10.1892	St. Michael	Alice Maud
Hartland Annie	f	7.5.1902	Coventry	Doris
Hartley Daisy Melda	f	17.10.1929	46 South Street	Hartley Dorothy
Hartop M. A		22.2.1862	N. F. A	Not registered
Hartshorn Alice Maud	m	7.2.1930	2 Radford Circle, Coventry	James Richard

Harvey Annie	m	11.4.1912	Coventry	Ernest
Harvey Ethel	m	7.7.1917	33 Mickleton Road, Earlsdon	Idris Sidney
Harvey Louisa	f	27.4.1918	91 Much Park Street	Alice
Harvey Louisa	m	6.12.1923	6ct 20h Much Park Street	Alfred
Harvey Mabel	m	10.4.1921	8ct 2h Gosford Street	Frank
Hastings Hilda	m	2.2.1925	The Green, Exhall	Herbert
Hatfield Winifred	f	22.12.1922	The Charterhouse, London Road	Georgina May
Haughton		29.4.1862	N. F. A	Not registered
Hawtin Hilda Violet	f	1.2.1929	57 Leicester Street	Hilda Doreen
Haycock Mabel		26.9.1926	20 Welford Place, Lockhurst Lane	Not registered
Hayes Annie Elizabeth	m	12.1.1921	2h 2ct Much Park Street	Percy
Hayes Dorothy		21.7.1927	3 Byron Street	Not registered
Hayes Esther		13.12.1892	St. Michael	Not registered
Hayes Jane	m	19.12.1927	32 Gosford Street	Michael John
Hayes Sarah Ann	m	19.1.1893	St. Michael	Leonard Robert
Haynes Charlotte	m	4.5.1912	Coventry	Harry
Haynes Margaret	f	23.6.1925	45 Thomas Road, Foleshill	Mavis
Haynes Margaret	f	6.5.1921	26 Smith Street	Evelyn Margaret
Haynes Mary Ann	m	22.7.1885	N. F. A	Thomas Rushton
Healey Kathleen N	f	16.5.1929	41 Bond Street	Sheila
Healey Laura	f	7.5.1915	11ct 9h Gosford Street	Hilda
Heath Margaret	f	28.4.1928	2 South Avenue, Tile Hill Lane	Margaret Eileen
Heathcote Daisy	m	23.3.1920	Hearsall Croft, Broad Lane, Whoberley	Alfred Ernest
Hemmings Francis		21.12.1901	Coventry	Not registered
Hemmings Rose Beatrice	f	24.9.1916	104 Little Park Street	Constance Grace
Hendry Annie	m	14.2.1929	4 Stanley Road	Dennis
Hendry Fanny May	f	24.7.1921	3ct 1h Tower Street	Joan Marguerite
Hewitt Alice	f	21.12.1896	St. Michael	Jessie
Hewitt Elizabeth	f	30.9.1919	14 King Georges Avenue	Emily
Hewitt Ellen	m	7.10.1889	St. Michael	David
Hewitt Rose	m	23.10.1926	Nuneaton Poor Law Institution	Ernest

Hewitt Theresa	f	28.7.1905	Coventry	Hannah Elizabeth
Hickman Mary Ann		27.1.1892	St. Michael	Not registered
Higgerson Annie	m	16.10.1928	Lenton Hurst, Stoke Green	Charles Victor
Higgins Thomas and Emma	m	17.4.1886	N. F. A	Thomas Charles
Higginson Alice	m	10.10.1923	43 Station Street West	Stanley Kenneth
Higginson Rose	f	17.10.1918	Hostel 15, Holbrook Lane	Evelyn
Higginson Ellen	f	13.3.1896	Holy Trinity	Ellen
Hill Edith May	f	10.9.1929	11 Gas Street	Elsie May
Hill Emily	m	4.8.1883	St. Michael	William
Hill Evelyn Lucy	m	21.7.1925	Girls Friendly Society Lodge, Foleshill Road	Robert
Hill Florence Dorothy	m	29.12.1924	12 Meadway, Stoke	William Albert
Hill Florence Edith	f	23.8.1926	Hill Farm Cottages, Sowe	Edith Stella
Hill Jane	f	24.5.1926	3 Stoneleigh Terrace	Irene
Hill Jane	F	24.5.1926	3 Stoneleigh Terrace	Patricia
Hill Laura Louisa	m	19.4.1918	325 Stoney Stanton Road	Frederick Clive
Hill Laura Louisa	m	19.4.1918	325 Stoney Stanton Road	William Henry
Hill Marjorie Evelyn	f	9.8.1928	141 North Street	Marjorie Gwendoline
Hill Sarah E		19.6.1916	Stretton under Fosse	Not registered
Hindle Ethel Sarah	f	15.2.1929	251 Swan Lane	Joan Edith
Hinds Kate and Thomas Charles	f	7.8.1891	St. Michael	Kate Elizabeth
Hine Caroline	m	8.10.1895	St. Michael	Frederick
Hipkiss or Reading Rachael	m	21.12.1923	47 Hartlepool Road	Herbert
Hipkiss or Reading Rachael	m	21.12.1923	47 Hartlepool Road	Stanley
Hitchcock Annie	m	19.1.1894	St. Michael	Bernard Millerchip
Hobday Beatrice	m	7.9.1929	6 Cow Lane	Dennis
Hobday Lily	f	14.6.1921	Pinley Green Farm	Lily
Hobday Rosaline		20.1.1925	Spinney Cottage, Coundon	Not registered
Hoderin Sarah Ann	m	11.7.1881	St. Michael	Beridge Fletcher
Hoderin Sarah Ann	m	27.5.1883	St. Michael	William Henry
Hodgkins Sarah Ann	m	10.1.1912	Coventry	Ernest Edward
Hodgkiss Elizabeth	m	2.5.1898	Holy Trinity	Arthur Maleaty

Hodierne Clara	f	19.1.1890	St. Michael	Gertrude
Hodierne Clara		27.1.1888	St. Michael	Not registered
Hodierne Sarah Ann		6.1.1889	St. Michael	Not registered
Hoey Theresa	m	11.12.1903	Coventry	William
Hogan Margaret	f	31.8.1929	68 Spon Street	Margaret
Hoggins Minnie		15.5.1907	Coventry	Not registered
Holland Isabel	m	18.1.1929	62 Days Lane	Roy
Holland Minnie Alice	f	11.10.1928	Nuneaton Poor Law Institution	Edith Ivy
Holland Unity	m	11.4.1918	Y.W.C.A. Hostel, Park Road	Charles Eugene
Hollins Charlotte	m	20.2.1879	Holy Trinity	Not registered
Hollyland Sarah	m	29.8.1885	N. F. A	William Henry
Holman Florence		15.2.1921	64 Holyhead Road	Not registered
Holmes Charlotte	m	9.6.1908	Coventry	Herbert
Holt Elizabeth	m	22.3.1915	38h Wellington Street	John
Holton Margaret	f	16.2.1930	Craigmore", Broad Lane	Margaret
Holyland Sarah	m	24.5.1889	Holy Trinity	George Hughes
Holyland Sarah	f	8.9.1865	N. F. A	Sarah
Hone Mary Ann	m	2.11.1911	Coventry	Richard
Hooson Gladys Lilian	m	1.8.1928	117 Earlsdon Avenue	Bernard
Hope Florence Maud	f	30.6.1929	3 Littlefields	Florence Eva
Hopkins Elsie Emily	f	26.2.1927	46 Gas Street	Elsie
Hopper Bessie	f	9.4.1920	344 Stoney Stanton Road	Hester Elizabeth
Horden Harriet Patience	f	7.11.1908	Coventry	Rose
Horncastle Grace	m	15.4.1928	1 Hertford Square	Eric
Hornsby Suzetta	f	3.6.1928	6 Freehold Street	Catherine
Horsfield Sarah		8.10.1860	N. F. A	Not registered
Horton Alice		24.2.1896	St. Michael	Not registered
Horton Christiana Elizabeth	m	10.6.1912	Coventry	William
Horton Christiana Elizabeth	m	24.7.1910	Coventry	Cecil Albert
Horton Rose Ann	m	12.2.1928	268 Munition Cottages	Donald
Howarth Jane	f	2.11.1893	St. Michael	Jane
Howe Annie	m	14.4.1918	2 Trafalgar Street	William

Howe Harriet		12.11.1910	Coventry	Not registered
Howe Jennie	f	14.3.1930	70 Cox Street	Jennie
Howe Mary	f	27.6.1924	96 Godiva Street	Irene
Howes Elizabeth	f	10.2.1930	52 St. John's Street	Joyce
Howeth Kate		23.3.1917	25 Swan Street	Not registered
Howley Mabel	f	29.12.1924	25 Spon Street	Louie Mary
Hubbard Elizabeth	m	20.5.1891	St. Michael	Thomas Percy
Hubbard Elizabeth	m	9.2.1893	St. Michael	John Parsons
Hughes Kathleen	m	1.6.1921	16 Colony Cottages	William
Hughes Laura		28.4.1900	Coventry	Not registered
Hughes Margaret	m	17.7.1900	Coventry	Arthur
Hughes Mary Elizabeth	f	15.7.1909	Coventry	Florence May
Hughes Olive May	m	18.1.1929	58 Fisher Road	Siriol
Hughes Violet	m	3.8.1928	110 Walsgrave Road	Graham
Humphries Annie		28.8.1900	Coventry	Not registered
Humphries Ida	m	10.6.1927	Pinley Gardens	Frank
Hunt Edith	m	7.9.1904	Coventry	Joseph Herbert
Hunt Elsie	f	16.9.1928	25 Widdrington Road	Irene Edith
Hunt Elsie	m	7.10.1927	3 Wests Buildings, Stoney Stanton Rd	Joseph Edward
Hunt Elsie Doris	f	31.5.1928	51 Freehold Street	Margaret Edith
Hunt Florence	f	22.11.1928	52 Humber Avenue	Daphne Florence
Hunt Sarah	m	14.11.1898	St. Michael	Alfred John
Hunt Sarah Ann	f	19.4.1904	Coventry	Ethel
Hunt Sophia	f	5.4.1919	7 Newdigate Road	Margaret
Hunter Sophia		7.2.1892	St. Michael	Not registered
Hutchinson Gertrude	f	15.5.1915	28 Cox Street	Phyllis
Hutchinson Gertrude Florence	f	26.5.1916	1 Gilbert Yard, Brook Street	Phyllis May
Hyam Lily	m	22.3.1927	138 Widdrington Road	Frederick Norman
Hyde Beatrice	m	26.9.1925	16 Upper Well Street	Eric
Hyde Beatrice Mary	f	2.3.1924	27 The Jetty, Broad Street	Joan
Hyland Maud Kathleen	m	20.10.1928	106 Godiva Street	Leonard Ambrose

MOTHER'S NAME	M/F	D.O.B.	ADDRESS	CHILD'S NAME
Ilsley Ada May	f	5.9.1927	3 Vauxhall Street	Eileen Freda
Ilsley Margaret	m	29.1.1928	5ct 4h Spon Street	John
Inckle Christina		18.6.1917	90 Cross Road, Foleshill	Not registered
Ingram Elizabeth	f	11.12.1904	Coventry	Annie
Ingram Elizabeth		17.4.1889	St. Michael	Not registered
Ingram Elizabeth	m	29.6.1886	N. F. A	Percy
Ingram Emma	f	27.7.1893	St. Michael	Hannah
Ireland Ada	f	15.3.1927	57 Eden Street	Joyce
Irons Dora	f	27.3.1926	Meriden Union	Murial Eileen
Isham Mary Ann	m	20.5.1915	34ct 4h Gosford Street	Arthur
Isham Myra Annie	f	17.6.1918	104 Little Park Street	Mary Joan
Isherwood Nellie		8.8.1924	66 Gorton Road	Not registered
Isley Ivy Selina	m	24.2.1930	20 David Road	George
Ison Louisa	f	11.4.1894	Holy Trinity	Harriet
Ison Louisa	f	31.5.1896	Holy Trinity	Louisa

MOTHER'S NAME	M/F	D.O.B.	ADDRESS	CHILD'S NAME
Jackson Hilda	f	27.2.1929	23 Gilbert Street	Joan
Jackson Lilian	m	18.1.1926	142 Cox Street	Cyril
Jackson Lily May	f	8.8.1922	1ct 9h The Burgess	Elsie May
Jackson M. Ann		27.2.1862	N. F. A	Not registered
Jakeman Annie	f	29.1.1930	63 Paynes Lane	Mary
James Edith	f	5.1.1910	Coventry	Evelyn
James Lilian May	f	29.8.1917	Hostel 6, Holbrook Lane	Glory
James Mabel	m	29.3.1929	St. Faiths Shelter	Gerald
James Mary	f	2. 6.1927	318 Munition Cottages	Edith
James Mary and Albert	f	1.10.1899	Holy Trinity	Druie
Jarvis Elsie May	f	3.3.1929	138 Broomfield Road	Sheila
Jeacock Hilda	m	4.8.1926	72 Canterbury Street	Eric Ernest
Jeffs Maud	m	12.11.1925	24 Peel Street	Jack
Jenkins Lucy Annie	m	15.3.1912	Coventry	Hugh Durrey Henry
Jennings Clara	m	7.2.1912	Coventry	Arthur Leedham
Jewkes Hannah	m	10.6.1928	1 Rydes Row, Arley, nr Coventry	Cyril William
Joad Sarah Ann	f	4.6.1928	17 Field Row, Stoke Heath	Agnes
Johnson		12.9.1860	N. F. A	Not registered
Johnson (Wheatley) Louisa & Henry	m	7.5.1912	Coventry	John Henry
Johnson Lilian E and John	f	27.11.1909	Coventry	Hilda Mary
Johnson Lizzie	f	15.3.1880	St. Michael	Ada
Johnson Lizzie		3.3.1888	St. Michael	Not registered
Johnson Rachael	m	22.1.1927	38 Lower Wellington Street	Norman
Johnson Winifred	m	28.8.1925	St. Faiths Shelter, Holyhead Road	George Henry
Jolliday Madge	m	5.2.1927	Kings Head Hotel	Albert Edward
Jones Alice		31.1.1930	18ct 2h Spon Street	Not registered
Jones Ann	m	3.8.1892	St. Michael	William Henry
Jones Annie	m	10.12.1913	Coventry	Arthur
Jones Blanche	f	4.12.1929	2 Barras Lane	Alexandra
Jones Caroline		9.4.1919	52 George Street	Not registered
Jones Clara	m	31.1.1882	St. Michael	Frank

Jones Daisy	f	6.8.1928	20ct 13h St. John's Street	Gladys May
Jones Elizabeth	f	24.10.1893	St. Michael	Annie Elizabeth
Jones Ethel Maud	m	5.6.1929	138 Nicholls Street	Trevor
Jones Florence Dorothy	f	24.3.1926	344 Stoney Stanton Road	Florence May
Jones Hannah	m	30.11.1875	Holy Trinity	James
Jones Harriett	f	19.7.1925	37 Starley Road	Doreen
Jones Jane	f	21.2.1886	N. F. A	Alice Jane
Jones Mildred	f	9.2.1930	155 Whoberley Avenue	Olive
Jones Sarah	m	16.4.1880	St. Michael	John
Jones Sarah	m	3.3.1897	St. Michael	Walter Burdock
Jordan Elizabeth	m	16.9.1916	Guild Road	Arthur
Judd Ada Maud	m	13.11.1909	Coventry	Richard William
Judd Annie	m	31.3.1898	St. Michael	Will
Judd Emily	f	14.6.1884	St. Michael	Florence May
Judkins Julia	m	31.1.1916	11, London Road	Arthur
Julian Elizabeth Alice	f	28.3.1928	Meriden Union	Gwendoline May

MOTHER'S NAME	M/F	D.O.B.	ADDRESS	CHILD'S NAME
Kavanagh Lizzie	m	3.3.1903	Coventry	Ernest Francis
Keatley Edith Bessie	m	8.8.1920	26 St. Patricks Road	Francis William
Keeley Mary Catherine	m	13.7.1927	33 Bridge Street, Coton, Nuneaton	Frederick
Keene Florence	f	22.6.1918	20 Munition Cottages, Holbrooks Lane	Margaret Ethel
Keight Sarah Jane and Walter	m	23.12.1911	Coventry	John Henry
Keight Sarah Jane and Walter	m	23.12.1911	Coventry	Walter
Kelley Francis	f	12.10.1901	Coventry	Florence
Kelly Jane	m	14.8.1860	N. F. A	William
Kelsey Harriet		11.2.1860	N. F. A	Not registered
Kemp Amy Elizabeth	f	22.6.1928	St. Faiths Shelter	Gladys Mary
Kennings Elizabeth	m	8.8.1911	Coventry	William
Kerrane Euphemia Queenie Maud	m	12.7.1928	Kenwood House", Beacon Road	Peter
Key Emma	m	14.4.1903	Coventry	Thomas Henry
Key Emma	m	18.12.1906	Coventry	Albert
Keyte Edith		28.8.1921	Beech House", Allesley	Not registered
Kimberley Esther	f	07.04.1878	Holy Trinity	Alice
Kimberley Esther		26.10.1880	Holy Trinity	Not registered
King Doris May	f	26.8.1929	Meriden Union	Margaret
King Florence	m	14.4.1921	238 Foleshill Road	Joseph William Arthur
King Florence	m	26.3.1923	328 Foleshill Road	William Henry
King Florence M	f	26.6.1915	4 Cow Lane	Florence May
King Nellie H	F	18.5.1919	85 Stoney Stanton Road	Marjorie May
Kiteley Louisa and William Henry	m	19.9.1903	Coventry	Albert
Klinche Edith Harriett		27.9.1897	St. Michael	Not registered
Kyte Harriett	f	09.08.1875	Holy Trinity	Unknown

MOTHER'S NAME	M/F	D.O.B.	ADDRESS	CHILD'S NAME
Labosta Antonia		11.11.1918	6ct 9h Well Street	Not Registered
Lafferty Mary	m	5.4.1918	104 Little Park Street	Vincent
Lakin Florence	m	11.2.1893	St. Michael	Frederick
Lane Florence E	f	18.11.1883	St. Michael	Florence Elizabeth
Lane Sarah Ann	f	6.2.1886	Holy Trinity	Elizabeth
Langley Beatrice	f	29.6.1933	73 Moat Avenue. G.R.M.H	Margaret
Langley Dorothy	m	2.1.1928	31 Thornhill Road	Charles
Larne Emma	f	26.6.1881	St. Michael	Jessie
Law Gladys	f	30.8.1929	36 Wright Street	Jean
Lawley Florence Rose		11.5.1921	N. F. A	Not registered
Lawrence Mary	f	12.10.1855	N. F. A	Sarah
Lax Sarah		28.1.1861	N. F. A	Not registered
Leach Bertha	f	13.5.1920	Angel Hotel	Mary Doreen
Leadbetter Eileen Ann	m	3.9.1928	12 Common Way	James
Leadbetter Eileen Ann	m	8.3.1930	7 Common Way, Stoke	Thomas
Lee Alice	f	22.9.1921	168 George Street	Joan
Lee Dora	m	11.9.1927	Parkside	Raymond Philip
Lee Gladys	m	24.7.1927	16 Adelaide Street	Stanley
Lee Hilda	m	18.10.1929	4 Vincent Street	Alfred
Lee Sarah		15.9.1866	N. F. A	Not registered
Leech May Ann	f	9.3.1888	Casual pauper	Minnie
Leeson Rebecca	m	9.7.1855	N. F. A	William
Lennox Agnes	m	19.12.1920	51 West Orchard	John
Lester Florence	m	3.8.1918	104 Little Park Street	Roland William
Lewin Lilian	m	2.10.1915	27 Castle Street	George
Lewin Lilian Eliza	m	4.5.1919	37 Castle Street	Harry
Lewis Emily A and Samuel	m	18.10.1904	Coventry	George
Lewis Jessie Ethel		7.7.1927	39 Lower Ford Street	Not registered
Lidgett Florence M	f	24.5.1928	29 Redcar Road	Ida Mary
Lidgett Lilian	m	16.11.1916	9 York Terrace	Herbert
Lidgett Rachel	m	2.1.1914	Coventry	Harry
Lilley Elizabeth	f	13.5.929	50ct 1h Spon Street	Veronica Ellen

Limm Margaret Louisa	m	10.6.1918	109 Much Park Street	William George
Lindsay Florence	f	24.9.1928	11 London Road	Edith May
Line Frances Sarah Jane	m	25.11.1924	28 Bishop Street	Arthur
Lines Martha	m	7.9.1916	b/o 142 Cox Street	John
Lines Rose Evelyn	f	4.7.1927	4 Lamb Street	Rose Evelyn
Lingard Jessie	m	28.4.1929	32 King Richard Street	Ronald William
Lissaman Ann	m	1.7.1855	N. F. A	Thomas
Livermore Gladys	m	29.8.1927	44 Gas Street	John
Livermore Hilda	m	17.6.1927	127 Corporation Cottages	John
Livesey Lily		16.11.1928	137 Colony Cottages	Not registered
Livesley Lily Florence	f	12.2.1924	137 Colony Cottages	Hilda
Lloyd Ada	m	2.5.1907	Coventry	Edward
Lloyd Ada	f	27.8.1904	Coventry	Heather
Loakes Ada	f	17.11.1918	52 St. John's Street	Amy Loudon
Loasby Florence	f	10.7.1929	101 Brook Street	Kathleen Evelyn
Locke Elsie Maud	f	19.4.1925	New Street, Castle Bromwich	Eva Primrose
Logan Eva	m	3.10.1929	Caister Bungalow, Pinley Gardens	John Edward
Lord Florence	m	1.5.1917	3ct 7h Greyfriars Lane	William Henry
Lord Lily	m	30.9.1928	6h 2ct Chauntry	Leslie
Lord Murial	m	27.9.1925	86 London Road	William Charles
Lord Winifred	f	17.5.1929	36 Cromwell Street	Pauline Winifred
Louse Sarah	f	5.5.1928	23h 1ct Leicester Street	Kathleen May
Love Hilda	f	27.12.1929	5 Priory Street	Joyce
Love Margaret	m	12.1.1922	38 Freehold Street	Peter William
Lovell Harriett	m	18.10.1915	140 Stoney Stanton Road	Cyril Edwin
Lovell Kate	f	13.5.1918	11 Hill Cross	Edna Violet
Lovett Lily		24.7.1922	17 Upper Well Street	Not registered
Lovett Sarah Jane	f	20.6.1928	11 London Road	Constance Sylvia
Lowe Ellen Gertrude	f	28.12.1928	52 Stoney Stanton Road	Thelma
Lowkes Ann		09.08.1878	N. F. A	Not registered
Lucas Annie	m	12.12.1925	10h 38ct Gosford Street	Dennis Thomas
Ludford Mary Ann	f	6.9.1905	Coventry	Lily

Lynch Jane	f	22.1.1901	Coventry	Mary Jane
Lynes Ada	f	23.4.1895	Holy Trinity	Rose
Lynes Ellen	f	11.1.1926	Minworth, near Bullring, Birmingham	Margaret
Lynes Sarah	f	18.12.1887	Holy Trinity	Emma Elizabeth Higgitt

MOTHER'S NAME	M/F	D.O.B.	ADDRESS	CHILD'S NAME
Mace Maud Florence	m	28.10.1926	27 Lower Nelson Street	Dennis
Macey Bessie	f	5.11.1928	5 Paradise Street	Georgina
Malloy Annie	m	7.11.1918	16 Stanley Road	Frank
Mann Elizabeth Alma	m	28.4.1929	Meriden Union	Jack
Mann Frances	f	25.2.1930	bk 494 Stoney Stanton Road	Sheila
Mansell Lilian	m	23.12.1918	Deasy, House Hostels	Desmond Hugh
Mapley Elizabeth	f	3.5.1881	St. Michael	Elizabeth
March Gladys Elizabeth	m	25.7.1921	110 Avon Street	Philip Stanley
Marklow Ruth	m	1.12.1918	104 Little Park Street	Reginald
Marks Minnie	m	15.8.1919	44 Harnall Lane East	Frank Pearson
Marlow Martha	m	18.10.1929	8 St. Thomas Road	John
Marsh Gertrude	f	12.11.1928	22 New Street	Lester Hazel
Marshall Alice	m	13.11.1918	12 St. John's Street	Eric Humphrey
Marson Hannah	f	21.11.1929	1ct 1h Henry Street	Gwendoline
Marston Helen Maud	f	15.2.1918	106 Gosford Street	Cora
Mason Hannah	m	4.2.1918	Hostel 6, Holbrook Lane	William
Maspers Sarah Lizzie	f	29.2.1928	76 Leicester Causeway	Mary
Masser Mary Ann	f	15.6.1925	48 Haunchurch Road, Stockingford	Doreen Barbara
Mather Lilian	f	20.9.1929	2ct 9h Whitefriars Street	Hazel Lilian
Mathews Alice	m	5.10.1922	18 Union Street	Norman
Mathews Eliza and John	m	23.11.1893	St. Michael	Sidney William
Mathews Eliza and John	m	26.3.1887	N. F. A	Samuel
Mathews Eliza and John	m	27.12.1888	St. Michael	John
Matthews Agnes	m	23.9.1916	30 Humber Road	Herbert
Matthews Doris	m	12.11.1928	10ct 13h Far Gosford Street	Eric
Matthews Doris	f	5.11.1927	10ct 13h Far Gosford Street	Hilda Nellie
Matthews Elizabeth		3.5.1915	9 Primrose hill Street	Not registered
Mavis Elizabeth and John	f	30.3.1890	Casual pauper	Kate

Maxwell Mary T	f	11.7.1922	7 Narrow Lane	Kathleen Teressa
Maycock Florence Grace	m	31.3.1930	15 Cope Street	James
Maycock Violet	m	16.5.1918	2ct 1h Fleet Street	John Henry
McCall Annie	m	14.9.1924	22 Henrietta Street	Donald
McCall Lily	m	21.4.1898	St. Michael	Horace
McCarthy Florence		13.10.1911	Coventry	Not registered
McCarthy Florence	m	26.1.1906	Coventry	Frederick
McDermott Florence	m	20.11.1922	12 Trafalgar Street	Patrick Thomas
McGorry Fanny and Patrick	f	24.1.1899	St. Michael	Henrietta
McLeaman Rose Kathleen		30.1.1922	156 Terry Road	Not registered
McTighe Alice Maud	f	12.11.1923	42 Coundon Road	Mollie
McTighe Marjorie	f	11.6.1928	28 Union Street	Mary Sheila
McVeigh Janet	m	7.7.1918	Hostel 17, Holbrook Lane	Stanley
Meakin Emma	f	24.12.1899	St. Michael	Emma
Meaney Edith May	f	26.10.1927	4 Barrack Place, Smithford Street	Dorothy
Maspero Sarah Lizzie	f	26.10.1925	76 Leicester Causeway	Elsie Kyrie
Mee Christina	m	26.11.1929	St. Martins, Beacon Road	Alexander
Merricks Maud	f	30.12.1927	1 Tower Street	Florence
Middleton Phyllis	f	10.6.1926	Nuneaton Union	Edith
Milburn Hilda	f	23.2.1929	39 Queens Road	Hilda
Miles Ellen	f	7.11.1918	8 White Friars Street	Alice
Miles Florence	m	24.4.1927	4h 3ct Gosford Street	Herbert Watkins
Miles Hannah	m	02.08.1877	St. Michael	Not registered
Miles Jane	f	16.10.1900	Coventry	Alice
Miles Jessie	f	9.7.1929	33 Bedford Street	June
Miller Alice Mary	m	13.8.1928	93 Raglan Street	Walter
Miller Emily	m	14.6.1895	Holy Trinity	John Robert
Mills Jane	f	18.10.1876	St. Michael	Not registered
Mills Julia	f	20.04.1877	Holy Trinity	Not registered
Milward Sarah Elizabeth	m	6.7.1918	18 Paynes Lane	Thomas
Moakes Violet May	m	16.12.1929	47 New Street	George

Moakes Violet May	f	18.12.1927	11 Raglan Street	Violet
Mobley Susan Agnes	f	12.9.1905	Coventry	Winifred Margaret
Molesworth Harriett Lavinia	f	18.2.1926	169 Corporation Cottages	Edith
Molesworth Harriett Lavinia	f	18.2.1926	169 Corporation Cottages	Vera
Monington Rebecca	m	28.1.1889	St. Michael	William
Moody Doris Milbourn	f	27.3.1929	117 Highland Road	Mary
Moore Caroline	m	15.11.1875	St. Michael	William Thomas
Moore Clara	m	21.10.1918	1 College Lane, Stratford on Avon	Francis
Moore Emma Elizabeth	m	24.12.1892	Holy Trinity	William
Moore Gertrude M	F	22.5.1927	69 Freehold Street	Ida May
Moran Annie Maria	f	29.12.1913	Coventry	Eliza
Moran Elizabeth	f	14.03.1876	Holy Trinity	Not registered
Morgan Adelaide Edith Ellen Terry	m	17.12.1928	25 Chauntry Place	Terence
Morgan Louisa	f	1.2.1928	48 Monks Road	Beryl
Morgan Sarah	f	10.03.1877	Holy Trinity	Not registered
Morley Alice E	F	28.6.1929	55 Richmond Street	Hazel
Morley Nellie	f	9.9.1926	Nuneaton Union	Nellie
Morris Ada		11.3.1908	Coventry	Not registered
Morris Ethel Mary	f	30.7.1909	Coventry	Irene
Morris Mabel A		28.7.1916	40 St. Michael's Road	Not registered
Morris Mabel A	f	28.7.1916	40 St. Michael's Road	Barbara Irene
Morris Sarah Elizabeth	f	8.9.1918	B Block, Whitmore Park	Sarah Elizabeth
Mortimer Alice Elizabeth	m	24.12.1927	33 Cox Street	Christopher George
Morton Henrietta	m	31.12.1892	St. Michael	Spencer
Mott Harriett	m	1.6.1925	68 Corporation Street, Nuneaton	Kenneth
Mott Minnie	m	27.5.1921	b/o 99 Queen Victoria Road	John Robert
Mott Minnie	m	7.4.1926	4ct 12h Much Park Street	Robert George
Mowe Harriett	m	2.5.1859	N. F. A	Henry
Muddiman Hannah	m	28.12.1853	N. F. A	William

Mulliner Ellen Elizabeth	f	28.3.1920	24 St. Margaret's Road	Doris Nellie
Mullins Mary	m	19.12.1914	31 Whitefriars Lane	Thomas
Mullis Florence	m	12.11.1896	Holy Trinity	Alfred James
Murphy Margaret		21.11.1861	N. F. A	Not registered
Murphy Mary	m	28.9.1917	Hostel 20, Colony 1, Holbrooks Lane	David
Murray Bridget	m	17.2.1930	20 Beech Tree Avenue, Lime Tree Park	John Patrick

MOTHER'S NAME	M/F	D.O.B.	ADDRESS	CHILD'S NAME
Naylor Lucy Mary	f	20.11.1917	Hostel 4, Holbrook Lane	Winifred May
Neal Eliza Ann	m	18.10.1929	2ct 1h Albion Street	Richard
Neal Mildred	f	6.6.1907	Coventry	Phyllis Florence Mildred
Neale Florence	f	21.6.1927	St. Faiths Shelter, Holyhead Road	Dorothy
Neale Minnie	m	25.4.1928	20 Craven Street	Derick Arthur
Neilson Florence	f	16.7.1919	44 Harnall Lane East	Margaret
Nelms Ann	f	1.5.1855	N. F. A	Mary Ann
Newcourt Hannah		31.1.1867	N. F. A	Not registered
Newey Florence	f	4.7.1895	St. Michael	Esther
Newman Annie	m	6.10.1916	15 Barras Lane	Frederick
Newman Elizabeth	m	12.8.1880	St. Michael	Charles
Newman Maud		31.1.1929	95 Munition Cottages	Not registered
Newton Josephine E. J	m	1.10.1925	335 Longford Road, Longford	Richard
Nicholls Elsie	m	5.3.1929	4ct 2h Cox Street	Raymond Maurice
Nicholls Mary	f	18.6.1911	Coventry	Mary
Nicholls Mary	f	22.6.1904	Coventry	Violet
Nichols Emily Jane	m	4.7.1921	11 Blythe Road	William Amos
Nixon Ivy Alice	m	24.11.1929	44 Swanswell Street	Bernie
Nixon Ivy Alice	f	8.4.1927	44 Swanswell Street	Eileen Mary
Noakes Gladys		14.8.1916	139 Narrow Lane	Not registered
Nolan Emily	f	22.5.1928	56 Whitefriars Lane	Edith May
North Eliza		28.11.1889	Holy Trinity	Not registered
North Eliza		3.12.1891	Holy Trinity	Not registered
North Eliza	f	5.5.1886	N. F. A	Eleanor
Norton Gladys	m	16.1.1929	Nanty Glyn", South Avenue, Stoke Park	Sydney Samuel

MOTHER'S NAME	M/F	D.O.B.	ADDRESS	CHILD'S NAME
O Donnell Winifred	f	12.4.1882	St. Michael	Not registered
O Donnell Winifred	m	3.2.1886	N. F. A	Charles
Oakley Annie Elizabeth	m	4.12.1910	Coventry	Harold Sidney
Oakley Eliza May	m	26.12.1929	Inglenook", Brandon Road	Lawrence
Oakley Elizabeth May	m	28.11.1927	429 Foleshill Road	Alford Raymond
O'Brien Margaret	m	30.5.1920	5 Passes Row, Station Street West	Michael Thomas
O'Brien Sarah Agnes	m	24.9.1928	2 Little Fields, Stoke Heath	Patrick
O'Conner Evelyn May	m	11.3.1930	8ct 3h Bond Street	Thomas
O'Hare Miriam	f	30.5.1928	71 Leicester Place	Sheila Margaret
O'Reilly Kathleen	m	3.2.1930	St. Faiths Home, Coventry	Eric
Orr Jane		14.1.1908	Coventry	Not registered
Orton Alice May	f	13.11.1921	31 Cobden Street	Irene May
Orton Jane	f	13.10.1865	N. F. A	Mary
O'Shea Florence	f	24.8.1917	51 Little Park Street	Mary Josephine
Overton Mildred	m	19.10.1918	68 Munition Cottages	Percy John
Overton Susan	f	10.3.1898	Holy Trinity	Edith
Owen Daisy Maud	m	5.4.1929	113 Chantries, Harnall Lane East	James
Owen Evelyn Georgina	m	7.6.1927	41 Springfield Road	Richard George
Owen Evelyn May	m	27.8.1926	70 1/2 Gilbert Street	Lionel

MOTHER'S NAME	M/F	D.O.B.	ADDRESS	CHILD'S NAME
Packer Selina		16.5.1862	N. F. A	Not registered
Pallett Kate Elizabeth	f	9.12.1910	Coventry	Gladys Maud
Palmer Ada	m	16.6.1926	Leicester Place, Leicester Street	Bernard
Palmer Elizabeth Annie	f	13.4.1929	Lindley House", Newby Road, Wyken	Ellen
Palmer Mary Ann	f	8.3.1929	25 Swan Street	Nellie Agnes
Parker Alice	f	23.5.1919	4 Boston Place, Lockhurst Lane	Gladys
Parker Annie	m	10.6.1897	Holy Trinity	Charles
Parker Annie	m	10.6.1897	Holy Trinity	Edward
Parker Edith Ellen	f	9.9.1915	Sylverdale", Eaton Road	Edith
Parker Hannah		7.2.1863	N. F. A	Not registered
Parker Vivian		1.9.1862	N. F. A	Not registered
Parkes Lily	m	23.2.1920	18 Binley Road	Terence
Parkinson Ada	m	16.4.1929	19 Cope Street	Ivor
Parnell Lilian	m	1.11.1927	57 Coventry Street	Douglas
Parnell Florence and Walter	f	. 1.1.1911	Coventry	Phyllis Nora
Parnell Florence and Walter	f	2.4.1906	Coventry	Ivy
Parrott Beatrice	m	28.1.1929	19 Cope Street	Peter
Parrott Violet May	m	23.1.1929	2 Queen Victoria Road	William
Parry Rose Edith	m	10.12.1899	St. Michael	George Clifford
Parsons Sarah Agnes	f	17.7.1924	34 Much Park Street	Joan
Partridge Annie		26.10.1918	12 Hawkins Road	Not registered
Patrick Clara	f	21.4.1915	9 Britannia Street	May
Pattison Rebecca	f	28.12.1898	St. Michael	Norah
Pavey Edith Ellen	f	19.4.1919	104 Little Park Street	Eileen
Paxton Sarah Ann	f	23.12.1919	320 Stoney Stanton Road	Iris
Payne Catherine H	f	1.5.1911	Coventry	Elsie May
Payne Florence May	m	14.1.1929	71 Humber Avenue	John
Payne Florence May	f	21.8.1927	71 Humber Avenue	Hazel
Payne Freda	m	11.8.1923	11 London Road	Kenneth Stanley
Payne Primrose E	m	26.2.1918	2 Barr's Hill Terrace	George Frederick
Payne Sarah	f	23.12.1883	St. Michael	Ellen

Peabody Constance	f	29.10.1929	2ct 4h East Street	Mary
Peach Kate	f	20.1.1912	Coventry	Florence
Peach Kate	f	29.12.1907	Coventry	Ada
Peach Kate	m	8.4.1906	Coventry	Richard
Peak Irene	f	29.11.1929	46 Barker Butts Lane	Dorothy June
Pearman Frances Bertha	m	21.9.1927	38 Highfield Street	David Richard
Pearson Rose	m	11.7.1900	Coventry	Thomas
Pearson Rose	f	23.12.1897	St. Michael	Elizabeth
Pegg Frances Laura	f	23.9.1928	27 Cromwell Street	Doreen
Pegg Mabel Doris	f	6.12.1928	27 Cromwell Street	Doris
Penn Florence	m	14.12.1915	N. F. A	James
Pepper Phoebe Hannah	f	30.8.1886	N. F. A	Phoebe Hannah
Perkins Gladys	f	5.10.1928	25 Humber Road	Lydia
Perrin Lucy Elizabeth	m	8.9.1908	Coventry	John
Perry Nancy May	f	28.3.1929	30 Fowler Road	Murial May
Pettitt Harriet	m	13.9.1855	N. F. A	Charles
Phelps Dorcas	m	31.8.1927	Green Wagon", Pinley Gardens	Cyril
Phillips Annie	f	6.11.1921	62 Mulliner Street	Evelyn Annie
Phillips Mary Ann	f	28.1.1899	Holy Trinity	Elsie
Phipps Alice		1.3.1913	Coventry	Not registered
Phipps Ellen Louisa	m	29.12.1910	Coventry	George
Pickard Sarah Ann	m	9.5.1887	Holy Trinity	Henry
Pickering Annie		4.7.1917	Hostel 31, Holbrooks Lane	Not registered
Pickering Florence Elizabeth	f	16.4.1908	Coventry	Violet Rosina
Pickering Rosaline May		17.6.1929	Maria House, Parkgate Road, Foleshill	Not registered
Pickford Florence	m	23.12.1929	28 Hill Street	Arthur
Piggott Sophia	f	20.11.1886	N. F. A	Not registered
Pitt Maty Elizabeth	f	29.4.1929	45 Queensland Avenue	Barbara
Pittaway Elsie Alice Mary		25.5.1921	58 New Street	Not registered
Plume Nora	m	25.3.1927	40 Smith Street	Ronald Alfred
Poland Amelia and James	f	12.11.1896	Casual pauper	Elizabeth
Pontin Nellie Ellen	f	1.10.1912	Coventry	Charlotte

Poole Charlotte	f	16.7.1921	1 Warwick Avenue	Kathleen Mary
Poole Gladys	f	21.9.1929	135 Narrow Lane	Doreen Elizabeth
Poole Jane	m	15.3.1855	N. F. A	William
Poole Selina	f	16.11.1929	3 Short Street	Joyce
Poole Selina		7.3.1921	3 Short Street	Not registered
Popplewell Gertrude	m	29.4.1928	3ct 1h St. Agnes Lane	Edward
Porter Eleanor	m	26.7.1918	117 Richmond Street	Raymond William
Portlock Florence Lilian	m	27.12.1927	144 Foleshill Road	John
Portlock Florence Rosina	f	4.12.1921	85 Stoney Stanton Road	Irene
Portlock Florence Rosina	m	4.12.1924	299 Munition Cottages	Dennis
Portman Ethel May	m	22.11.1929	5 Priory Street	William
Poultney Rose Ann & William Henry	m	25.11.1887	St. Michael	Christopher
Poulton Ivy Margaret	m	9.4.1926	Foleshill Union	Arthur Reginald
Powell Agnes Amelia	f	11.5.1920	65 Much Park Street	Gladys May
Powell Emma	f	8.12.1927	144 St. Georges Road	Mavis
Powell Gertrude	f	29.7.1929	20 Spring Street	Dorothy Edith
Powell Theresa	f	21.3.1890	St. Michael	Ellen
Power Annie	f	10.12.1926	5 Mill Terrace, Godiva Street	Joan Hannah
Power Annie	f	31.12.1925	4 Vernon Street	Annie
Poweth Agnes Amelia		19.10.1917	65 Much Park Street	Not registered
Powis Edna May	m	24.11.1929	Rosewood", Pinley Gardens	Albert Charles
Powner Ethel May	m	30.1.1930	14 Skinners Yard, Bell Green	Peter
Pratt Elizabeth	m	24.5.1929	159 North Street	James
Pratt Elizabeth Jane	m	8.11.1927	24 Winchester Street	Eric
Pratt Emily	m	17.6.1896	Holy Trinity	Arthur
Pready Polly	f	20.3.1889	Holy Trinity	Polly
Prestidge Ida Gladys	f	23.6.1925	Carol Green, Berkswell	Pamela Dorothy
Preston Alice M	m	26.11.1919	21ct 13h St. Johns Street	Bernard
Preston Florence Annie	f	10.2.1930	21h 13ct St. John's Street	Brenda

	M/F	D.O.B.	ADDRESS	
Price Bertha Patience	m	1.7.1926	Coventry and Warwick Hospital	Leslie Frank
Price Elizabeth	m	18.11.1921	3 Chapel Street	John Henry
Price Elizabeth	f	29.10.1904	Coventry	Winifred
Price Elizabeth		29.10.1904	Coventry	Not registered
Price Lizzie	m	26.7.1891	Holy Trinity	John
Price Minnie	m	18.1.1914	Coventry	James
Pritchard Ann	f	16.9.1860	N. F. A	Ann
Probert Florence	m	7.6.1929	Nuneaton Union	Derrick
Probin Amy	f	27.3.1904	Coventry	Minnie
Probin Beatrice	m	12.3.1929	12 Silver Street	Derrick
Proctor Theresa	m	29.8.1926	104 Caludon Road	Sydney
Purnell Violet	m	13.1.1930	62 Avon Street	Raymond
Purver Ann and Thomas	f	8.6.1892	St. Michael	Harriet
Putman Gladys Evelyn	m	23.1.1929	5ct 6h Smithford Street	Gordon Newton

MOTHER'S NAME	M/F	D.O.B.	ADDRESS	CHILD'S NAME
Quinn Phoebe Eliza	m	15.9.1929	17 Marlborough Road	Roy
Quinney Ethel	m	5.7.1916	30 Bright Street	John Edgar

MOTHER'S NAME	M/F	D.O.B.	ADDRESS	CHILD'S NAME
Raby Eliza Jane	f	12.6.1880	Holy Trinity	Annie
Raby Mary A	m	21.9.1881	St. Michael	William
Raby Sarah Ann	m	18.8.1882	St. Michael	Charles
Rafferty Gladys Clara Bell	f	10.4.1928	35 Cobden Street	Gladys Margaret
Rainbow Edith Hilda	f	20.9.1927	2 Gulson Square	Edith
Rainbow Mary Ann	f	21.04.1878	St. Michael	Alice Mary
Ramsdale Esther	f	21.04.1878	Holy Trinity	Annie Maria
Randle Edith	f	29.7.1927	Nuneaton Poor Law Institution	Edith Joyce
Randle Ellen	f	8.6.1922	3 Albion Street	Mary
Randle Martha	m	5.6.1883	St. Michael	Walter
Randle Ruth	m	6.6.1928	Nuneaton Poor Law Institution	Frederick
Randle Violet Irene	m	25.12.1920	N. F. A	Noel
Rattigan Ethel	f	4.11.1929	78 Richmond Street	Rita Grace
Raven Florence	f	1.11.1920	2 Whitehorse Yard, Days Lane	Winifred Maud
Rawlin Amelia Elizabeth	m	6.12.1916	49 Henrietta Street	Arthur
Rawling Ethel	m	22.2.1916	26 Spon Street	Frank
Rawlinson Edith May	m	15.2.1928	114 Sovereign Road	Kenneth Ivor
Rea Fanny Gertrude		22.5.1913	Coventry	Not registered
Read Ada	f	23.3.1901	Coventry	Doris
Reader Eliza	m	23.8.1889	St. Michael	Henry
Reader Mary Louisa	m	7.8.1908	Coventry	Frederick
Reading Daisy	f	10.4.1929	Meriden Institute	Beryl
Reading or Hipkiss Rachael	m	21.12.1923	47 Hartlepool Road	Herbert
Reading or Hipkiss Rachael	m	21.12.1923	47 Hartlepool Road	Stanley
Reaves Elizabeth A	m	14.6.1884	St. Michael	Not registered
Reaves Elizabeth A	m	14.6.1884	St. Michael	Not registered
Reddan Sarah	f	8.5.1929	13 Ford Street	Margaret
Reddington Florence Edith	f	10.3.1929	44 Glendower Avenue	Jean Margaret
Redfern Kate	f	2.5.1926	9h 3ct Well Street	Kathleen

Redgrave Caroline	f	07.03.1876	St. Michael	Ada
Reechia Antonia	f	24.7.1922	7ct 9h Well Street	Mary
Reeves Alice	f	21.8.1929	90 Station Street East	Pearl
Reeves Dora May	f	14.10.1917	26 Charterhouse Road	Dorothy
Reeves Elizabeth	f	22.12.1916	128 Harnall Lane East	Violet
Reid Phyllis May	f	19.2.1930	Nuneaton Union	Kathleen May
Renton Sophia	m	14.2.1922	5 Conduit Yard	Louis Eric Valentine
Revel Mary Elizabeth	m	10.11.1905	Coventry	Charles Nicholas
Rhodes Annie	m	14.1.1885	St. Michael	William John
Richardson Ann	m	8.3.1854	N. F. A	Henry
Richardson Annie Elizabeth	m	9.11.1921	3 Field Row, Brays Lane	William Jefferies
Richardson Daisy	f	19.1.1929	28 Leicester Street	Joyce Rosina
Richardson Elizabeth and Albert		29.5.1906	Coventry	Not Registered
Richardson Lucy May	m	17.2.1929	194 Eagle Street	Harold
Richardson Minnie	m	27.3.1928	299 Munition Cottages	Lionel
Rigby Emily	f	27.5.1920	54 Leicester Street	Margaret Emily
Riley Catherine and Tom	f	30.4.1915	28ct 1h Gosford Street	Doris
Riordan Florence	m	20.6.1929	28 Hurst Road	Peter
Roach Dorothy		2.12.1912	Coventry	Not registered
Roadnight Sarah Jane	m	19.10.1905	Coventry	Arthur Thomas
Robbins Ethel	f	26.3.1922	26 Smith Street	Ada
Robbins Hetty	f	12.7.1929	26ct 3h Gosford Street	Olive
Robbins Winifred Elizabeth	m	12.11.1929	Nuneaton Union	Clifford
Roberts Jennie Ann	f	13.7.1927	Meriden Union	Margaret
Roberts Sarah and William	m	19.11.1892	St. Michael	Bertie
Robinson Alice Beatrice		26.9.1926	4h 6ct Castle Street	Not registered
Robinson Clara	m	22.11.1891	N. F. A	Ernest Edward
Robinson Edith		24.12.1890	St. Michael	Not registered
Robinson Edith		9.5.1888	Holy Trinity	Not registered
Robinson Edith Evelyn	m	31.5.1929	48 Maycock Road	Lewis

Robinson Elizabeth	m	6.4.10905	Coventry	Arthur
Robinson Emily	m	26.10.1876	St. Michael	Not registered
Robinson Gertrude Ann		25.9.1929	49 Trentham Road	Not registered
Rodgers Harriett	m	31.12.1926	St. Faiths Shelter	Norman
Roe Elizabeth Harriett	f	13.12.1927	Ryton Lodge Farm, Ryton	Beatrice May
Roebuck Marjorie	m	15.10.1927	St. Faiths Shelter	Arthur Leslie
Rogers Maria	m	20.11.1919	63 Berkley Road	Dennis
Rogers Nellie	m	22.7.1927	44 Grove Street	Maurice
Rollason Jennie Beatrice	f	19.3.1917	12 Nelson Street	Jennie
Rollason Nora	f	29.8.1927	3ct 4h East Street	Norah
Rollins Daisy	f	20.11.1918	b/o 23 Weston Street	Gwendoline
Rollins Emma	f	24.4.1909	Coventry	Gertrude
Rollins Ethel Louisa	f	17.5.1925	Tile Cross, Marston Green	Vera Mary
Ross Dorothy	m	13.4.1921	47 Mayfield Road, Earlsdon	Clifford
Rossiter Violet Clara	f	30.7.1928	49 King William Street	Joan
Rostram Florence	m	31.3.1930	39 Westminster Road	Reginald
Roughton Florence Gertrude	f	12.9.1929	1 Ena Road	Elizabeth Ellen
Rouse Annie	m	16.2.1899	Holy Trinity	Walter James
Rowley Amelia		1.10.1918	37 Allesley Old Road	Not registered
Rowley Charlotte	f	30.8.1881	St. Michael	Amy
Rowley Lilian		13.7.1927	8 Kent's Buildings, Days Lane	Not Registered
Rowley Rose		31.5.1862	N. F. A	Not registered
Rowthorn M. A		16.3.1868	N. F. A	Not registered
Rumball Sarah Elizabeth	f	17.3.1914	Coventry	Alice
Russell Annie	f	26.2.1906	Coventry	Ellen Beatrice
Russell Daisy	m	30.11.1928	165 Whoberley Avenue	Robert Peter
Ryan Mary	f	20.11.1884	St. Michael	Mary
Ryan Mary Cecilia	m	30.5.1917	Ashlea" Binley Road	Christopher Ronald
Ryde Louisa Gladys	f	22.11.1926	102 Mulliner Street	Doreen
Ryley Sarah		22.11.1866	N. F. A	Not Registered

MOTHER'S NAME	M/F	D.O.B.	ADDRESS	CHILD'S NAME
Sabiston Emeline		19.7.1918	7 Common Way, Stoke Heath	Not registered
Sadler Elizabeth	f	3.1.1868	N. F. A	Eliza
Sammons Rose Heritage	f	8.12.1927	25 Waverley Buildings, Days Lane	Mary
Samson Annie	m	23.3.1928	St. Faiths Shelter	Angus
Sanders Annie Elizbeth	m	1.1.1928	65 Vernon Street	Dennis
Sanders Emma Amelia		25.11.1926	80 Blythe Road	Not registered
Sanders Gertrude Alice	m	3.7.1928	9 Bond Street	Bertram
Sanders Hilda Nellie		25.3.1921	13 Herbert's Row	Not registered
Sanders or Bassett Rosalina	m	23.12.1901	Coventry	William Charles
Sargent Jane	f	28.2.1867	N. F. A	Mary
Satchwell Lydia	m	21.11.1905	Coventry	Leonard
Satchwell Maud H & Richard H	m	12.8.1913	Coventry	Herbert
Saunders Harriett		8.4.1906	Coventry	Not registered
Saunders Mary	f	1.5.1902	Coventry	Dorothy
Savage Alice		28.5.1914	95 Holyhead Road	Not registered
Savage Edith Radcliff	f	3.5.1922	11 London Road	Clarice
Saville Jessie	f	26.7.1918	28 Union Street	Brenda
Sawyer Edith	m	21.1.1926	Coton Infirmary	William George
Scanlon Harriett	f	6.3.1906	Coventry	Elizabeth Maud
Schofield Hilda Mary	m	14.4.1929	18ct 7h Spon Street	Raymond
Scott Charlotte	m	9.12.1924	24 Cow Lane	Selwyn
Scrivener Ellen	f	25.7.1914	Coventry	Rachel Elizabeth
Scrivener Fanny		21.8.1892	St. Michael	Not registered
Scrivener Martha and John	f	29.1.1893	St. Michael	Ellen
Seaborn Gladys	f	4.2.1918	17 Munition Cottages, Holbrook Lane	Sylvia
Seageley Elizabeth	f	27.3.1921	8 Bull Yard, Hertford St.	Joan
Seaman Winifred	f	20.6.1929	31 Church Cottages, Arley	Doreen

Seaman Winifred Kezia	f	11.8.1925	31 Church Cottages, Arley	Clara Kezia
Sedgeley Elizabeth	m	19.11.1928	27 Barns Heath Hostels	Norman
Seeley Emily	m	20.8.1887	Holy Trinity	William Thomas
Sephton Florence Kate		6.8.1909	Coventry	Not registered
Sharman Elsie Elizabeth	m	15.11.1927	7 Stoke Aldermoor	George Albert
Sharp Maud Mary	f	5.4.1927	St. Faiths Shelter, Holyhead Rd.	Ellie Mary
Shaw Edith Emma	f	19.10.1909	Coventry	Rose Ethel
Shaw Elizabeth	f	25.12.1921	4h 8ct Greyfriars Lane	Kathleen
Shaw Mary	m	19.2.1892	Casual pauper	Thomas
Sheasby Violet Annie	m	22.11.1921	115 Narrow Lane	Jeffrey George
Sheen Bessie		2.9.1920	N. F. A	Not registered
Sheers Lilian Maud	f	15.4.1928	5 St. Agnes Lane	Lilian Maud
Shelley Martha Jane	m	27.5.1921	7 Chapel Street	William John
Shellington Josephine	m	14.7.1918	18 Ordnance Hostels	William
Shenwick Hilda	m	5.7.1928	Nuneaton Union	William
Sheriff Lily	m	17.1.1903	Coventry	Albert
Sherriff Martha	m	14.2.1929	3ct 3h Bond Street	James
Shipley Julia and Joseph	m	30.4.1908	Coventry	John
Short Harriett (nee Large)	f	29.11.1884	St. Michael	Ada
Short Isabella	m	31.10.1911	Coventry	Bryan
Shortland Annie	m	12.3.1911	Coventry	Bertie Lewis
Shufflebotham Lilian	f	14.9.1928	19 Newnham Road	Lillian
Shuttleworth Eliza	m	16.4.1885	St. Michael	Samuel Henry
Sidwell Ann		24.4.1866	N. F. A	Not registered
Sidwell Florence Beatrice	m	17.6.1917	2ct 3h Hertford Place	Ronald Arthur Dance
Sidwell Martha	f	16.8.1867	N. F. A	Eliza
Sillito Violet	f	19.1.1930	7 Drapers Fields	Margaret Edith
Simister Annie Rebecca	m	11.1.1918	Coventry and Warwick Hosp.	Arnold
Simmonds Ellen	m	3.4.1925	248 Munition Cottages	Frank
Simmonds Mary Ellen	m	13.9.1925	Chilvers Coton, Nuneaton	Albert

Simmonds Mary Ellen	f	3.5.1927	Nuneaton Poor Law Institution	Irene May
Simmonds Sarah	f	11.11.1880	Holy Trinity	Alice
Simmonds Sarah	m	31.3.1883	St. Michael	Charles Henry
Simmons Mary		11.11.1859	N. F. A	Not registered
Simms Grace Irene	f	5.2.1928	141 Churchill Avenue	Elsie Clarice
Simpson Florence	m	15.5.1925	140 Colony Cottages	Bernard Alfred
Simpson Mary		9.3.1862	N. F. A	Not registered
Sims Sarah E		2.11.1907	Coventry	Not registered
Skelsey Eliza Ann	m	18.9.1906	Coventry	John Henry
Skelsey Florence	m	20.2.1913	Coventry	Leonard
Skinner Louisa	f	5.7.1929	18 Hill Street	Doreen
Slade Elizabeth	f	4.1.1928	7 Union Street	Colleen
Slater Florence	f	26.3.1928	40 George Street	Florence
Slater Nora	f	9.3.1930	180 Corporation Cottages	Patricia
Sly Ann	f	06.09.1877	St. Michael	Lucy
Sly Ann	m	19.11.1881	St. Michael	Frank
Slyde Alice Maud	m	11.2.1926	6 Bayley Lane	William Robert
Smith Agnes Elizabeth	f	5.6.1912	Coventry	Beatrice
Smith Alice	f	3.6.1921	12ct 1h Thomas Street	Alice
Smith Amelia	m	15.3.1889	Casual pauper	Cornelius
Smith Ann	m	14.4.1854	N. F. A	John
Smith Annie Elizabeth	m	9.4.1917	104 Little Park Street	Rudolph Arthur
Smith Beatrice	m	3.12.1915	1 Warwick Avenue	Arthur
Smith Charlotte Elizabeth	m	17.1.1913	Coventry	Ernest Walter
Smith Eliza	f	30.8.1882	St. Michael	Amy
Smith Ellen	f	30.1.1901	Coventry	Elizabeth
Smith Ellen	m	8.7.1894	Holy Trinity	Bertie
Smith Ellen and David	m	27.11.1902	Coventry	John
Smith Elsie	m	15.9.1925	11 Upper Well Street	Stanley
Smith Emily	m	16.8.1914	14 Yardley Street	Walter
Smith Emma	m	22.9.1900	Coventry	William
Smith Emma and Henry	f	22.6.1893	Casual pauper	Fanny
Smith Florence	m	23.2.1904	Coventry	Charles

Smith Florence May	m	20.3.1927	15 Silver Street	Allen John
Smith Hilda		17.5.1926	2 b/o 22 New Street	Not registered
Smith Jane	m	10.5.1892	Casual pauper	Henry
Smith Josiah and Elizabeth	f	27.7.1855	N. F. A	Sarah
Smith Kate	f	13.1.1911	Coventry	Edith
Smith Kate	m	6.2.1901	Coventry	Joseph
Smith Keziah		20.6.1911	Coventry	Not registered
Smith Lily (proper, Emily Jane Sadler)	m	19.8.1916	42 Villiers Street	Frederick
Smith Lizzie	f	30.4.1914	1 Norton Street	Gertrude Ellen
Smith Margaret	m	5.1.1930	135 Spon Street	Percy Ralph
Smith Mary Ann	f	18.8.1917	2 Leicester Street	Cecilia
Smith Mary Ann	m	22.8.1855	N. F. A	Thomas
Smith Mary Ann Priscilla	m	30.7.1912	Coventry	John Isaiah
Smith Mary Jane	m	24.7.1885	N. F. A	William Henry
Smith May	m	26.7.1913	Coventry	David
Smith Sarah	m	11.10.1880	St. Michael	Henry
Smith Violet Elizabeth	m	1.1.1927	St. Faiths Shelter	Richard
Soden Lily	m	13.9.1929	1 Brewery Street	Alfred Walter
Southam Jane	m	5.6.1882	St. Michael	William
Spare Elizabeth	f	23.6.1927	32 Cromwell Street	Violet
Sparkes Eliza	m	10.02.1877	Holy Trinity	Not registered
Sparkes Eliza	m	26.06.1878	Holy Trinity	William Henry
Sparkes Lilian	m	21.12.1925	35 Whitmore Park Cottages	Leonard Jack
Spatcher Florence Kate	f	19.2.1929	195 Aldermans Green	Betty
Spelcey Charlotte	m	10.1.1891	Holy Trinity	Joseph
Spencer Amy Mary	f	30.6.1909	Coventry	Marjory
Spencer Eliza	m	29.1.1886	N. F. A	Alfred
Spencer Eliza Ellen	m	6.5.1911	Coventry	Lancelot Alwyn
Spencer Mary Ann	f	11.4.1854	N. F. A	Sarah
Squires Alice	f	5.6.1904	Coventry	Doris
Stafford Kate	m	21.11.1911	Coventry	Thomas
Stanley Elizabeth		30.3.1891	Holy Trinity	Not registered
Stanley Florence	m	21.12.1914	N. F. A	Albert

Stanley Florence Annie	m	17.1.1917	4h 6ct Castle Street	Harold
Stanley Lizzie	f	16.5.1899	Holy Trinity	Elizabeth
Starley Annie	m	4.5.1921	Brentford Union	John Marshall
Statham Sarah	f	30.1.1929	24 Binley Avenue	Dorothy Edith
Steane Emma		18.5.1867	N. F. A	Not registered
Steane Martha Ann	f	31.1.1912	Coventry	Mabel Ellen
Stear Lilian	f	16.2.1930	54 Hillside	Marjorie
Stephens Emma	m	30.9.1903	Coventry	Arthur
Stephens Sophia	m	7.3.1917	6 Hostel, Holbrooks Lane	Albert Cecil
Stevens Emma Maria & Alfred Chas	m	30.6.1910	Coventry	Frank
Stock Ethel	m	7.6.1924	20 The Butts	Eric Bowes
Stock Minnie	f	27.2.1928	502 Foleshill Road	Clarice
Stokes Hilda Rose	f	21.7.1919	N. F. A	Phyllis May
Stoneman Kate Susan	f	28.10.1928	Achill", Tile Hill Lane	Kitty
Stratton Alice	f	9.6.1928	22 Craigsend Avenue, Binley	Dorothy Betty Ruth
Stretton Florence	f	21.1.1927	1ct 3h Cow Lane	Brenda
Stringer Lucy Fanny	f	23.3.1927	317 Munition Cottages	Albert George
Sturman Kate	f	14.12.1928	St. Faiths Shelter	Betty May
Sturman Phyllis	m	11.10.1929	54 Cambridge Street	Victor Walter
Styles Florence	m	21.8.1929	2ct 2h Warwick Lane	Herbert
Stynes May	m	11.5.1929	20 Harnall Lane West	Richard
Summerfield Mary Annie	m	7.1.1923	34 Queens Road	Reginald
Summers Ann	m	25.3.1906	Coventry	Victor
Sutton Ada Harriett		31.7.1923	83 Wright Street	Not registered
Sutton Florence	m	12.2.1922	5 Chapel Street	Ronald William
Sutton Selina	m	24.5.1900	Coventry	Arthur
Swain Florence	m	4.4.1929	10 Oaks Yard, Longford	Albert
Swain Louisa Alice	f	9.9.1911	Coventry	Doris
Swain Rebecca	f	3.7.1854	N. F. A	Rebecca
Swann Mary Lavinia	m	2.8.1917	15 Coniston Road, Earlsdon	William Joseph
Swindell Dora	f	16.12.1926	5 Meadow Street, Nuneaton	Rachael Edith

MOTHER'S NAME	M/F	D.O.B.	ADDRESS	CHILD'S NAME
Tallis Florence	m	17.12.1929	271 Munition Cottages	Gilbert
Tallis Florence		4.5.1925	N. F. A	Not registered
Tandy Elizabeth Catherine	m	14.5.1928	Oakfield", Warwick Avenue	Charles William
Tarheege Mary	m	14.8.1892	St. Michael	Albert
Tasker Catherine Edith	m	30.7.1928	30 Monks Road	Thomas
Taylor Ann	f	4.3.1882	St. Michael	Ethel
Taylor Eleanor Annie	m	20.2.1924	32 Alma Street	George
Taylor Eleanor Annie	f	24.3.1929	325 Lythalls Lane	Joyce
Taylor Elizabeth	f	16.5.1928	5ct 7h Gosford Street	Eileen Annie
Taylor Elsie	f	28.9.1927	115 Colony Cottages	Barbara Beryl
Taylor Elsie May	f	2.12.1926	37 Lord Street	Annie
Taylor Elsie May	m	28.8.1928	32 Hill Street	Phillip Horace
Taylor Emily	m	12.2.1889	St. Michael	John William
Taylor Ethel	m	9.2.1930	1, Brown Van, Pinley Gardens	Raymond
Taylor Evelyn	f	24.5.1929	30ct 15h Hill Street	Irene
Taylor Flora		3.2.1911	Coventry	Not registered
Taylor Florence	m	21.9.1913	Coventry	George
Taylor Gladys	f	17.10.1927	Sunrise Caravan", Pinley Gardens	Gladys Joyce
Taylor Hilda May	m	26.8.1917	479 Stoney Stanton Road	Ronald
Taylor Lilian Frances	f	17.11.1906	Coventry	Mabel Dorothy
Taylor Lizzie	f	14.2.1912	Coventry	Maud
Taylor Lizzie	m	20.9.1914	91 Norton Street	Kenneth
Taylor Lucy	m	17.4.1900	Coventry	George Percy
Taylor Maria		17.1.1868	N. F. A	Not registered
Taylor Mary Elizabeth	f	6.12.1911	Coventry	Louisa
Taylor Olive	f	7.7.1929	Victoria", Fir Tree Avenue	Alma
Teasdale Florence Maud	m	25.3.1930	42 Providence Street	Alec
Thomas Alice	f	16.10.1922	Nuneaton Union	Sarah Jane
Thomas Alice Elizabeth	f	9.6.1918	85 Gosford Street	Alice Elizabeth

Thompsell Daisy	f	23.8.1929	56 Craven Street	Betty
Thompson Amelia	f	2.2.1854	N. F. A	Amelia
Thompson Amy	m	11.11.1912	Coventry	John Thomas
Thompson Ann and William	f	16.10.1893	St. Michael	Sarah Amy
Thompson Sarah Ann		7.12.1924	6h 1ct Swanswell Terrace	Not registered
Thompson Susannah	m	18.3.1883	N. F. A	Not registered
Thorley Frances Emily	m	28.11.1928	91 Holyhead Road	Charles Edward
Thorpe Annie	f	19.5.1927	40 Gas Street	Edith
Thurstan Rebecca	m	20.1.1880	St. Michael	Joseph Henry
Tibbey Gertrude	m	29.1.1909	Coventry	Richard Frederick
Tierney Nora	f	13.3.1927	318 Corporation Cottages	Nora
Tilsley Florence May	m	29.7.1927	114 Eden Street	Frank
Timms Nita Violet	f	23.1.1923	75 Little Park Street	Norma
Tinsley Mary	f	22.6.1855	N. F. A	Eliza
Tipper Clara	m	16.9.1914	2a Conway Square, Spon End	Cyril Ernest
Tipper Clara Ann	m	22.12.1912	Coventry	Sidney
Tisdale Ada Eliza	m	1.9.1928	3 Whoberley Cottages, Tile Hill	Alan Victor
Todd Ethel Lydia	m	9.5.1923	47 East Street	Frederick Richard
Toney Elizabeth	m	10.1.1912	Coventry	Francis Bernard
Toney Elizabeth and John	f	15.1.1905	Coventry	Gladys May
Toney Elizabeth and John Henry	m	10.1.1909	Coventry	Albert Victor
Toney Lizzie & John Henry	m	1.10.1899	St. Michael	William Henry
Tonks Lucy	f	22.2.1926	Nuneaton Union	Edith
Toogood Amy	m	3.6.1903	Coventry	George
Tooth Louisa	m	23.1.1930	13ct 4h St. John's Street	Alfred Ernest
Tranter Ada	f	1.3.1914	Coventry	Gladys
Tranter Eileen	f	4.3.1930	13 Waveley Road	Jean
Treddle Caroline M	f	29.7.1929	Armadale Bungalow", Pinley Gardens	Edna May
Treen Hilda Mary	m	28.10.1915	10 Spencer Road	Sidney Arthur

Trickett Eliza	m	27.2.1867	N. F. A	James
Tromans Ethel and Rueben	m	12.2.1910	Coventry	David
Troughton Harriet	f	18.2.1889	Holy Trinity	Sarah Elizabeth
Troughton Sarah	f	9.12.1893	Holy Trinity	Florence Gertrude Day
Tunnicliffe Alice M	f	28.5.1906	Coventry	Lily
Turbitt Mary	f	9.10.1860	N. F. A	Eleanor
Turner Elizabeth		29.8.1859	N. F. A	Not registered
Turner Rose	f	1.3.1926	150 Munition Cottages	Nora Grace
Turner Rose	m	4.5.1927	7 Gilbert Place, Brook Street	Bernard Robert
Turner Ruth	m	26.9.1928	Meriden Union	Philip
Turrall Catherine	f	29.8.1900	Coventry	Mary Ann
Turrall Ellen M	m	1.7.1892	Holy Trinity	Joseph
Turrall Ellen Maria	f	2.8.1890	Holy Trinity	Ellen
Turrell Mary Ann	m	24.12.1878	Holy Trinity	George James
Twigger Henrietta	m	05.10.1875	Holy Trinity	John William
Twynham Annie Doris	f	12.12.1926	50 Stoney Stanton Road	Marjory
Tyers Emily		30.9.1928	288 Grange Road, Longford	Not registered
Tyso Mary		22.4.1889	St. Michael	Not registered

MOTHER'S NAME	M/F	D.O.B.	ADDRESS	CHILD'S NAME
Unsworth Doris	f	27.9.1923	40 Swanswell Terrace	Aileen Elsie Florence

MOTHER'S NAME	M/F	D.O.B.	ADDRESS	CHILD'S NAME
Vanstone Beatrice	f	24.7.1920	66 Thomas Street	Murial
Vanstone Bessie	f	22.5.1922	104 Little Park Street	Kathleen
Varney Mary Ellen	f	14.3.1897	Holy Trinity	Gertrude Alice
Vernon Emma	f	23.7.1885	N. F. A	Rose
Vernon Rose Mary	f	20.4.1929	52 Hill Street	Joyce
Vickers Elizabeth	m	13.9.1929	17 Nethermill Road	Ethel
Villiers Harriet		10.4.1899	St. Michael	Not registered
Viner Ellen	m	21.7.1901	Coventry	Alfred
Viner Sarah Ann	m	2.5.1881	St. Michael	Arthur

MOTHER'S NAME	M/F	D.O.B.	ADDRESS	CHILD'S NAME
Wagstaff Eutey		2.10.1865	N. F. A	Not registered
Wain Elizabeth		17.6.1862	N. F. A	Not registered
Wain Sarah	f	15.11.1882	St. Michael	Louisa
Wainwright Nellie	m	16.2.1927	108 Heath Road	Graham Leslie
Wainwright Nellie Elizabeth	m	6.1.1929	108 Heath Road	Horace Sydney
Wakefield Eleanor Louisa	f	31.8.1891	St. Michael	Lily
Walden Rose	m	8.1.1893	St. Michael	Robert
Walford Ellen	f	19.5.1905	Coventry	Evelyn
Walford Ellen	m	19.5.1905	Coventry	Henry
Walker Ada Mary	f	25.4.1910	Coventry	Winifred May
Walker Ann		27.12.1861	N. F. A	Not registered
Walker Doris	m	22.9.1926	St. Faiths Shelter, Holyhead Road	Alan
Walker Doris	f	4.1.1928	58 Holyhead Road	Mavis
Walker Gladys Mary	m	30.6.1921	98 Highfield Road	William Henry
Walker Rose		14.1.1912	Coventry	Not registered
Walters Edith	m	21.5.1926	149 Whitmore Park Cottages	Alfred
Walters Emma and Henry	m	24.9.1893	Holy Trinity	William
Wanley Mary Ann	m	10.3.1893	Holy Trinity	James
Wanley Mary Ann	m	5.8.1903	Coventry	Harry
Wanley Mary Ann	m	7.1.1896	St. Michael	William Henry
Want Nelle	m	14.2.1920	18 Paynes Lane	Kenneth Valentine
Ward Amelia	m	23.1.1889	Holy Trinity	Walter
Ward Edith May	f	21.6.1927	Nuneaton Poor Law Institution	Edith
Ward Elizabeth	f	29.4.1914	26 Upper Well Street	Elizabeth
Ward Fanny	m	28.12.1878	Holy Trinity	Ernest Herbert
Ward Florence	m	22.7.1929	2ct 1h Hertford Street	Dennis
Ward Frances	f	14.11.1928	129 Corporation Cottages	Florence May
Ward Harriet	f	24.4.1880	Holy Trinity	Lucy Elizabeth
Ward Maria	m	17.10.1896	St. Michael	Arthur James
Ward Mary	m	27.1.1929	13ct 6h Far Gosford Street	John
Waring Ivy Alice	m	22.5.1928	180 Cross Road	Ernest

Warner Evelyn	m	15.5.1929	7ct 1h Greyfriars Lane	Derrick
Warner Evelyn Emily	m	1.5.1928	22 Swan Lane	Norman
Warren Nancy Elizabeth	f	19.4.1929	N. F. A	Margaret Rose
Warren Phyllis Eugene	m	18.5.1928	37 Broomfield Place	Robert Dennis
Warren Violet Ellen	m	17.7.1927	10 Duke Street	Derick Baden
Warwick Mary	m	8.4.1867	N. F. A	David
Warwick Norah	m	14.12.1927	14 Swanswell Terrace	Dennis
Waters Ellen	f	28.12.1887	St. Michael	Emma Elizabeth
Watkins Beatrice Maggie	m	19.12.1929	9ct 1h Butts	Frederick Brian
Watkins Elsie	f	13.6.1927	5 Church Street	Mavis June
Watkins Emma Amy	f	4.10.1911	Coventry	Fay
Watson Doris	f	14.2.1927	22 Cromwell Street	Eveline
Watson Doris	f	14.3.1927	22 Cromwell Street	Doris
Weaver Beatrice	m	1.11.1918	395 Stoney Stanton Road	Edgar
Webb Mary and Richard	m	10.2.1886	St. Michael	John James
Welby Margaret		19.1.1923	60 Spon Street	Not registered
Welby Margaret		9.4.1926	54a Boston Place, Lockhurst Lane	Not registered
Weldon Eliza	f	26.7.1886	N. F. A	Alice
Wells Julia	f	30.8.1882	St. Michael	Alice
West Caroline	f	09.01.1876	Holy Trinity	Florence Ada
West Edith	m	18.3.1892	Holy Trinity	Herbert Whynout
West Kate	m	11.3.1887	Holy Trinity	Joseph
Westley Henrietta		11.11.1865	N. F. A	Not registered
Weston Emily Violet	m	5.12.1906	Coventry	Ronald Edward
Weston Florence Mary	f	17.2.1909	Coventry	Hilda May
Whailing Irene	f	30.10.1929	53 Hillside, Stoke Heath	Hazel
Whinmill Beatrice May	m	17.7.1928	77 Much Park Street	Peter
White Jane	f	19.7.1866	N. F. A	Eva
White Lily	m	7.12.1929	22 Queen Victoria Road	John
White Sarah Ellen	m	11.2.1901	Coventry	William
White Sarah Ellen	f	11.2.1901	Coventry	Annie

Whitehead Mary Ann		18.4.1862	N. F. A	Not registered
Whiteman Margaret	f	27.12.1927	42 Much Park Street	Margaret
Whitwell Annie	m	19.3.1880	St. Michael	Tom
Worrall Emma	f	13.6.1881	St. Michael	Emma
Wigmore Beatrice	f	16.6.1921	219 Sovereign Road	Catherine Mary
Wilkes Dorothy May	f	28.1.1918	202 Melbourne Road	Eva May
Wilkes Lilian	m	31.3.1930	17 Dreppell Street	Wilfred
Wilkins Agnes Bertha	m	29.5.1917	104 Little Park Street	Joseph Harry
Wilkins Gladys	m	2.4.1928	1 Freeth Street	Albert William
Wilks Susannah (nee Williams)	f	13.11.1884	St. Michael	Mary Elizabeth
Williams Caroline	f	21.4.1910	Coventry	Joan May
Williams Clara	m	12.8.1914	7h 2ct Cook Street	Frederick Thomas
Williams Daisy	f	17.3.1916	15 Eaton Road	Edith
Williams Hilda		22.9.1928	272 Munition Cottages	Clancy
Williams Hilda	f	27.7.1925	2 Munition Cottages	Gladys
Williams Olive Frances	f	10.4.1909	Coventry	Gladys May
Williams Thresa Esme	m	3.4.1929	218 Whitmore Park	Donald Edward
Williamson Sarah	m	12.7.1878	Holy Trinity	John
Willis Ivy	m	4.10.1928	3 Shakespeare Street	James
Wills Gwendoline	m	1.5.1927	57 Colchester Street	Albert Edward
Wills Irene	f	16.8.1923	11 London Road	Pamela
Wills Mary	m	4.6.1854	N. F. A	William
Wilson Amelia Bennett	m	18.5.1927	83a East Street	Ronald
Wilson Charlotte	f	8.9.1908	Coventry	Nora
Wilson Doris	m	18.11.1929	31 Greyfriars Lane	Francis
Wilson Easter Ruby	f	25.12.1929	40 Whitefriars Street	Loraine
Wilson Edith	m	17.8.1905	Coventry	Thomas Henry
Wilson Edith Lucy	f	1.11.1928	164 Spon Street	Edna May
Wilson Edith Lucy	m	1.11.1928	164 Spon Street	John
Wilson Elizabeth		4.5.1860	N. F. A	Not registered
Wilson Flora	m	4.4.1912	Coventry	Edward
Wilson Flora and William	f	1.8.1908	Coventry	Flora

Wilson Lily Nora	f	19.6.1921	25 Swan Lane	Edith
Wilson Mary	f	7.2.1930	13 Smith Street	Mary
Wilson Matilda	m	19.10.1923	Binley, nr Coventry	William Frank
Wilson May Mary	m	18.10.1916	Lockhurst Lane	Michael
Wilson Selina and William	f	30.10.1914	2ct 1h Swanswell Street	Lily
Windham Jane		19.10.1862	N. F. A	Not registered
Windsor Lucy	f	16.4.1928	103 Whitmore Park	Theresa Evelyn
Winkett Mary Elizabeth	f	13.12.1926	Meriden Union	Edith Alice
Winterburn Elizabeth		11.1.1929	Bairyana", Warwick Avenue	Not registered
Wood Eliza	m	18.1.1914	Coventry	William
Wood Elizabeth	f	18.6.1854	N. F. A	Caroline
Wood Fanny	m	14.9.1877	St. Michael	William
Wood Jessie	m	17.1.1918	B Block, Whitmore Park	Roland
Wood Rose Elizabeth	f	16.11.1926	9ct 6h Well Street	Betty
Wood Sarah and John	f	28.6.1893	St. Michael	Sarah Ann
Woodfield Ada		5.9.1915	N. F. A	Not registered
Woodfield Laura	m	2.5.1925	152 Corporation Cottages	Frank Stanley
Woodfield Mary Jane	m	17.2.1883	St. Michael	Alfred
Woodfield Rebecca		10.9.1861	N. F. A	Not registered
Woodhouse Mary	m	6.2.1927	13ct 9h St. Johns Street	Cecil
Wooding Elsie	f	28.5.1928	7 Plough Yard, London Road	Margaret
Woodman Nellie	f	28.2.1914	Coventry	Norah
Woodrow Jane		19.9.1865	N. F. A	Not registered
Woodward Elsie	m	29.8.1927	9 East Street	Walter
Woodward Mary	f	4.2.1859	N. F. A	Rebecca
Woodward Sarah	m	27.2.1886	N. F. A	William
Woodward Sarah	f	6.12.1882	Holy Trinity	Lucy Emma
Woodward Vina and William	f	16.2.1909	Coventry	Leonora Phyllis
Wollaston Hilda May	m	18.3.1928	31 Meadow Street	Kenneth Raymond
Woolley Ada Dorothy	f	1.1.1922	64 Paynes Lane	Hilda May

Woolley Gladys Maud	m	15.6.1928	54 King Edward Avenue	Thomas
Wootton Emily	m	7.5.1889	St. Michael	James
Wootton Ethel Beatrice	f	14.7.1925	1 Mattock & Spade Yard, Jordan Well	Ethel Beatrice
Wright Ada	m	1.7.1920	138 Bolingbroke Road	Walter
Wright Blanche Evelyn Elizabeth	m	24.6.1928	25 Gulson Road	Cyril
Wright Elizabeth	m	14.8.1914	31 George Street	William
Wright Ethel F	f	19.7.1929	20ct 9h Much Park Street	Mavis
Wright Hannah	m	20.2.1919	194 Eagle Street	William Thomas
Wright Hilda Mary	f	15.11.1927	70 Mulliner Street	Violet Hilda
Wright Rose Hannah	f	16.11.1882	St. Michael	Amy
Wyatt Fanny Elizabeth	m	9.12.1903	Coventry	William Thomas
Wyatt Iris	m	25.9.1928	11 Cope Street	Norman George
Wyatt Martha Ann	m	26.5.1913	Coventry	Walter Drakeford
Wykes Florence	m	23.2.1923	1 Grove Street	Dennis
Wythe Violet	f	5.3.1929	142 Cross Road	Edith Gwendoline

MOTHER'S NAME	M/F	D.O.B.	ADDRESS	CHILD'S NAME
Yardley Emma		16.5.1893	St. Michael	Not registered
Yardley Kate	f	24.6.1926	St. Faiths Shelter	Margaret
Yardley Margaret	f	12.07.1876	St. Michael	Not registered
Yardley Maria	m	3.8.1859	N. F. A	John
Yardley Maria		9.1.1863	N. F. A	Not registered
Yates Emily		17.2.1891	St. Michael	Not registered
Yates Emily		25.8.1895	Holy Trinity	Not registered
Yates Emily	f	29.3.1899	St. Michael	Edith
Yeats Dinah	m	31.3.1925	30 Monks Road	Harold
Yedvabrick Florence	m	3.2.1930	6 Engleton Road	William
York Lucy	m	11.11.1898	St. Michael	John
Young Alice	f	11.4.1918	24 Hostel, Holbrook Lane	Irene

www.ingramcontent.com/pod-product-compliance
Lightning Source LLC
Chambersburg PA
CBHW060842280326
41934CB00007B/893